Mayflower Bastard

ALSO BY DAVID LINDSAY

House of Invention:
The Secret Life of Everyday Products

The Patent Files:
Dispatches from the Frontiers of Invention

Madness in the Making:
The Triumphant Rise and Untimely Fall
of America's Show Inventors

THOMAS DUNNE BOOKS
St. Martin's Press ✺ New York

MAYFLOWER BASTARD

A Stranger Among the Pilgrims

DAVID LINDSAY

THOMAS DUNNE BOOKS.
An imprint of St. Martin's Press.

www.stmartins.com

Endpapers courtesy of the Public Record Office

Richard More's signature courtesy of the Peabody Essex Museum

Title-page photograph of Richard More's gravestone courtesy of Tom Stanley
© 2002; More is the only "First Comer" whose burial place is known.

ISBN 0-312-26203-5

First Edition: November 2002

10   9   8   7   6   5   4   3   2   1

TO MY MOTHER, *Helen Lindsay*,

WITH MUCH, MUCH LOVE

Contents

Acknowledgments

THE NUMBER OF PEOPLE who shepherded me through this book are legion. I owe a great deal to them all. They include Steve Dodson and Holt Parker, who provided me with a near instantaneous translation from Renaissance law Latin; David Greene, the editor of *The American Genealogist,* who pursued a hypothesis of mine with selfless alacrity; D. E. Wickham, archivist at the Clothworkers' Company in London; Nicole Rioles, archivist at the Peabody Essex Museum; Dr. Alaric Faulkner, a superb archaeologist of the Maine coast; Paul Mahoney at the Massachusetts Archives; the county archivist at the Northamptonshire Record Office; Harman Clark, for his information on the Southold More family; Ken Murray, keeper of the Woolnough family flame; Karen Mullian; Penny Fussell; and Caleb Johnson, who went beyond his normal duties in running the Mayflower Web Pages to lend his considerable historical perspective.

I also owe an abiding debt to the staffs at many institutions I consulted, among others, the Public Record Office, the Guildhall Library, the Society of Genealogists, the New York Public Library, the Shropshire Records and Research Centre, the New-York Historical Society, New York University's Bobst Library, Yale's Stirling Library, and the Peabody Essex Museum.

Winnifred Pierce, my second cousin, did the fundamental work in establishing our lineage to Richard More; without her tenacity and insight, there literally would have been no book for me to write. Special thanks must also go to Marian Roberts, archivist of the More family papers, and Justin Coldwell, the current heir of Linley Hall, for opening their books and their doors to a prodigal American writer; to Anne McNaught, for tolerating my obsessions while in London; and to Mrs. Buckley, for her hospitality at the College Hill Guest House.

Then there are those who simply cannot be thanked enough. Goran Dordevic heard it all and lived to tell the tale, as did my good friends Craig Marsden and Jim Scott. Chick Bills and Christine Lidrbauch not only enlightened me about archaic seafaring customs but rescued me from a moment of penury with grace and good humor. Donald F. Harris and Iris L. Harris were incalculable boons and the most perfect guides imaginable for my trip to Shropshire. Generous of spirit, vigilant of fact, they made my explorations into the depths of the seventeenth century an incomparable pleasure.

My editor, Ruth Cavin, was, and is, simply amazing: tireless, enthusiastic, rigorous, big-hearted and, above all, right. The same, and much, much more, can be said of my mother, to whom I dedicate this book. And of course, for Claudia even superlatives fall short: if the heart is where reading and writing truly take place, then this book was, in some inarguable sense, originally written by her. All dishonor to me if I have erred in the translation!

And many of you being immediate Successors, cannot but be very sensible what these New-England Liberties have Cost your Progenitors, some of them having buried their Estates, all of them their bones in these Foundations, and left you now in Possession, that if you should put Contempt upon their Adventures, their Courage, Wisdom, Zeal, and Self-Denial, by Under-prizing these Inestimable Infranchizements, and slight them . . . God may then put you to learn the Worth of them at that School where they Learnt it; and I am sure you will pay dear for your Tutoring if it comes to that.

—JOHN WISE, 1717

Preface

THIS IS NOT A BOOK about a famous person. Richard More appears to us through the haze of centuries as a minor character on the world stage, a Shakespearean bit player allotted no more than two or three lines of dialogue. He left behind no great works, no heroic deeds, only a smattering of entries in a few crumbling documents. Ordinarily, such a person would not command our attention; like countless others who have lived throughout the ages, he would simply melt into the crowd. Richard More, however, bridged a significant gap in American history.

When the average person thinks of the Puritans, two distinct images generally come to mind. One is of the *Mayflower* passengers, having survived the high seas and a raging sickness, celebrating their first Thanksgiving dinner. The other is of ordinary citizens being hanged from the trees of Salem on insupportable charges of witchcraft. It would be hard to imagine a greater contrast: an idealistic community persisting through every adversity, and a vengeful community consuming its own. How did the one event lead to the other? Were these completely separate worlds, or was there a connection between the two?

The life of Richard More presents a rare opportunity to answer that question. Thrown onto the *Mayflower* at the tender age of five, he more than survived—he was still alive almost eight decades later, when he witnessed a close acquaintance meet his doom in the Salem witch trials. Between those events, he was a sea captain, which gave him a broad view of the English-speaking world (broader than that of the typical planter or smithy) and something of a special status as well. The sailor enjoyed great liberties in his day, and More availed himself of them freely, until he went too far and was forced to live under a cloud of secrecy. Yet for all that, he was forever considered one of the First Comers, one who had been there at what, even during his lifetime, came to be called the Ancient Beginning.

He thus became a kind of repository of the many conflicts of a fledgling culture. By looking through his eyes, we may glimpse a century in all its particulars and, at the same time, perceive how incompatible views of the world warred within one individual. Like few others, Richard More represents the myth and counter-myth of America—the wellsprings of our current patriotism and dissent—on an eminently human level.

Of course, in a book about a man who died more than three hundred years ago, the very notion of a common humanity is thrown into doubt. So much has changed in the interim: dress, customs, speech, governments—even the stars in the sky have shifted from their places. In that time, our understanding of seventeenth-century Massachusetts has drifted as well and, inevitably, has been shaped to fit the needs of the present. Add the gaps and ambiguities in More's life and one is presented with a task that begins to resemble paleontology.

Or, to bring the metaphor home, seafaring. When the captain of a ship offers the wheel to a new hand, he will sometimes give nothing in the way of instruction but the casual remark "Don't hit anything." That has been my goal in writing this book. The waters that Richard More passed over were wide and deep, mostly uncharted and often draped in fog. In navigating them, I have tried my best to stick to the channel and keep the rudder from getting fouled.

In so doing, I have labored to keep my claims as conservative as possible. It may be of some comfort to know that I had to throw away a great many suppositions, some of which were exciting enough. For a time, William Shakespeare hovered within view (thanks to a publisher named Richard More who liked to print swans on his covers), as did the Renaissance composer William Byrd, for having a daughter-in-law named Katharine More. And I surely would have liked to believe that Richard More's bigamous wife was, in fact, a certain woman who ended up bewitched in Massachusetts, if only it could have been so.

The same holds true for the less glamorous calls. The name Richard More appears often in colonial literature, and although in many instances the identity behind it was either certain or completely unknown, almost as many others fell into a gray area. Faced with these, I made my evaluations, and devil take the hindmost. The result is the one story I felt could be written, out of the many that could not. Whether, after attending to the scruples of historical record, I have succeeded in "bringing it to life," as the expression goes, is no longer my business. Already the winds have changed, the years fallen off, and the tale is under way. . . .

Introduction:
The Casting Out

Old Captain More having been for many years under suspicion and a common fame of lasciviousness at least some degree of incont[in]ency and therefore was at several times spoken to, by sundry brethren and also by the Elders in a private way, because for want of proof we could go no further. He was at last left to himself so far as that he was convicted before justices of the peace by 3 witnesses of gross unchastity with another man's wife and was censured by them. On July 1, after the morning sermon, 5 Elders acquainted the Church with it, 2 of the brethren were sent to him to require him to come in the Afternoon which he did, speaking in some relenting way, and submitting to the Church and so a publicke Admonition was consented to by the vote of the brethren, which was pronounced by the Pastor charging him the blame and shame of a scandalous Sin being a gross breach of the 7th commandment not fit to be named, and that aggravated by his being formerly privately admonished, and he was now in his old age, etc., then he was delivered from the Lords table and required to repent as Revelation 2:21.

—*The Records of the First Church of Salem*

A COMMON FAME: that was the heart of it. You had heard of his exploits, and what you had not heard could always be gleaned from the gossips: legends of the First Comer in your midst. There he was, an old salt in his tavern, slowly taking on the aspect of a landmark, while the preachers exhorted you to hearken to the glories of the Ancient Brethren, who had risked all for your comfort, who had dared to dream of a world where God and man spoke as one. And yet the old captain—one of the Ancient Brethren himself—seemed to be following another path altogether, direct to its sordid conclusion, even in his seventies. Everyone talked, everyone pointed—there, that house, right by the Old Burying Ground, he's old enough to be buried there himself.

That fame, common or not, set the captain apart from the others, and certainly from you. Indeed, although I say "you," your identity has been carefully concealed from me. You might be a teenaged girl, a middle-aged cooper, or a righteous mother—the records do not say. I cannot claim to know your name, your loves or aspirations. All I can say with any confidence is that your life at that time was confused, within and without—a slipping, sliding, eroding sensation. For that reason alone, I should be slow to blame you. In a broken time you sought a small purchase, some faint recognition, if only from the magistrates.

And so down on your knees you went, peering through a knothole in the pine (and how convenient that the knotless oak had gone out of style) into another world, of sailors and drunks, travelers and strangers, their talk deformed by the peculiar argot of the sea.

But what power there is in the eye! Sight is God-given and finds grace when it perceives God's signs in return; in this your covenant held true. Once the signs of decline were revealed in their fullness, all that remained was for you to describe them aloud, and by something akin to magic, the old man was summoned before the Salem court (he still able to remember the days when the site was bare land) to answer for his crime of "gross unchastity with another man's wife." His head bowed, his censure received.

And then the rest of it, for once the court was done, it was the church's turn to have at him. One Sabbath lecture that summer, the elders stood and spoke plainly and secured a vote for the casting out.

You must have been present for that. Having played a central role in his capture, you would not have missed his confession. But how powerful was your vision, really, I wonder? After two of your fellow churchmen had left the meetinghouse and gone to bring him to conscience, was your inner eye able to fill out the scene, to travel beyond the beams, out the door and along the streets to the waterfront—or is it only now, through my infernal science, that the scene can finally come to life?

On July 1, 1688, while you waited in your pew, Captain Richard More sat in the gloom of his moribund tavern, with little to do but contemplate his long, multifarious existence. These reflections had their counterpart in geography, for his house was situated in such a way as to create two distinct panoramas—one behind him, signifying life, and the other before him.

Richard did not have to turn around to know what course the ships were taking in Salem Harbor that day, in casual disregard for the edict against traveling on the Sabbath. He knew the route as well as he knew how to breathe—had, in fact, been engaged in both activities for almost the same length of time.

In the beginning, as he could well recall, a spit of land had jutted out from Salem Neck, just above the turn where his own wharf lay. Soon enough, however, the trees were cleared from the neck, and the wind blew hard across Elvin's Point until eventually it breached the land and cleared a north channel, which was straighter and better during spring tides. Then, with Richard's old age, the wind had had its way again and closed the North Channel, this time with sand, and again vessels had only one road— along the South Channel, down toward Giggles Island and then out into the harbor, and from there to sea.

In short, Richard belonged to the world at his back. Once having shipped out, he was in complete control. In his fifty years as a mariner, he had never lost a vessel, nor had any sailor brought charges against him.

The land, however, was another story. The home fires did not burn bright in July 1688. By the time you found him out, he had sold or bequeathed every plot of property he owned. Even the two-story house in which he sat had been mortgaged to a neighbor. The signs visible through the front window were just as clear: in the graveyard, several of his family members rested beneath silhouetted stones (the winged angel of death cut into their peaks), while before them the figures of the churchmen grew larger as they approached.

The captain's appearance in the darkened doorway made for a striking contrast with his summoners. He in his tarred breeches and dreadnought jacket, and the churchmen in their steeple-crowned hats and sweeping cloaks—the scene might have been ripped from a child's primer: Humility Confronts the Debauched.

Immutable as any test of faith, then, the allegory proceeded. Richard had never been accused by the church before, had never been asked to reveal his soul in public, but he had seen it countless times and knew there was little alternative now. After his adversaries had explained their mission, he collected himself and prepared to meet his accusers.

It was not far from his home to the meetinghouse—down the path that would later become Charter to St. Peter, then Church Street, and a block or two farther from there—but even that short distance held clues for the discerning eye. It had not been so very long ago, after all, that the church elders had described immoral behavior as "disorderly walking," and as a sailor, Richard had a wobbly gait that matched the expression exactly. On they walked, the churchmen purposeful in their stride, Richard walking disorderly, as if deranged (though his face said otherwise), the party as a whole falling into a kind of mock unison of land and sea as they came within earshot of the church bell and began to step in time.

The bell. As a measure of how far Richard More had fallen from grace, that was probably the surest sign of them all. You knew it instantly as the voice of God, each peal boring into the conscience of the sensitive listener. You had heard it many times, everyone had, its reach describing the radius of the congregation, and Richard and his escorts did not stop until they heard it as loudly as you did.

Their boots thudded the steps, bone-dry from the long drought that had sent the preachers calling for public fasts, and the door swung open. Each pair of eyes was trained on the doorway.

Someone swatted a fly.

There is a moment in every man's life when he feels that his entire store of memories, opinions, grudges, beliefs, and darkest desires is hidden from the world by only the few centimeters of bone that cover his head. Walking into the meetinghouse, Richard had available to him a gallery of images that few others could boast: of remote wilderness, of pestilence and mutiny, wars and cruel ironies, of a thousand women—none of whom, on closer inspection, was the one who had vanished. And then there were those things that had formed him without his knowledge, long ago, in a world almost no one could recall, which he himself could not remember, much less convey to you, sitting there in your pew.

You heard every word, his voice ringing flat against the rafters until there were no more words to be said and the minister, citing Revelation, formally barred him from the Lord's Supper; and then at last, as the captain departed, cut off from the church—a man hove into the darkness—the bell took up its tolling again.

But you must have wondered, too, at what lay behind his words, which in the end were only patterned after the general model: the providence of God, the depravity of man, more or less.

Was the old captain pretending, as so many others had? Was it simple dissembling—some dastardly act of familism—while unregenerate thoughts swam in his blood? Or, alternatively, was there some textured truth within him, some redemptive tale that failed to pass the sieve of convention? Could you hear, for example, buried deep in his voice, the strangled belief that history is but a chain of confessions derailing the destinies of its inhabitants, from mother to child, ad infinitum?

But perhaps I say more than I realize. If you could fly by witch's broom across the ages to where I sit, you would be amazed at how unbroken that chain has been. Here, on this peculiar perch of the twenty-first century, ordinary people bare their sins in public every day, through a popish device called a "television"—a cheap catharsis that prevents the airing of any tragedy worthy of the name. We still demand moral solvency, and still the demand derails us.

What, then, of the bell that rang above your head? Could you hear in its fading tones a second meaning—the tolling not just of the captain's depravity but of his failure to be avenged as well? In its overtones the impossibly twisted story of his life sprang into the air, became mingled with the story of the New World itself, and then died away. If you could have picked that tale from the wind, would you really have been so quick to condemn him?

I wonder. Wonder and shuffle my papers, with their own diminutive wind. . . .

Mayflower Bastard

1

Swan Song

But to his son and heir his house and land he assigned,
With an old will and charge to hold the same bountiful
mind,
To be good to his neighbors and to his tenants kind,
But in the ensuing ditty you shall hear how he was in-
clined;
Like a new Courtier of the King's . . .

—"The Old Courtier of the Queen's"
(traditional English ballad)

THE STORY BEGINS LONG AGO, before you were born, in a tunnel. The tunnel was supposed to have opened behind the fireplace at Larden Hall, threading its way beneath the sheep-spotted hills of Shropshire, a mere stone's throw from Wales, and emerging some ten miles distant, at Wenlock Priory. That no one has ever found such a tunnel hardly makes any difference. Its very impossibility was the point of the fable, because it said that the land was wrong and, since every gentleman was of the land in those days, that a particular gentleman had been wronged by his wife in that tunnel, which could not have been true, because there could never have been such a tunnel, and thus the children could never have been. There are less economical ways to protest the violation of marriage vows.

Admittedly, Katharine More had never expected to find herself in such a bind. The youngest daughter of a local bailiff who had built Larden Hall with his own hands, Katharine had grown up assuming, quite naturally, that one of her elder brothers would live to be heir. But Jasper More had kept a loose house, like the new squire in the ballad of the day, and he had spent much of his time dunning the locals to fill his own coffers while his children ranged as they would. In 1607 the price of their freedom was named: Katharine's elder brother got into an argument over a woman and, in the duel that followed, was felled by a pistol shot. With Katharine's sisters already married and her other brothers dead of disease or fate, she was thrust to center stage of the household, with responsibilities she had never imagined as hers. And that she was in no position to take on.

Neither you nor I will ever know if she and Jacob Blakeway were already in love by that time. There are documents that hint at the truth—the lease for the farmland that the Blakeways rented from the Mores, with Samuel More's signature firmly affixed to the back; the confusion decades later as to the exact time and place that Samuel and Katharine were wed; the look of the road leading down from their official wedding site to the town where the Blakeways lived, a wild, overtangled stretch that resembled a ravine more than a place to set foot in for any conceivable business. . . . But these are mute clues to a question that remains unanswerable, the question that lies at the heart of all stories, as it must for yours as well: When and where, the sages ask, does love begin?

Marriages, on the other hand, are more easily tracked. (Indeed, perhaps that is why matrimony exists.) On her wedding day, Katharine was already twenty-three years old—roughly the same age that her grandmother Jane Pemberton had been two decades earlier when she sat for a portrait by Holbein, a miniature revealing the proud swan of the family coat of arms.[1] Jane had been a headstrong woman, keeping her maiden name after marriage, and Katherine may well have searched that very painting for resemblances that day. Was her neck as straight? Her face as gaunt? Her hand as delicate? Was her gaze the same mixture of determined and plaintive?

At some point, consciously or not, Katharine must have seen her grandmother's ambiguous expression staring back from the mirror, for her husband-to-be was hardly a swan. Samuel More was her fifth cousin, of that there can be no doubt, but he had none of the fine looks of her side of the family. Nor could he boast of his own father's features: Richard More the elder had a splash of the raffish about his eyes, and a thin nose that, underscored as it was by a spare mustache, suggested wit. Samuel's face, on the other hand, was pudgy, his best expression slightly embarrassed, his eyebrows pinched in worry.

It appears that their parents were not unaware of a lack of passion between the two and that the wedding was accordingly dispatched with some desperation. Arranged marriages, for openers, were all but archaic by that time. Though this one had the undeniable virtue of keeping the More estates in the family, the terms also bespoke a certain cold practicality. Unlike many unions, which saw the parents of the bride agreeing to "table" the couple—that is, to house them—Samuel and Katharine's marriage settlement specifically asked for the arrangement to be conducted "without tabling," thus allowing Samuel to remain at his own Linley Hall, ten miles to the west of Larden Hall, at his leisure. The iciness shows through in the family finances as well: the new-lyweds were given separate yearly allowances of twenty pounds each, as if to emphasize the unimportance of inquiring too closely into each other's affairs.

The wedding took place on February 11, 1611, in the Shipton church, under the conventional square wooden tower. Katharine and Samuel spoke the words of promise and faith and forever, the Anglican minister blessed their union, and the fact was re-corded in the parish records. Everything else then began to hap-pen off the record—or, if you prefer, in the tunnel.

IN SOME WAYS, little has changed in this border county since your day. The roads, though paved now, are still largely empty.

The sheep are still there, too, their shaggy wool giving them the aspect of wandering strays. Shropshire today is still very far from the tensions of world events, and still quite conservative in its politics.

When I made a pilgrimage there, my guide was Donald L. Harris, a retired schoolteacher and the preeminent authority on Richard's early childhood. A man of brisk opinions and generous impulses (who with his wispy white hair and square jawbore a marked resemblance to my grandfather), Don showed me around, allowing me to lock horns with him on arcane historical disputes as we went.

One of our requisite stops was, of course, Larden Hall—or rather, what is left of it. The original Larden Hall stood until 1968, when it was dismantled and delivered to a Texas outfit called Canterbury Interiors, which apparently turned around and sold it off piecemeal. The new Larden Hall is a specimen of serviceable brickwork dropped into a spectacular pastoral, inhabited by a Mrs. Jones. When I was introduced as the descendant of the first tenants, she chirped, "My! You're looking well!"

The original manor, located behind Mrs. Jones's home, was not looking at all well, however. The rooms where Katharine played out her flamboyant drama and where her son Richard crawled, then walked, have been reduced to a whiskery stone hutch about the size of a walk-in cooler, studded with unexpected doorknobs.

Don offered the only postmortem possible. "It's a shame is what it is," he said.

The other ancestral home—the one that passed down from Samuel's side of the family—has fared considerably better. An eighteenth-century Palladian manor some few miles west of Larden Hall, Linley Hall radiates stability, if not grandeur. Approaching it, one passes a serene pond stocked with swans.

But there are peculiarities beneath this stately exterior. Upon entering the front door, I immediately became aware of a gruesome sight. High above me, on the stairwell wall, hung a still life depicting an assortment of fowl, all of them dead. At the center of this painting—and clearly its subject—is a swan, still bleeding from a wound at its neck.

This seemed to me to be someone's idea of a sick joke, because the swan was, and is, the symbol of the More family. Traditionally it appears on the coat of arms, in the impossible argot of heraldry, "Sable a Swan argent beaked and legged Or, a bordure engrailed of the last," and is accompanied by the motto *Deus dabit*, meaning "God will provide." Usually, the swan is not portrayed as being dead.

I had come to Linley Hall to research a portion of the More family papers—a welter of documents in boxes, most of them gathered by Sir Jasper More, the heir of Linley Hall until his death a few years ago. During my visit, Justin Coldwell, the present heir, managed to project a splendid imitation of English gentry—casual, indifferent, immeasurably droll.

"Ahh, Richard More," he said, consulting the ceiling before handing me a plate of Italian artichokes. "Wasn't he the one who went to America and behaved dreadfully?"

I immediately felt at ease around Justin, so later that day, when he offered me a ride back to the bed-and-breakfast in nearby Shrewsbury, where I was staying, I took the opportunity to ask him about the painting.

"Yes, well, dead animals are cheaper than live ones," he quipped, gripping the wheel with his gloves. It was by the Dutch painter Pieter van Oordt, he said, and had been housed in Spain just before Justin bought it on auction at Christie's.

I asked him if the swan's fate was a conscious comment on how he felt about the family.

"Well, aren't you a clever boy!" he replied without dropping a beat. The dead swan, he explained, symbolized the end of the More line, because he was descended from a collateral branch. With the confidence only true gentry can muster, he added, "I'm actually sort of an impostor, you see."

I thought about that for a moment. Then, well aware of my American accent, I said, "You know, I *am* a direct descendant in the More line—from Katharine's side. Think I should I get myself a painting of a living swan?"

Justin was most amused at the idea. He continued to chuckle the rest of the way to Shrewsbury, where he dispatched me with the utmost civility. From there he hastened onto a train to London, where, it seemed to me, he had some terribly unimportant appointments to keep.

In that, he was keeping up on an old, old tradition.

IF, as the bard put it, all the world's a stage, then London in the 1610s was stage center. In the previous century the rural manors had been the lifeblood of the culture, but at the dawn of the seventeenth century (granted, I speak of the times before your Ancient Beginning), London was exploding with vitality. The textile monopolies of Elizabeth's reign had produced a wealthy merchant class (to which the mothers of both Samuel and Katharine belonged), and from the cloth they yielded came an array of fashions so diverse as to suggest costumery rather than dress.

What an outpouring of popish pretense there was! Ruffs grew so large that their diameter was restricted at royal occasions, literally to allow enough berth for people to enter and exit a room. In Cheapside, the profusion of fabrics was such that "even those of base birth and below the yeomanry in standing, went daily in silks, velvets, damasks, taffetas, and such-like," making it impossible, as some noted loudly, to know anyone's rank on the street.[2]

Of course, where there are costumes, actors soon must follow, and so they did. It was not uncommon for country squires—and Samuel More was exactly that—to be away from their manors, hobnobbing in London, for two years at a stretch. By 1633 so many squires were abandoning the home fires that a law was passed requiring them to spend at least part of the year on their estates.

Samuel, even in his unformed adolescence, was as avid a city-goer as any, and just as keen on making his way in the world. His specific entry came through the Zouches, a family of considerable influence at court. Sometime before 1616, when Samuel began to "forbear" his wife—a verb meaning "to avoid"—he took a position as the personal secretary to Edward, Lord Zouch, a post he kept until his lordship's death in 1625.[3]

If Samuel needed a change from his situation at home, Lord Zouch provided a first-rate opportunity. Zouch had spent his youth on the Continent as a self-admitted wastrel, and he continued in that vein well into his maturity—abandoning a wife who did not please him, reigning over the Council of the Marches of Wales like a despot, even deigning to be interred in the end beside his wine cellar, a decision that his friend the playwright Ben Johnson made hay of in his epitaph:

> Wherever I die, oh, here may I lie
> Along by my good Lord Zouche,
> That when I am dry, to the tap I may hie,
> And so back again to my couch.[4]

Because he could offer the thrill of stag hunting at his country-seat in Bramshill, Zouch also attracted the ever wavering attention of King James.[5] Zouch's favorite cousin, Sir Edward Zouch, further sharpened the royal interest with masques at his city residence, a fine-brick palace not far from Woking that had formerly been a getaway for Edward IV, Henry VII, and Henry VIII.

These were nighttime affairs: on a nearby hilltop, a tower with a kind of lantern acted as beacon to guide King James on his way.[6] Some years before Samuel arrived in London, one such affair—typical in kind if not in measure—began with an actress toppling into the lap of the king of Denmark and ended with the characters of Love and Charity "sick and spewing" from alcohol poisoning. "The entertainment and show went forward," a friend of Lord

Zouch's had remarked, "and most of the presenters went backward, or fell down; wine did so occupy their upper chambers."[7]

Falling in with the Zouch retinue, Samuel could easily drown his worries in the pageantry of it all—and "abandon a wife who did not please him" in the bargain. Love threw up, Charity gagged, and a country squire had a chance in life.

But you were interested in confessions; let us move to them.

ALMOST EVERYTHING that is known about Richard More's early childhood comes from a document written by Samuel in 1622 in response to a petition by Katharine to Lord Chief Justice James Lee, which demanded an explanation for what had become of her children. Katharine's petition has since been lost, and Samuel's Declaration does not entirely fill in the gaps. Crucial information is missing, and the sequence of events as described is maddeningly vague. Samuel's Declaration also represents the point of view of an angry man, with no particular need to see his wife's position. Say, then, that it provides enough evidence to be more than a blank slate, and enough mystery to encourage the taking of sides.[8]

As Samuel began to forbear his wife, his wife began to have children in rapid succession. Her first child, Ellen, was born on May 12, 1612. A son, Jasper, followed on August 8, 1613. Perhaps things continued to go smoothly between the Mores even then. But by the time Richard More was baptized, on November 13, 1614, a cruel physical fact was becoming all too plain. As Samuel put it, there was a "likeness and resemblance of most of the said children in their visages and lineaments of their bodies" to a certain Jacob Blakeway, "a fellow of meane parentage & condicon."

Men will make their bid at immortality in the hearts of women, and Jacob Blakeway, in choosing Katharine for a lover, was one of the few who succeeded for only that reason. The son of Edward

Blakeway, Jacob was baptized on July 25, 1583, in Stanton Long Parish, a community immediately to the south of Shipton. In 1608 he and his father renewed the lease on a parcel of sloped land owned by Katharine More's father, Jasper. Jacob later apparently worked it in some capacity, although he lived in nearby Brockton. Later on, the lease ended up among Samuel's effects with his own signature affixed to the back—an elegant way of stating who was really boss.

Other than these facts and a few scattershot appearances in Samuel's Declaration, history has little to say of Jacob. He appears only as a distant figure on the landscape, his muscular outline stirring the heart of the wife and, eventually, making the husband's blood boil. We may, however, ponder those "visages and lineaments" of which Samuel wrote, and find ourselves resting on the eyes. Samuel's portrait shows a man with dark eyes—dark green perhaps, but probably brown, as his father's eyes clearly are in *his* portrait. We might infer, then, that Jacob's eyes were blue.

An uneasy sequence is thus suggested. Like all children, Richard More did not look like anyone in particular when he was an infant. The damning evidence—say, a small nose that contrasted with the Pinocchio-like protuberances of Samuel—already written in the faces of Ellen and Jasper, would not yet have been apparent. For the moment, Samuel could only look upon the young Richard with a suspicion of what he would *become*.

Before he knew how to speak, Richard More was being observed not in wonderment but for the crime he symbolized a crime that was only slowly coming into view. Would his lineaments confirm the portent of those eyes gazing up from the cradle, or would they contradict it?

THE ROLE Jacob Blakeway played in history remains a sensitive subject in Shropshire to this day. Everyone freely admits that he

and Katharine had an affair, the sultry rhythms of which produced several illegitimate children. Yet some things are still too
disturbing to be asserted.

On our continuing tour, Don Harris took me next to the church
in Shipton, where Richard More was baptized. I stood at the bap-
tismal font, resting my hands on its edge, and tried to imagine a
baby's skin against its coarse texture. Before leaving, I entered my
name into the church register as a descendant of Richard More.

So far, so good. From there, we proceeded to the church where
Blakeway was baptized, in nearby Stanton Long. We walked
around inside for a moment, feeling the coolness of the stone walls
and otherwise absorbing the atmosphere of posterity. As in Shipton, I leafed through the church register and stopped at the page
where the writing ended. Picking up a pen, I signed my name.
Then, below it, I wrote, "Descendant of Jacob Blakeway."

I heard Don try to suppress gasp. "They'll probably tear that
page from the book!" he said as we got back to the car.

The idea of tearing a few pages from the church records may
well have crossed Samuel's mind as well, once his suspicions were
aroused. Yet, oddly, he did nothing to vent his rage. He did not
lay a rough hand on his wife, even though his law—unlike mine,
or yours for that matter—would have permitted it. He did not
even show any renewed interest in settling down at Shipton. Instead, he simply warned Blakeway away from his wife and asked
her friends to keep an eye on her.

Of course, it could not have helped when word of Samuel's
domestic problems reached the ears of the London elite. The point
was not his broken heart; he did not show the remotest interest
in being near his wife. What made the matter intolerable was the
physicality of it: the children looked like someone else. They carried the message of his shame wherever they went, and as time
went on, they were likely to carry it farther afield. Samuel all but
admitted as much later when he wrote that their very existence
caused him a loss of "preferrment"—that is, his chances for ad-

vancement into the upper ranks at court. And yet he seemed intent on running away from his problems whenever he could.

Up to a point, that is. According to his statement, his troubles—his "vexacions," as he called them—began in 1616. It can be no coincidence that this was the same year that he turned twenty-one and thus, as the eldest son, gained control over the combined estates of Linley and Larden. And over the children of his wife as well. Such were the laws in the old country: if a woman's husband stood on English soil at the time her child was born, he was considered the father, no matter what the secrets of the night happened to be. Samuel did not have to control his wife, or even assert his manhood, when the law could do it for him. He had been waiting for his moment, and it would soon be at hand.

Sometime about February 1616, Samuel returned from London to Shropshire, riding, as was usual for a gentleman, in a four-wheeled carriage with open sides, attended by a coachman and two footmen. To get to Shropshire, one traveled north, either by Oxford and High Wycombe or by Banbury and Aylesbury, to Warwick—a two-day journey that covered a distance of 120 miles. His estate lay one day further off and was reached by smaller roads that branched away from the main route to Chester. Looking out on the English night from that last country tavern (not ten miles from the house where the relatively unknown playwright William Shakespeare lay dying), Samuel had plenty to ponder.

And then the time for pondering was over. Once in Shropshire, Samuel sat down with his father, Richard More of Linley, and they formally exchanged the family holdings, father to son.

But perhaps you would not say "formally." Perhaps you would say deviously. The handoff, after all, was achieved through the pretense that Richard was suing his son. For this unfilial act, Samuel received nine hundred pounds and, tangentially,

50 messauges, 14 cottages, 11 toftis, 2 mills, 1 dove cot, 50 gardens, 50 orchards, 1200a of land, 200a of meadow, 600a of pas-

ture, 300a of wood, 300a of furze and heath and 40s worth of
rent with appurtenances in Linley, alias Linlege, Beache, Norton,
Peldradley, Beachmoore, Upper Larden, Nether Larden, Shipton, Brocton, Moorehowse, Sifton Wall, Under Eywood, Ben-
thyes, Moore and Mooreswood, with free warren and view of
the frankpledge with appurtenances in Linley, and the advow-
son of the church of Moore in the manor of Downton with appurtenances and 10 messauges, 10 gardens, 10 orchards, 50a of
land, 100a of meadow, 50a of pasture, 200a of woodland, 500a
of heath and furze with appurtenances in Downton and Bur-
rington Herefordshire.[9]

Samuel was now in possession of his land, and a man in possession of land was able to *act*.

By this time Katharine was seven months pregnant with her
fourth child and quickly progressing from rotund to bedridden.
That Samuel stayed his hand at this moment suggests a certain
tolerance for the sanctity of motherhood. It also suggests an almost
unbearable pressure mounting in the More family.

When the day finally came, Katharine sat in what was known
as an "obstetric chair"—an otherwise ordinary stool with the bottom cut out, leaving only the rim to catch the weight of her hips.
The back of this chair was girded with whatever clothing or rags
were at hand. The midwife, her hands anointed with almond oil
or the "oyle of white Lyllies," leaned close to Katharine's ear and
whispered "sweet woordes."[10] Then, drawing from a prayer book
of the day, *The Monument of Matrones*, by Thomas Bentley, husband and wife began to intone her sins—nominally those of general motherhood, though for them, a set of charged accusations
under cover of cosmological truth as well.

We can almost hear the grimness creeping into Katharine's
voice as she recited:

Shall I be the grave of my child: Shall I give death the fruit of
my bodie, for the sins of my soule; and my fourth born for the
transgressions of my youth?[11]

And grimmer still the irony postpartum, as she cautioned herself in the third person, to "cast not thy minde upon ruffians lest
thou destroy thine heritage."[12]

Did either Samuel or Katharine drop the farce at any point to
name the specific transgressions? If so, the baptism of Mary More
was nonetheless entered into the Shipton parish register on April
16, 1616, and as with the other three More children, that book
solemnly records Samuel as the father. Yet Katharine's admission
to Samuel could not have come much later than that moment,
because the More family shifted abruptly into more troubled waters.[13]

A headstrong woman like Katharine was not apt to have confessed of her own volition, or even under pressure from Samuel.
Perhaps Blakeway, unable to resist temptation, came sniffing
around the house to see his newborn child. A masked but loving
glance, a certain quality of touch—at that point, there would have
been no hiding it. At any rate, Samuel, no longer deferring to a
pregnant woman, felt emboldened to accuse Katharine outright.

When he did so, he discovered just how strong a force his wife
really was: Katharine snapped back that *he* was the impostor, that
she and Jacob were actually the ones who were married! They
had, she insisted, a "precontract."

A precontract was actually a fairly strong defense. In England
at the time, no ceremony was required for a marriage to be valid.
A man and a woman had only to say to each other, "I receive you
as mine," to be married. It was not an engagement. Having ut-
tered their vows, neither person could marry anyone else without
committing bigamy. They did, however, need to be able to produce at least two witnesses to their vows, and Samuel understand-

ably asked her to produce them. Katharine, unable to do so, shrugged and told Samuel that "it was all one before god."

But it was not all one before the law. Four days after the baptism of Mary, Samuel took an action known as cutting the entail, which involved the immediate repudiation of Katharine's children and their disinheritance from any rights to the combined More properties. This feat accomplished, he placed the children under the care of one of his father's tenants in Shipton and put Katharine on an allowance of twenty "marks" a year (though this sum may have actually represented her original allowance, to which she was presumably still entitled), on the condition that she stay away from Jacob. Then he quit Shropshire altogether, to live more or less permanently with Lord Zouch in London.

This is some stunningly swift maneuvering for a man who had sat idle through five years of unhappy wedlock. But Katharine was not entirely unprepared, either: she, too, could avail herself of those labyrinthine laws of old.

On the day that Samuel disinherited the children, the elder Richard More agreed in writing to maintain "the grandchildren of the said J.M. [Jasper More] for the 21 years."[14] This careful mention of Katharine's late father served, among other things, to keep a fifty-pound annuity flowing from his fortune into the hands of Katharine's childless uncle, Matthew Smale, for as long as her male children lived.[15] For all intents and purposes, young Jasper and Richard More were the only living shoots of the Larden family line, and as long as that continued to be so, Katharine could expect an ally—and perhaps some small dispensation—from her uncle, who, in addition to having no heirs, lived in far-off London. She would need that alliance, because the worst was still to come.

According to Samuel's Declaration, sometime between April and June, Katharine went to the tenant's dwelling into which her children—Richard, Jasper, Ellen, and Mary—had been sequestered and, in a hail of murderous oaths, "did teare the cloathes from their backes."

Did tear the clothes from their backs. Unless Katharine was certifiably psychotic, which she is demonstrably not in her actions elsewhere, this ripping and tearing must refer to a heartbreaking tussle in which she tried to regain custody of her children.

And yet, seeing that the children were in danger, the elder Richard all but condemned them to it. Samuel's Declaration uses the word *forbear* again here:

> Samuel's parents were continually vexed & grieued they forbearinge to take the sd children into their house to avoide her slaunders (yf it should have pleased god to visit any of them wth death) of beinge murtherers of them: and wth all to shunne the continuall sight of their great grief of such a spurious broode.

In some ways, the inclusion of this passage in Samuel's Declaration is the most revelatory thing about it. Why, after all, would his father be more concerned for the children's well-being in his own house than in his tenant's dwelling? Wouldn't he be responsible either way, because of his agreement to maintain (clothe, feed, house) the children until they turned twenty-one? And weren't the children in greater danger at the tenant's house, where physical conflicts were manifestly taking place? That the elder Richard agreed to maintain the children under duress, then refused to take reasonable steps in that direction, almost cries out that he did not want them maintained. The Linley Mores were dreaming of dead swans.

For the next four years, the More children lived under the weight of this dream, in the house of a tenant who, if kindly or cruel, was not as well-to-do as the masters of Larden and Linley. No more wandering through the palatial rooms of Larden Hall; the architecture shifted now to the thatched roof and the lean-to.

When this period began, Ellen was approaching the age of four and Jasper the age of three—both sufficiently grown to remember the fight between their mother and their caretaker. Not so for

Richard, who at one and a half would later only be able to recall the tearing of clothes and the hurling of "slaunders" as a feeling, a signal tightening of the skin.

But sometime during those years, Richard became old enough to walk and therefore to wonder at the strange rocks that littered the soil around his new home. Groaned up from some antediluvian orgy, these stones still bore the marks of an age when Shropshire lay beneath the Atlantic: bits of shale with seashells neatly imprinted, rib by rib, as if sending a message from the coast.

Richard was beginning to get his education.

WHEN KATHARINE claimed that her love for Jacob was "all one before god," she was, in effect, saying that their precontract was valid with or without witnesses. Intentionally or not, this was a departure from standing matrimonial law, not least because her insistence on the validity of her precontract automatically made her marriage to Samuel an act of bigamy. As a result, Samuel was able to file charges against Jacob in the Court of the High Commission.

Did your own church elders ever speak of that court, I wonder? Did they tell how Archbishop Laud had used it as an instrument against the Puritans, how it resembled, and was often compared with, the Spanish Inquisition? No jury, no lawyer, judges having the right to ask defendants almost anything, then imprison them in roofless shelters in winter, shackled, starved, all for a religious belief?

One did not want to be a defendant in the Court of the High Commission—and Samuel knew it. He had filed the same charges with another court, the Council of the Marches of Wales, where Lord Zouch reigned unquestioned. Why not leave the matter there, unless he hoped to frighten the devil from Katharine and her overactive Jacob?

If Samuel had meant to extract a confession, he achieved his aim admirably. Through the help of an unnamed friend (perhaps that uncle again), Katharine and Jacob were granted an audience before the chancellor of the diocese of Hereford—a local bishop who was legally answerable to the High Commission—in hopes of avoiding an appearance before the High Commission itself.

At first, the couple sought, as Samuel put it, to "obteine a divource and to marry (as it seemeth)." But this line of defense must have failed, because before passing out of the bishop's jurisdiction, they obtained a commutation of sentence, "to free the said Blakeway from any informacon in the high Commission court for the said offence." Though the "said offence" is not specifically named in Samuel's Declaration, the commutation of sentence amounted to a charge of adultery, which would seem to point to bigamy as the original charge.

Their confession, translated from Renaissance law Latin:

> 14 June 1616, Both the aforementioned James [Jacob] Blakeway and the previously mentioned Catherine More were convicted, against who(m) a title [the main heading in the law code] or a criminal charge of living an incontinent life or adultery had been brought; they confessed that they had together, often, and on repeated occasions lived an incontinent life and committed adultery together.[16]

As compensation, the lovers had their penalty reduced to a twenty-pound fine, as long as they stopped seeing each other. Samuel, however, pressed onward, and it came out during a trial before the High Commission that Katharine and Jacob were still meeting "in secret and obscure places." Caught out in a lie, their response was to get a pardon from the king.

Royal pardons, like baronetages, were currently available for a fee,[17] so it must have been Katharine who secured theirs. It is also here that we get the first glimmers of the children's future: the man who signed Jacob Blakeway's pardon, Henry Marten, was doing double duty in 1616 as a judge of the High Court of Admiralty, which handled cases related to the high seas and the colonies.[18]

As far as Samuel was concerned, he and Katharine could continue to go about their lives separately: there was no need for a divorce. The lovers were making any such arrangement increasingly difficult, however. In fact, the real wonder is that, for all the furniture broken, Katharine and Jacob found a way not to produce any more children. Pardon in hand, Jacob began to strut with impunity before "Samuell's friends" and actually to inhabit the Larden estate, which quite obviously belonged to Samuel. As for Katharine's friends, whom Samuel had asked to be his eyes and ears, they proved to be worse than useless: rather than monitoring the lovers, they actually began to assist them in their revelries. And if any of them was among the witnesses who later proved "the very act of adultery," as Samuel claimed, he was doing something more than assisting!

Thus was an estimable estate wrecked as the blue-coated servants waited on their imperious mistress and her intrepid lover. To complete the air of the day:

> With a new hall where the old hall stood,
> And a new chimney that burns neither coals nor wood,
> And a new shovel-a-bord table whereon meat never stood . . . [19]

Eventually, seeing that tolerance would never serve, Samuel again roused himself from his torpor, and again, the critical violation was not of his heart but of his property. At least that was how he put it: Jacob had been carousing "about the howses & about the grounds of the sd Samuel." Accordingly, he charged Jacob with trespassing, breaking and entering, and other "enormities." For "treadinge his grasse," Samuel assessed the damage at ten pounds, a modest sum that belied more serious charges behind the thousand-pound claim.

The trial began in early 1619. Jacob pleaded not guilty and managed to hold his ground until charges of adultery (those handy "other enormities") were brought and a jury found against him to the sum of four hundred pounds. Suddenly the lovers were cornered.

Did Jacob steal away without a word in the middle of the night? Did he go at Katharine's bidding, so as not to suffer along with her? Did he say good-bye to his children, each in turn, whispering solemn promises through rum-soaked breath?

The records offer no clue other than Samuel's remark that Jacob ran—"to prevent execucon fledd." The appearance of Henry Marten's signature on his earlier pardon suggests that he may at some point have been presented with the option of forced emigration— that is, deportation to Virginia as a bond slave. But if that is what happened, Jacob must have changed his name or died en route, because he has not surfaced in any of the New World records. For all intents and purposes, Richard More's natural father vanished from the face of the earth.

Having gained the upper hand both emotionally and legally, Samuel now filed for divorce in the Court of Audience. Toward the end of June 1619, husband and wife were again involved in litigation. Katharine, fighting on her own behalf for the first time, prolonged the proceedings with what Samuel deemed "friuolous allegacons" but may well have been attempts at a better settlement for herself and her children. In any event, she failed and the divorce was awarded in June or July 1619. (The records for this case have perished.)

We next come upon Katharine appealing the divorce in the High Court of Delegates, with no abatement of stamina whatsoever. Crying "Crocadills teares," as Samuel put it, she insisted that her family had brought good money to the marriage. Samuel countered that her family had brought less than was promised— only one hundred pounds a year—and that, furthermore, Katharine's father had been spending part of that amount all along. (The elder Jasper More had died in January 1614, but his widow, Elizabeth, continued to receive a dispensation.)

Back and forth they went, then back and forth again. Katharine must have relocated to London for the trial—perhaps to her uncle Mathew Smale's manor in Paddington—because the Act Books record no fewer than twelve actions for their case between late December 1619 and July 8, 1620, when it was finally dismissed. This was ostensibly the longest time she had ever been more than a few miles away from her sons and daughters. For Samuel, already a Londoner, the trial was a burden of another variety: as he pointed out later, he had been compelled to pay the costs for both sides.

Certainly, the ordeal was exhausting for both of them. But their tribulations were still not at an end, because there remained in Samuel's possession a gaggle of children whose very sight disgusted him. And that he simply could not abide.

2

Religious Company

It may be demanded how it came to pass that so many
wicked persons and profane people should so quickly
come over into this land . . . There were sent by their
friends some under hope that they would be made better;
others that they might be eased of such burdens, and they
kept from shame at home that would necessarily follow
their dissolute courses.

—William Bradford, *Of Plymouth Plantation*

THE IDEA of sending Katharine's children away was already in the air, if not the record books, while her appeal
was in progress. Indeed, it seems that her appeal and the
preparations for a transatlantic voyage could have been linked
through the courts themselves. The Court of Delegates, which
heard Katharine's appeal, had a long-standing relationship with
the High Court of Admiralty, on which Judge Henry Marten sat,[1]
and at least two of the four commissioners who decided Katharine's appeal—Sir William Bird and Dr. Barnabe Gooch—had connections beyond the seas as well.[2]

The circumstances of Barnabe Gooch, master of Magdalen College,[3] are particularly compelling. On July 23, 1620—two weeks
before the *Mayflower* sailed—the Privy Council (the king's inner
circle of advisers) proposed the formation of the Council for New
England to oversee the colonization of "northern Virginia," an

area that effectively covered all of America north of present-day Long Island.[4] Not long after, Barnabe Gooch became secretary of this council,[5] and eventually the council awarded him a land patent in New England—one of the so-called Palatinate Patents. Interestingly enough, this tract corresponded closely to the area where the *Mayflower* passengers settled: an indistinct stretch between Boston Harbor and Rhode Island.

Gooch, one may assume, was already abreast of colonization attempts by the time Katharine stood before him in court.

The same must be said for Lord Zouch, who was not only Samuel's employer but a peer of Gooch's. In addition to his longstanding position in the Virginia Company (the older company from which the Council for New England sprang as an offshoot), Zouch was a member of both the Privy Council and the Council for New England. As late as June 13, 1619 (by which time Jacob Blakeway had lost his case against Zouch's secretary and disappeared to points unknown), Zouch and his fellow Privy Councillors were looking to settle "a Plantation upon the River of the Amazones in the West Indies."[6] On his own charge, Zouch sent a ship, the *Silver Falcon*, to Virginia that same year and commissioned its captain in a letter dictated to "Sa: Mores."[7]

Shipping marginal citizens off on perilous voyages was not an alien notion to Samuel's employer, either. The Privy Council had been sending condemned prisoners to various budding English colonies since 1617, if not earlier.[8] Lord Zouch's cousin Sir Edward, as Knight Marshall, had been assigned on at least one occasion to ship "an hundred dissolute persons" to Virginia.[9] These hapless souls were to be apprenticed to a trade or entered into servitude, although the implicit plan was to rid England of its troublemakers.

From Henry Marten to Barnabe Gooch, with the rhyme of a Zouch ever present in the background—this was a network of highly placed connections, to which one must surely add the elder Richard More, Samuel's father, who had a stake in the Virginia Company as early as 1618–19, when his name appears on a list of investors along with his in-laws Thomas and Roger Harris.[10] If Samuel More wanted to have four waifs shipped off as indentured servants, he certainly had the ability to set such a plan in motion. The entire weight of English power stood behind him, ready to be unleashed whenever he gave the word.

Yet strictly speaking, this is not what happened to the More children.

SOME HAVE SUGGESTED that Samuel deliberately chose to send the children on the *Mayflower* because of the religious makeup of its passengers. This interpretation rests mainly on Samuel's claim, in his Declaration, that he placed the children in the hands of "honest & religous people" and on his later activities as a Puritan during the English Civil War.[11]

The reasons for such an argument are understandable. What is at stake is the origin myth of a nation, your tale of the Ancient Beginning from which everything else has flowered. Any aspersions cast on this story can serve only to weaken it, and so to weaken the values it represents: bravery, determination, idealism. Unfortunately, the events of 1620 do not really allow Samuel the latitude to be noble. If anything, they portray a man in a hurry.

In December 1619, when Katharine's appeal began, the people who some centuries later came to be known as the Pilgrims had been in contact with the Virginia Company—the corporation legitimized by the king to settle in "northern Virginia"—about a voyage to the New World, but they had yet to express any desire in having outsiders go with them. Nor was their ability to sail certain until February 1620, when they received permission from the Virginia Company. And it was not until later again, on some uncertain date after June 11, that Londoners of any religious persuasion were invited to sail on the *Mayflower*.

On June 19 either Samuel was preparing to accompany the ailing Lord Zouch to Bath or he was already there, and there he was still on July 8, when Katharine's appeal was finally over and done with.[12] As if to make his lack of interest in the proceedings patently clear, Samuel had not particularly bothered to attend Katharine's appeal while it was in progress, either: one of the lawyers on the case asked that he be threatened with excommunication if his nonappearance continued.[13] Whatever his religious disposition, he did not have much chance to become aware of the *Mayflower*.

Two options present themselves. Either Samuel entered into the agreement in the middle of June—that is, *before* the Court of Delegates had rejected Katharine's appeal of the divorce, which looks rather cynical of him—or he clinched the deal from Zouch's country retreat near Bath, a fairly remote locale for handling fast-breaking developments.[14] Of course, he may have taken the virtues of the *Mayflower* passengers into consideration, but this was mostly a matter of good luck; the emphasis was on the *next* ship out rather than on the best one.

Control from a distance, allowing the engines of the law to do his work for him—this sort of behavior is certainly in keeping with the actions of a man who could move to London at the height of his marital crisis. Katharine, on the other hand, had rejected her arranged marriage, flown in the face of the law, and carelessly flaunted her passion, and so, of course, in the final hour she pleaded with everything she had.

The minutes to her appeal contain precious little beyond boilerplate, because the judges at the Court of Delegates typically did not record their cogitations.[15] It is known, for example, that Katharine sought alimony[16] but not whether she got it, or whether it was the amount she wanted. It is also known that the divorce was definitively upheld, but not why. Nevertheless, the drawn-out nature of the case speaks to a fierce tenacity, and if credit is to be laid anywhere, it must go to Katharine for extracting from the court, whether directly or by sheer attrition, something resembling an inheritance for her children.

The agreement signed by Samuel did not stint on terms. For an enterprise in which the minimum investment was ten pounds per person (double for those who paid for provisions), Samuel paid a whopping one hundred pounds and made the "spurious broode" full partners in the planned colony, with the promise that they "should be sufficiently kept and maintained with meate drink apparrell lodginge and other necessaries and that at the end a seaven Yeers the[y] should have 50 acres of land a peece in the Countrey of Virginia."

This contract was highly unusual, perhaps even unique in the British colonies. Though a fifty-acre allotment was standard for planters—that is, for the people who actually went to colonies like Virginia, as opposed to the adventurers, who bankrolled such expeditions—it was usually the case that planters were over the age of sixteen. But here was a case in which unwanted children stood equal with the adults.

If Katharine had lost her lover and her family—and with them, any kind of comfortable life for herself—she had nonetheless secured for her children that fundamental, all-important thing: land of their own.

The extra twenty pounds (over and above the double share for each child) seem to have been purely the work of Thomas Weston—a man who, as we shall see, was both quick of tongue and short on cash. Yet Samuel made no complaint about the cost this time. When word came that Katharine's histrionics were at an end, Samuel immediately sent word to Shipton for one of his cousins, Paul Harris, to transport the four More children to London, and specifically into the care of Weston, the organizer of the *Mayflower* voyage. Then, exhausted from years of calumny and legal wrangling, he rejoined his lord and tried to forget the entire ordeal.

On July 13, 1620, five days after the divorce appeal was rejected, Lord Zouch wrote instructions to Samuel from the London suburb of Clerkenwell, requesting him "to receive back a gelding, which Mr. Lougher seized, but is now willing to restore."[17]

Zouch's secretary was apparently getting back into the swing of things. Still, it must have smarted whenever Samuel recalled that, thanks to his ex-wife's machinations, one of London's confidence men had fleeced him. A hundred pounds! Two years later he was still referring to Katharine as "that wicked woman."

None of this was known to the More children, of course, as they stood by a coach in Shropshire that had not produced their mother, waiting to be carried off to London. (Given the speed with which Samuel acted, she had next to no time to get to Shropshire—if she knew of the need to rescue her children at all.) As a member of the "other side" of the family, Paul Harris, the adult charged with transporting them, would not have been one for consoling words.[18] No, now was the time for the sturdy old servant accompanying them to leap in with vast reserves of awkwardness and inaccuracies. Their mother was descended from kings, they were special people in a special time, they were going somewhere exciting and magical—and Mr. Weston, oh yes, Mr. Weston was a fine man, a fine fine man, they would see—the ruse becoming more and more strained throughout the interminable ride and the stops at local inns, until at last the fantastic panorama of London came into view and, exhausted beyond exhilaration, they pulled up to a house in the busy ward of Aldgate.

The coach stopped, and Paul Harris got out. Presently, the children were delivered into the hands of a stranger. A bond exchanged hands. Then—just as quick as that—Harris rattled off in the carriage, leaving Ellen, Jasper, Richard, and Mary More behind in their latest alien abode.

THE MORE CHILDREN remained in Weston's house for a short time, perhaps only a week, yet the stay remained vivid enough in Richard's mind that he remembered it more than half a century later.

Small wonder. Few historical figures have been better fitted for the role of wicked uncle than Thomas Weston. Born in Rug\, England, about 1576,[19] Weston was admitted into the Ironmong\ Company on March 21, 1611, and apparently never mongered any iron again. In 1615 he persuaded Edward Pickering, at the time a shopkeeper in Cheapside, to become his agent in Holland, and together they began importing a variety of nonconformist tracts that were too seditious to be printed at home (nonconformism referring to any view antithetical to the Church of England).

That was about as innocent as Weston ever managed to be. In early 1619 another of his business agents, Philomen Powell, imported thirty tons of alum, unloading it at night to avoid customs duties. Unfortunately, Powell got caught, and when the alum was confiscated, a pair of shortchanged buyers took their case to the Exchequer Court.

While this was going on, Weston did what he did best under pressure: he left the country. Specifically, he made a trip to Leiden, Holland, where Pickering had recently married a woman belonging to a Puritan sect called the Separatists. These were the Englishmen and -women living in exile for their religious views and hoping to gain passage to America with the Virginia Company. Weston, never one to miss the main chance, convinced the Separatists to deal with him instead and promptly drew up articles of agreement.

There was nothing unusual about the financing of Weston's enterprise, dubbed the Merchant Adventurers. The Virginia Company had drawn up similar stipulations and then found a group of colonists who would labor to meet them. The only problem with Weston's scheme was that he had no capital to get the thing started.

Meanwhile, Pickering was beginning to make noises about unpaid debts, which put Weston in a more desperate way again. Hoping to attract more adventurers to the Virginia voyage (and so to pay Paul with Peter's front money), he amended the articles of agreement with the Separatists, striking two clauses: one that gave planters two days a week to do as they wished, another that let them keep their own houses at the end of seven years. This sudden alteration caused considerable anxiety among the Separatists, and when Robert Cushman, their agent in London, agreed to the changes without their consent, he earned their harsh condemnation.[20] Though Richard was blissfully unaware of it, his promised fifty acres had been summarily thrown into limbo, and there they would stay for forty years.

And still the worst of it was yet to come. By June 11 Weston had already chosen the larger of the two ships they would need. Three days later he abruptly withdrew his personal capital from the venture—perhaps to stimulate investment by others, perhaps because he panicked, or perhaps because he simply wanted to put the cheap back in Cheapside. Then he opened the voyage to all comers, and potential passengers with no connection to the Separatists began appearing in London with ten, twenty, or thirty pounds to invest.

The whole endeavor was a mess. There was no clear chain of command among the Merchant Adventurers, no agreement about the terms, and a stunning shortage of funding. Eventually, the London contingent took matters into their own hands and elected a man named Christopher Martin to head their effort, only to see Martin temporarily vanish to parts unknown.

It was into this shambles that the More children were dropped, needing some assurance that they were not destined for a beheading. To say they did not get it is an understatement. By Samuel's agreement, they were to be handed over first to Philemon Powell—whose background as a smuggler lent the entire process an unsavory air—and Robert Cushman, who jointly agreed to find them guardians from among the passengers. In the meantime, they stayed at Weston's house in Aldgate, watching the disaster unfold through their innocent eyes.

Exactly who their new parents would be was not obvious from the proceedings. Indeed, we can rest assured that the First Comers knew little of the circumstances of their last-minute charges until it was already too late to turn them away. By July 19, when the larger of the two ships arrived, the principal organizers of the voyage were all scattered over different cities—Southampton, London, Kent, Leiden. Weston himself was disingenuously approaching various parties to ask what was going on, "as if he were hardly an accessory to the undertaking," then cursing them behind their backs for refusing to accept his "reasonable" alterations to the articles. It takes very little imagination to picture Weston haggling over a shilling, then throwing in a discount for taking on a wayward brat.

The first to emerge as a taker was Edward Winslow. One of the few passengers with a claim to good breeding, Winslow was a young man from Droitwich, Worcester, with long, curly hair, a mustache, and dark eyes set somewhat far apart. A printer by trade, he had traveled to Holland, where he had joined the Separatists and helped William Brewster, who was both a printer himself and a leading figure among the community, in publishing their religious tracts.

Winslow also happened to be in London at a moment when the other potential guardians—that is to say, the other well-to-do passengers—were still at large. It thus fell to him to take the eldest of the More children, Ellen, under his wing.[21]

For all the turbulence the young Richard More had seen, this was the first time he had been separated from one of his siblings— a memorable rift for a child in any era. Richard would not soon forget the face of the man who took his sister away. On the contrary: whether by accident or design, he would find his life inextricably woven with Winslow's in the decades to come, as the consequences of his exile compounded.

All of that lay immeasurably far ahead, of course, as Robert Cushman escorted him and Jasper and Mary down to the dock in Rotherhithe, on the south side of the Thames, and onto a ship. Soon he was belowdecks, the lines were cast off, and they were

on their way, down the river to the coast and the English Channel—his first taste of the sea he had seen memorialized in the gray
stones of Larden Hall.

BY 1620 Southampton was no longer the thriving town it had been
the previous century. It did a respectable triangle trade in smoked
stockfish from Newfoundland and tobacco from Virginia, but
most of the traffic moved between nearby France, Newcastle, and
the Channel Islands. Into this sleepy port poured the disconnected
energies of the Merchant Adventurers project, with all the decorum of a failing theater troupe.

John Carver was already in Southampton on the nineteenth, and
so was ready to take Jasper, the second-eldest of the More children,
more or less immediately. Richard and Mary, however, were another story. For the moment, there was no one to take them, and
Cushman was sorely preoccupied. His first item of business was to
hand over seven hundred pounds to the resurfaced Christopher
Martin—part of which, it seems, came from Samuel More's last-
minute payment. At the same time, petty disagreements had to
be resolved and innumerable details sorted out, not the least of
which were the arrangements for the passengers due in from Holland. The last two More children were hardly a priority; they
would have to shift for themselves for the time being.

For a child who had spent the previous four years essentially
under lock and key, the chaos at Southampton surely presented
an intoxicating chance to make new friends. The strongest candi-
dates for companionship were clear enough. Although there was
a whole town's worth of children with whom Richard could debate the rules of nine men morris or the fine art of skipping stones,
only Resolved White, Bartholomew Allerton, and Bartholomew's
sister Remember were close to his age.

Did Richard forge an alliance with these children, whether in
play or in mute resignation, as children the world over do? Did

he find himself telling them, without quite understandi
meaning, the story of the man who had laughed and drank an
then stolen off in the night?

If so, he could certainly have pointed to the adults around him
for illustration. The London contingent was a proverbial motley
crew, and while waiting for the Leiden group to arrive, they had
little to do but spend a pound or two in the local taverns. That
some of Samuel More's money underwrote the merriment of this
group, with Richard receiving his first sip of beer from the same
coffers, is too tempting an idea to dismiss out of hand.

So it went for a week, with the thin distractions that have attended delays since the beginning of time, until at last the *Speedwell*, having departed Delftshaven, Holland, on July 22, put in at
Southampton and disgorged the Leiden contingent. The entire
company was now finally assembled by the sea, with two ships
riding anchor and ready to take them forward. Unfortunately, the
Speedwell had proved leaky on the voyage over and needed repairs. Again the passengers would have to wait.

During this latest delay, Cushman was able to conclude at least
one item on his agenda. Among the newcomers was the revered
Elder William Brewster, who stood out in the crowd with his vi-
olet cloth coat. (Ironically, it was the London group who dressed
in high-crowned hats and capes flung over the shoulders—the
"middle class" fashion of the moment—not the more pious Separatists from Holland.)

Cushman consulted with Brewster, and it was decided: there
being no one else who wanted them, Brewster would take the last
two More children in his charge and provide for them as he would
for the two sons he had brought along, Love and Wrestling.

Richard's entry into the Brewster family came at a peculiar
moment. Unlike the essentially secular Londoners, the Leiden
group retired behind closed doors at the least provocation, to pray
and undertake "fasts of humiliation," as they called them. Talking
among themselves, they also began to worry about the newcomers

nd to refer to them as the Strangers. It was Almost from the beginning, the Separatists presence of the Strangers would fray the unity had worked so hard to achieve. Richard, the child vas from the outset a cause for prayer and distress. the growing lack of cohesion among the passengers was the ꞈ il unresolved matter of the articles. Sometime between July 26 and August 3, Weston personally appeared in Southampton to discuss them. The Separatists, who had been expecting a full-court press of Merchant Adventurers, were disappointed to see him show up alone. They were more crestfallen again when Weston rejected their position and left in a huff, telling them that "they would have to stand on their own legs from now on." In a last-minute plea, the Separatists sent off a letter to the Merchant Adventurers in London, proposing a compromise: if there was no profit after seven years, they would gladly extend the arrangement.

But there was no time for a response. On August 5 the two ships were ready to sail. The passengers passed through the West Gate, a medieval arch carved in a high stone tower, and proceeded to the West Quay, where they gathered close to hear William Brewster read a letter from John Robinson, the separatist leader, who was staying behind with the majority of the congregation.

"I do heartily, and in the Lord, salute you all. . . ."

To a child's ear, the remainder was deathly boring. And yet there were prophetic tones in it that would affect the children present as much as anyone else.

"Whereas you are to become a Body Politic, using amongst yourselves Civil Government . . ."[22]

Though this was not the first time English colonists had talked about forming a government of their own (the idea had been broached in both Virginia and Bermuda), Robinson had special reason for believing that his flock would need it—Thomas Weston's special brand of chaos theory had seen to that. The peculiar makeup of the group—equal parts Saints and Strangers—made tolerance especially needful. Fully half of Robinson's letter was taken up with admonitions for everyone involved to turn the other cheek. "You are, many of you, strangers as to the persons so to the infirmities one of another, and so stand in need of more watchfulness in this way. . . ."[23]

A patchwork crowd of people standing by the sea, among them Ellen, Jasper, Richard, and Mary More, ages four to eight. Where were they? Where were they going? Where was their *mother?*

At that moment, back in London, Sir Edward Zouch was busying himself with preparing a royal entertainment. "The Bp. [of Winchester] will entertain the King like an emperor at Farnham," wrote the master fool to his cousin, Lord Zouch. "Cannot equal the Bishop's good cheer, but will give His Majesty and the Prince more mirth at Woking, and masques each night. Requests a leash of bucks and a brace of does from Odiham Park."[24]

Whatever lay in store for the More children, a brace of does was not going to be part of it. The pageantry of Jacobean England, the ruffs and damasks and brightly painted fans, the complex structure of the courts, the infinitely nuanced caste system, the Roman ruins scattered in the hills, the density and variety and theatricality of London life—all this lay at their backs.

When the five-year-old Richard More stepped off the West Quay, he brought nothing with him except a resemblance in visage and lineaments to Jacob Blakeway, a man already lost to the backroads of time. The only things he knew for certain were that his mother was wild and that his father—or the man with the power to act as one—was indignant beyond words.

As it turned out, these same qualities describe the two groups that had been thrown together around him. Together they were embarking on an adventure that, in time, would amplify Richard's childhood impressions and project them across a continent.

There was scarcely time for anyone to notice him as he daw-dled along the deck and disappeared into the hold. The anchor was raised, and the *Mayflower* slowly drifted away from England and toward the New World.

3

The Promised Land

I am a stranger and a sojourner with you: give me a possession of a buryingplace with you, that I may bury my
dead out of my sight.

—Genesis, 23:4

NO STIRRING CHOIR accompanied the departure from Southampton. The sails were raised and the anchors weighed, and everything immediately began to fall apart. For a child alert to every detail, it was a first-rate opportunity to learn how a seagoing voyage should *not* be conducted.

The *Mayflower* took the lead out of port, bearing some ninety of the passengers, with the thirty remaining souls following in the *Speedwell*. Trouble arose without delay. Before they had reached the tip of Cornwall, the *Speedwell* was leaking badly again, and the ships were forced to put in at Dartmouth.

No sooner had they set sail than Christopher Martin, the man in charge of the *Mayflower* passengers, began yelling at anyone who so much as peeped in his direction. At Dartmouth, Martin reached such a state of apoplexy that he required his passengers to stay in the hold for as long as the ship was anchored. Robert

Cushman, Martin's counterpart on the *Speedwell*, fared no better with the man on shore. Finally able to ask for an accounting of the seven hundred pounds, he found Martin unwilling to answer at all, much less explain: the money from Samuel More, meant to secure the inheritance of the four More children, was gone like a hat in a gale.

Meanwhile, on the *Speedwell*, a board some two feet wide had been so badly damaged that it could be pulled away by hand to let sea rush in. The crew was puzzled as to the cause of the leak, but the rumor was that Captain Reynolds was in no great hurry to spend a year in the new colony.

The two ships left Dartmouth on August 23 and made more than three hundred miles when again they had to turn back, this time to Plymouth, in Devon. With two aborted departures behind them, it was clear that the *Speedwell* had to be abandoned—it would never survive the trip. The trade-off for a safer passage was the reduction of the 120 passengers to about 100, who then had to be squeezed aboard a single ship. Through skullduggery or not, Captain Reynolds got to wave the voyagers good-bye from a Plymouth dock on September 6, 1620. Cushman remained on-shore as well, stricken with a grave illness and expecting at any moment to become "meate for ye fishes."[1]

The most acute emergencies now past them, the passengers faced the slower tensions brought on by the high seas, the hard-tack—and one another. For one thing, space was certainly tight. They had to make their own cabins belowdecks, and some of them were forced to sleep in the shallop—a small boat much like a dinghy. There was no room for children to run around except on deck, and this was not permitted, so Richard was essentially confined, as he had been so often before, to the vicinity of substitute parents.

From this vantage point, which he shared with his younger sister, Mary, he watched as the Strangers muttered oaths and the Saints cast their eyes to the deck boards in fervent supplication, humiliating themselves, as they put it, for the impurities within them that had brought on such violent fortune.

Richard's new father was an object of considerable interest, not only for Richard but for the congregation as well. A lawyer, printer, and former diplomat, William Brewster had nevertheless been in hiding from the king for several years because of his prominence as a nonconformist, and the attending separation from many of his fellow Separatists had found him often in dire straits.

In Brewster's telling, the story was filtered through the rarefying language of the Saints, but between the lines, it was still an exciting tale larded with vivid details: the printing of a treasonous Scottish text, the arrest of a common drunk who was mistakenly thought to be Brewster, the destruction of Brewster's press, and his last-minute appearance in London in disguise.

Nestled into the folds of his new mother Mary Brewster's dress, Richard had ample opportunity to hear this story told and retold, and to wonder at the impressive-sounding names interspersed throughout the account: the secretary of state, Sir Edwin Sandys, even Thomas Weston—the man who had put him up in London, to whom Richard could give a face. And he may well have taken solace in the tale's conclusion: If Brewster could disappear yet not be gone forever, then mightn't Jacob Blakeway reemerge someday, too?

Even more revelatory was Brewster's way of seeing the world. Unlike the adults Richard had encountered before—the materialistic gentlemen, passionate women, and humble servants of his border-county upbringing—Brewster was an idealist and a man of integrity. As a Saint, he belonged to an extremist sect of Puritanism, which had renounced the Church of England as hopelessly corrupt, a sodden corpse of ritual and outward pretense.

Indeed, Brewster considered mankind to be thoroughly depraved and doomed, except for the select few who, by the providence of God, were struck with grace. One could not even know, necessarily, who such people would be: the task was to be vigilant for the signs as they were revealed in the world, and especially in nature. Every dip of a sparrow or rumble of thunder meant something in the divine plan, if only one could read it.

As the ruling elder (as opposed to the pastor, who had stayed behind in Holland), Brewster was also expected to be the eyes and ears of the community. Others might daydream or talk, but he had to be on the lookout for the evil wrought by men.

This made for a strange relationship between guardian and ward. Whereas the aging Brewster was the leader of the Saints by popular acclaim, Richard was a young soul whose allegiances were as yet unformed. Would he take to the Saints' brand of peity, or would the forces from his past—of which Brewster must have known something—resurge and claim him? Certainly, there were temptations even aboard the ship that might yet bend Richard's soul into an unregenerate thing.

The crew, for one, could hardly have been more different in their outlook than the Saints. Rather than consulting Providence, they generally resorted to the knife. While the Saints huddled below in stricken terror, the sailors hauled and swore, and sometimes danced a mad dance on deck, in the belief that the exercise would ward off scurvy. To the strident proclamations of their passengers, the crew generally responded with curses and unpleasant advice.

THE MARITIME CULTURE has been remarkably well preserved through the ages. One of my friends, Chick Bills, is a first-rate skipper who, by some strange coincidence, is also a descendant of Robert Coppin, the pilot of the *Mayflower*. Chick is a stocky man, with a handlebar mustache and the ruddy complexion one gets from living, as he does, on a boat. A man of equal parts mirth and rage, he has certainly not lost any of the contumely of his seafaring ancestors. When I first told him about my interest in Richard More, he all but exploded.

"It's all the fucking Puritans' fault!" he bellowed. "They fucked it up for everybody else. I can't believe such a small group of people could get control of an entire country with such weird ideas. I remember when I was a kid and I first heard about this idea—that if you were doing well, it was because God loved you. I mean, how fucking stupid is that? For years after that, I was totally whacked, trying to figure that out."

There we were, several centuries down the line, the sailor incarnate spewing invective while I, progeny of a Stranger, listened and tried to locate my affinities. I don't imagine Richard, who became a sailor only seven years later, had as much trouble as I did. On the *Mayflower*, the wind was already singing in the shrouds.

Even the sailors were not the worst influence on Richard, however. Among the Strangers aboard the *Mayflower* was a man with his own rousing tale to tell of having fallen afoul of the king's pleasure.

In 1609 Stephen Hopkins had sailed for Virginia on the *Sea Venture*, only to be cast away in Bermuda. Hopkins, a clerk well versed in the Bible, had tried to persuade his fellow castaways that they were legally beyond the king's purview; no longer subject to English law, they could live as they pleased. Eventually, new ships were built, and the party sailed on to Virginia and then back to England, where Hopkins faced execution on charges of treason. Pleading for the well-being of his wife and children, he received a pardon and lived to see himself depicted as a drunken butler in Shakespeare's final play, *The Tempest*.

Hopkins was thus doubly worrisome to Brewster, who loathed the artifice of theater as he did the Devil. The Elder Saint was dealing with a known mutineer who had exercised his adventure in the Bermudas with a liberal dose of pragmatic duplicity. If it came to loggerheads, it would be hard to predict which worldview would prevail: the laissez-faire attitude of the Strangers and the sailors or the severe ideology of the Saints.

This question loomed large as the voyage progressed, with days alternating between mind-numbing doldrums and storms severe enough to crack the main beam amidships. John Howland, one of the passengers, was swept overboard and managed to keep hold of a topsail halyard even after he was "many fathoms under the water." Howland was rescued and lived many years. Not so the anonymous sailor who delighted in taunting the Saints, and then fell ill and died. Both events were quietly attributed to Providence.[2]

Suspicions shifted back onto the crew when they intentionally steered north. Had they been paid by authorities in Holland to avoid the projected site of New Amsterdam? Did their English king want them to settle a safe distance from the Anglicans then living in Virginia? Or was it simply a matter of contrary weather, as the sailors claimed? Every origin myth has its mysteries, and this is one of them: the Ancient Men may have been swindled, or they may have been guided by divine winds. But Richard surely noticed, even at his young age, that sailors had a practical authority that Brewster was powerless to overrule.

Land was sighted on November 9, 1620, and landfall made at the tip of Cape Cod on November 11. Before anyone could disembark, however, the passengers were confronted with a problem. In arriving so far north of Virginia, they would, like the *Sea Venture* in 1609, arguably be beyond the king's realm once they set foot on land. In the parlance of pirates, they would henceforth be "beyond the line." Hopkins's past returned en force, as some of the Strangers, realizing this, stirred up a mutiny.

It was a paradoxical dispute, to be sure. The Strangers, who thought of themselves as ordinary English subjects, militated for freedom, while the Separatists, whose position was in their very name, argued for fealty. Yet there was a certain logic underlying the paradox.

The Strangers, after all, were not operating according to any concerted plan; they were acting spontaneously, in the spirit of adventure. The Separatists, on the other hand, had taken great pains to make this voyage, with specific ideas about what they would do when they got to the other shore, and why. They were in for the long term and intended to keep their promise, even if it meant honoring a government that despised them.

In the end, the voices of loyalty carried the day, perhaps because the Saints continued to fast and pray for deliverance long after the undecideds had begun groaning for an end to the debate. Richard, watching from the sidelines, thus received his first inkling of the freedom that the high seas made possible. And he had occasion, too, to wonder at the sight of his foster father dipping his quill while the passengers craned their necks to see what he would write. . . .

In ye name of God, Amen. We whose names are underwriten, the loyall subjects of our dread soveraigne Lord King James by ye grace of God, of Great Britaine, Franc, & Ireland king, defender of ye faith, &c.

Haveing undertaken, for ye glorie of God, and advancemente of ye Christian faith, and honour of our king & countrie, a voyage to plant ye first colonie in ye Northerne parts of Virginia, doe by these presents solemnly & mutualy in ye presence of God, and one of another, covenant & combine our selves togeather into a civill body politick; for our better ordering & preservation & furtherance of ye ends aforesaid; and by vertue hearof, to enacte, constitute, and frame such just & equall lawes, ordinances, acts, constitutions, & offices, from time to time, as shall be thought most meete & convenient for ye generall good of ye Colonie: unto which we promise all due submission and obedience. In witnes wherof we have hereunder subscribed our names at Cap-Codd ye .11. of November, i in ye year of the raigne of our soveraigne lord King James of England, France, & Ireland ye eighteenth, and of Scotland ye fiftie fourth. Ano: Dom .1620.

This document, the Mayflower Compact, was signed by forty-
one of the adult males, roughly half of them Saints and half of
them Strangers. Even though the land was to remain an extension
of English soil, the government would be based on something
entirely different—not the embroideries of pedigree and impene-
trable custom, but the pealings of personal convictions.

They would need those convictions soon enough.

ON NOVEMBER 13, 1620, Richard turned six years old—a birth-
day and a new era in one. He himself did not know his own age
precisely, and if anyone else aboard did, it was of no interest compared to the main event of the day: the first shallop was sent out
to Cape Cod with a load of women eager to do some washing
after the arduous journey.

After this brief respite, the ship passed farther down the coast
to make for the Hudson but was beaten back by storms—or possibly by the desire of the sailors to steer clear of Dutch-owned
land to the south. The honors of sighting Plimouth Harbor fell to
my friend Chick's forebear, Robert Coppin. Thinking he had been
there before on a previous voyage, Coppin recommended that the
ship advance through a punishing downpour. In the end, he was
mistaken—the harbor was unknown to him—but neither Saints
nor Strangers nor sailors could endure much more, and so the
legendary community received its new home.

A scouting party bushwhacked and came upon the remains of
an Indian village, its inhabitants completely wiped out, as they
would later learn, by smallpox or something very like it. The hand
of Providence had delivered the perfect location, so the Saints declared, and construction of a common house commenced.

Meanwhile, death was making itself more clearly felt aboard
ship. While Richard and his younger sister, Mary, huddled close
to ward off the bitter winter cold, Mary Allerton gave birth to a
stillborn son. About the same time, one of the Billington boys

nearly sent everyone to their maker by shooting off a gun near an open gunpowder keg.

These incidents paled, however, in comparison with the growing signs of infection. Richard's elder brother, Jasper, all of seven years old, was among the first to fall ill, mumbling a string of words that trailed off into babble, despite the best efforts of Mary Brewster and the ship doctor to revive him. Before the voyage was technically over, Richard had experienced the death of a loved one for the first time.

And his first funeral as well. The *Mayflower* passengers could not afford to keep corpses on board, but with the shoreline so close, neither was it fitting to bury them at sea. And so Jasper's body was laid out in a shallop and slowly rowed to shore, through the jagged whitecaps of November, to be buried in the New World.

Tradition has it that the teenaged Mary Chilton was the first woman to step onto Plimouth Rock, although there is no proof, or even of whether the rock was actually used for disembarking. Indeed, over the years the rock has been made to carry more symbolism than it can possibly bear.

The occasion was momentous, however. In the words of future Plimouth governor William Bradford, "they fell upon their knees and blessed the God of heaven, who had brought them over the vast and furious ocean, and delivered them from all the perils and miseries thereof, again to set their feet on the firm and stable earth, their proper element."

The vast and furious ocean: that was something they could all agree on.

IN HIS FIRST DAYS at Plimouth, Richard's ears were filled with the sounds of saws and hammers as the colonists immediately started building separate houses. The stated reason for doing so was that self-interest would spur construction, although no doubt the Saints and the Strangers were eager to get some distance from one another as well. As long as they continued to be wedged in together in the common house, the frictions between them could only interfere in the struggle to survive.

Which was hard enough as it was. The colonists had squandered their time choosing a location while winter approached, and the temperatures can only be described as bitter.

When I visited Plimouth Plantation one February, I made the short walk along the shoreline from my hotel (something like one of your seventeenth-century taverns, but with the inevitable abominations that have proliferated since) to the site of the original colony. Before I was halfway there, I thought I would pass out from the cold. It was not at all difficult to imagine the exploratory trip in a shallop, undertaken in the first days of the settlement, when two of the passengers actually did pass out from the cold, their faces "glazed" with frozen mist.

Indeed, the Plimouth colonists were almost ludicrously ill-prepared for their mission. Even though the plan had been to make their way as fishermen (which news the king had received as a clever biblical allusion to the fishermen Jesus had picked as his disciples), they had neglected to bring the heavy fishing hooks needed for the task. Neither prayers nor curses were any substitute for knowing how to build houses or catch fish.

Nor were they adequate to stave off the "common infection." What this malady was is a little unclear—perhaps scurvy, typhus fever, infectious pneumonia, and fatigue rolled into a single scourge—but there is no doubt that it threatened to take everyone, down to the last soul. In the end, half of the party perished, and only six or seven were well enough to tend to the sick.

Oddly, or perhaps providentially, William Brewster remained the most able adult throughout. Thus, as children were expected to assist their elders in every circumstance, foul or fair, it fell to Richard, as Brewster's charge, to lend a hand in carrying the dead—his sisters Mary and Ellen and the countless others, Saints,

Separatists, and sailors alike—up to a rise just south of the common house, at dawn or dusk or midday, to clear the rocks and roots from the grave, to lay them to rest with their feet facing east, and to throw the black dirt over a coffinless shape while Brewster inveighed the simple words of Puritan eulogy: our Lord, grace, mercy, amen.

By the time the epidemic subsided, Richard was the only member of his family still alive, a Stranger among strangers and very far from home. How a six-year-old might handle such a moment cannot really be imagined, in that or any other time—what he did with the darkness, or with the peculiar brightness of the days that continued to break for him. This was the Ancient Beginning for Richard: the birth within him of something hard and unbreakable, and something wrong. To his first experience as the embodiment of a mysterious crime committed back in England, he could now add a peculiar variety of survivor's guilt—the sense of being chosen.

Because thou hast made the Lord, which is my refuge, even the most High, thy habitation; There shall no evil befall thee, neither shall any plague come nigh thy dwelling; For he shall give his angels charge over thee, to keep thee in all thy ways. (Psalm 91: 9–11)

But chosen for what?

WITH THE COMING of spring, the *Mayflower* returned to England with what was left of its crew, and the colony slowly clawed its way toward a semblance of normal life. On the burial ground, Richard helped plant seeds, so as to hide the community's tragedy from the Indians, and grain began to rise from the graves of Ellen, Jasper, and Mary More. Among the living, meanwhile, garden plots and houses took shape, and Plimouth Plantation soon

d four dwellings, seven other buildings, and even a few
nal streets.

Slowly the "body politic" began to crystallize as well. John
Carver, the first governor of the colony and the guardian of Richard's elder brother, Jasper, had died with the others, but several
of the community's leaders had survived, among them William
Bradford, who was elected governor in Carver's place, and Isaac
Allerton, who became governor's assistant under Bradford. To his
role as elder, Brewster added that of the colony's preacher until
such time as their pastor, John Robinson, could come and assume
his rightful role.

The Brewster family's move into their own house on Leiden
Street sometime in 1621 coincided with Richard's transition from
early to middle childhood. Shedding his gown (worn by all young
English boys) for his first pair of breeches, he began to spend less
time with Mary Brewster and more with her husband, who taught
him to read the Breeches Bible favored by the Saints and to pen
his own name.

This was in addition, of course, to his nearly constant work-
load. Richard, like all children in the colony, was expected to fetch
water; gather firewood, berries, and other wild plants; help preserve food; and plant and harvest with the rest. He was also expected to serve the Brewsters their meals, bowing when addressed
and retiring to a stool to eat his food after the others had finished.

Only when night came, as he slept on a straw mattress laid out
on the earthen floor, did Richard really have time to think for
himself. And there were so many things to figure out: the conversation of the adults, the clarity of the Plimouth water, the thick-
ness of the woods around them, and, now and then, if he dared
to think of it, the forbidding enigma of his guardian, confined to
his ornately carved wooden chair, poring over dense theological
passages by rushlight in preparation for the Sabbath lecture.

Richard's recourse to alternative perspectives was limited. As any natural child would, Wrestling Brewster probably regarded his foster brother as a threat, especially since they were the same age; he could not be depended on for much besides abuse. The only other reliable companions were the three children first encountered back in Southampton: Bartholomew and Remember Allerton, now ages eight and six, and Resolved White, a boy one year Richard's junior. Between daily chores, these were the children most likely to meet with Richard by the stream or in the woods to play out the unsounded vibrations of adult life.

There was, however, another culture among them that took special pleasure in the ways of children.

On March 22 Samoset, sachem of the Abenakis, arrived in the tiny village and stunned one of the colonists by addressing him in English. Stephen Hopkins put Samoset up at his house for a night and learned of his earlier meetings with European fishermen who frequented the Maine coast. That marked the beginning of personal relations between Plimouth and the native Americans, relations that soon became so close that one Wampanoag, Hobbamock, felt free to build a house just outside the plantation.

The Indians knew a great deal about survival—how to hasten crops along by planting fish in with the seeds, for example—and likely taught their secrets to Richard as they worked alongside him. Unlike the Separatists, they also played as easily as they worked, and were fond of games in general. When one of them named Squanto arrived, he lightheartedly brought along the gift of a dog. (A *dog!*) Certainly, mingling with the Indians presented none of the barriers imposed by an angry god, especially for the Stranger children, who were not well acquainted with an angry god in the first place.

The teenaged John Billington showed his own trust in the heathens by disappearing into the woods one day in late May. With Squanto going along as an interpreter, ten men set out from Plimouth on June 11, 1621, and found the boy in the hands of the

Nausets, a tribe that had attacked the colonists during their first days ashore. After a tense standoff, Aspinet, the Nausets' sachem, appeared.

"He had not less than a hundred with him," Edward Winslow later wrote, "the half whereof came to the shallop unarmed with him, the other stood aloof with their bows and arrows. There he delivered us the boy, behung with beads, and made peace with us, we bestowing a knife upon him, and likewise on another that first entertained the boy and brought him thither. So they departed from us."[3]

Here was a story that Richard, plodding through his day back in the village, heard again and again, with endless embellishment: the original rendition of "playing Indian." And while Billington's escapade no doubt excited Richard's envy, it also proved that a boy could survive for at least a month outside the borders of Plimouth Plantation.

As summer turned to autumn, the terror of the epidemic subsided, the weather withdrew its punishments, and, finally, the first harvest came. The famous event held that October was, strictly speaking, not a day of thanksgiving but a traditional harvest feast of the sort that the Strangers as much as the Saints were likely to put on. Bent on lavishness, the fifty colonists and some ninety Indians indulged themselves for three days with a tableau of vegetables, venison, fowl, possibly even swan—a veritable bounty of meat and drink.

The moment was not without its tension. Some say that the Indians were not invited at first, others that they were asked to sit separately from the English, as if unworthy.[4] Of course, these distinctions mattered little to Richard. After waiting on the adults, the children of Plimouth went off to eat in their own places anyway, and the natives, unaccustomed to the bizarre ritual of table dining, would have fallen in with them easily.

In this way, Richard found himself laughing and playing in close proximity with the tall and graceful Massasoit, sachem of the Pokanokets. Another frame from the pilgrim's progress: two very different individuals swept up in the festivities of the moment, one young, the other old, one blue-eyed, the other brown, neither of whom understood yet how deeply the force of dispossession would mark him.

Shortly after the harvest festival, the *Fortune* arrived, bringing another wave of settlers. Among the arrivals was Robert Cushman, who had languished behind in England on the brink of death, helpless to affect the outcome of the expedition. Now fully recovered, Cushman was of course eager to hear every detail of the previous year.

And what a year it had been! Disease and death, followed by new friendships and the first glimmerings of security, all taking place against the backdrop of an exotic continent—a tale of the glories of Providence indeed.

Still, there was a great deal to be done—most important, to attract more capital to the project. To this end, Edward Winslow gathered his various writings into an account of their annus mirabilis that downplayed the colony's difficulties. Cushman, who was planning to return to England on the *Fortune*, agreed to take this manuscript with him and have it published in London, that it might be read widely and so catch "new fish."

Despite their hardships, none of the original colonists had chosen to return to England on the *Mayflower*. Nor did they board the *Fortune* when it was ready to sail in November 1621. (Many of the original colonists did leave eventually, but not as a direct consequence of the initial difficulties.) Of course, not all the settlers had the same options. Brewster had sworn his pledge for seven years, and Richard was old enough by then to know that only one of those had passed.

And so, having been put aboard one ship with no say in the matter, Richard watched as another left without him. Plimouth was beginning to look less like an adventure and more like a permanent fact of life. If there was any hope of making contact with his former world, perhaps it lay in the *Fortune*'s cargo: the tale of his amazing adventures, fixed on paper for all to see.

Richard never knew how close that tale came to resting on the bottom of the ocean. On its way home, the *Fortune* was overtaken by French pirates and plundered of the goods sent as payment to the Merchant Adventurers. But fortunately, English texts were of little interest to the brigands, and on February 17, 1622, the ship arrived in London at last, with Cushman and the manuscript intact.

Published almost immediately, *Mourt's Relation* ("Mourt" being an apparently arbitrary pseudonym for Edward Winslow) was the first public account of what had become of the *Mayflower* party. In an age when colonization attempts were a matter of general interest, it was widely read. And the timing of subsequent events suggests that at least one of its readers was Katharine More, mother of the four hapless children who had been summarily dispatched from their pastoral home at Larden Hall.

4

A Mother's Wish

It is the sinfullest thing in the world, to forsake or destitute a plantation once in forwardness; for, besides the dishonor, it is the guiltiness of blood of many commiserable persons.

—Sir Francis Bacon, *Of Plantations*

W E LAST LEFT Katharine More in defeat before the Court of Delegates, while Samuel, suffering from no particular urge to inform her of his intentions, took the waters at Bath. A heartrending state of affairs, to be sure, but what happened next?

In the interest of understanding the Ancient Beginning, its width and breadth and height, let us try to determine if not what definitively did take place, at least how many obstacles—or how few—stood between the reunion of a mother and her child. In so doing, we may succeed mostly in providing a wish fulfillment for Richard (many years too late!) but we may also hope to map the limits of a particular variety of silence.

Very little is known about how Katharine lived after 1620, when her divorce appeal failed. Not a single piece of evidence of her has turned up in any of the parishes where her immediate family members lived, nor has her will been found. This is not surprising, since in her day a divorced woman was essentially regarded as a member of the criminal class. It seems likely that she stayed on in London at least for a time, though under what circumstances can only be surmised. She may have found safe harbor in Paddington with either of her uncles; reunited with her lover, Jacob Blakeway; or done something else entirely. The specter of prostitution certainly cannot be discounted.

On the other hand, Katharine was nothing if not tenacious; the stack of records from her appeal speaks eloquently to her ability to fight long after the battle was lost. Nor has the maternal instinct changed much over the centuries. All castigations of her character aside, it is impossible to imagine Katharine, a more pugnacious mother than many, not doing everything possible to discover the status of her children. And although there is no evidence that Katharine ever set foot in the New World, there is some evidence to suggest that she tried to.

Once the *Mayflower* sailed, the silence must have been excruciating. No doubt Katharine knew that her children had been deported, and knew the name of the ship as well. She had spent too much time in court to have missed these facts.[1] But what else could she expect to know of a voyage that had ended thousands of miles away?

Nothing—until the end of February 1622, that is, when Robert Cushman arrived in London and made haste to distribute *Mourt's Relation* as quickly and as widely as possible. Though this pamphlet was maddeningly vague in its particulars and obviously meant as propaganda—it told nothing of an epidemic, for example—it did describe a young boy (not named in the account!) who had been taken in by natives and then released with great ceremony. It also revealed that the vessel had arrived in a cold northern clime instead of in Virginia.

One can imagine Katharine's growing state of alarm. What was all this about cold winters and boys running off with Indians? Why had the vessel veered off course? Had this been planned in secret? And what did the call for more investors say about the stability of the colony itself? Had Samuel forgotten the deal he had made? Did he think he was off the hook? If so, he had another think coming!

Katharine had no power to bring her children home. She did, however, have the legal right to an explanation of Samuel's actions. Here the dates line up quite neatly, because an explanation is exactly what Katharine sought, sometime in early 1622, when she laid her petition before Chief Justice James Lee.[2]

With this, Samuel was pried out of his shell once again and forced to reiterate his agreement. Wearily and with a great suppression of bile, he relented:

In July ao dni 1620 by the appointmt and direccon of the said Samuell More the fower children of the Petitioner Katharine More were brought up to London by a servant of the father of Samuell and delivered to Philemon Powell who was intreated to deliver them to John Carver and Robert Cushman undertakers for the associats of John Peers for the plantacon of Virginia & to see that they should be sufficiently kept and maintained with meate drinke apparrell lodginge and other necessaries and that at the end of seaven Yeers the should have 50 acres of land apeece in the Countrey of Virginia for performance whereof they entered into Articles and they together wth one Mr. Weston an honest and sufficient Merchant gave bond to Mr. Paul Harries cosin germane of the said Samuell.

Samuel also used the opportunity of his Declaration to vent his spleen, albeit somewhat incoherently, complaining that Katharine could not "be contented to continue her lewd lief but still by complaints bringeth the [passages] of her lewd life to be published [i.e., publicized] in all places . . . wch yf there were any modesty lefte she would desire to hide and wch the said Samuell to his great grief is forced by way of his . . . defence to discover."

If Samuel could barely stand to be reminded that Katharine existed, that was fair enough. Then again, in the strategic realm of conjugal discord, rage was the best response Katharine could have wished for, to the extent that a hotheaded Samuel might lose sight of how much he was revealing. Certainly, Samuel's Declaration furnished Katharine with information she hadn't possessed before—most important, the names of the principal characters involved in the deportation.

On close study, Katharine's list of contacts fell into sequence. Philemon Powell had been the first (painful as it was to imagine) to take charge of her children when they stepped from the carriage, Robert Cushman the second, and Thomas Weston the third.

All these men were in town in the spring of 1622. Cushman was in some ways the strongest lead, since he had actually been in Plimouth and, indeed, had brought the news of events there to London. Unfortunately, Cushman was also one of the Saints, who manifestly counted "wicked women" (to use Samuel's phrase) in low regard. Katharine could not have gotten very far with him before their differing moral conditions barred the way.

Weston and Powell, however, were not likely to turn Katharine away. On the contrary, Weston had recently pulled out of the Plimouth enterprise and, with Powell's help, was soliciting adventurers for another project: a colony called Wessagusset, to be settled north of Plimouth with his own—that is to say, Katharine's—sort of people.

Weston thus represented a bundle of wild hopes. He could offer Katharine glimpses of those hectic days before the *Mayflower*'s departure, when her children had squeezed into the nooks and crannies of his house in Aldgate. Having been in frequent contact with the colony until recently, he might also have told her what he knew of their circumstances in Plimouth. And as an active colonizer, he perhaps could even have offered Katharine a berth on one of his ships—provided she could pay her way, that is.

As it happened, he was just then planning to send another two ships, the *Swan* and the *Charity*, with a larger load of passengers.[3]

Of course, developments could be more wild than hopeful where Thomas Weston was involved. For starters, he had no legal claim to the land at Wessagusset, which technically belonged to the Council for New England. And that was the least of it. Having been authorized on March 1, 1622, to convey a cannon to New England for use by the council, he sold it instead to Turkish pirates and pocketed the money. By late spring, Weston was an outlaw from the Crown, and in seeking him out, Katharine would have been hard put to find him.

Ironically, this very turn of events, while seeming to frustrate any further progress, closed a loop in Katharine's search. On May 31, 1622, the Council for New England ordered the forfeiture of Weston's ships. On the same day, the council appointed a new treasurer: none other than Barnabe Gooch, one of the commissioners who had sat on Katharine's appeal case.[4]

As the council's secretary, Gooch had already been faithfully recording Weston's follies, so he knew a great deal about the state of affairs in New England. Now, as treasurer, he had full access to the information regarding the whereabouts of Weston's ships. Most significant, the council was in the midst of planning its own colonization attempt in New England, in which Gooch expected to receive a rather large patent of land, not far from where Katharine's children had struck root.[5]

University masters and lewd women did not mix easily in Stuart England, yet Katharine had some advantages her contemporaries did not. During her drawn-out appeal, she had had time to familiarize herself with Gooch's comings and goings; he was someone she knew how to find. Indeed, Katharine had been required to file her petition (demanding Samuel's Declaration) with the King's Bench, and it is plausible that she had picked up that legal action where she had left off—with the four commissioners who had sat on her divorce appeal.

Having availed herself of a document that pledged her children fifty acres of land—at a time when it was known to the council that Plimouth would have trouble fulfilling that promise—Katharine could now entertain the notion of returning to Gooch without embarrassing herself. And within a few weeks' time, she could hope to add a trump card to her hand as well.

Again the timing of events is compelling. The Council for New England took legal control of Weston's ships on the last day of May. Before June was out, Katharine had screwed up her courage and approached Samuel, presently tending to his ailing lord, with a proposal. She would renounce her claims to Larden Hall if he compensated her with a respectable sum. After all she had been through, that wasn't too much to ask, was it?

Apparently not. On June 24, 1622, Katharine and Samuel severed all obligations to each other, save one. By law, neither one could marry until the other was dead. In return, Katharine received the tacit promise of three hundred pounds from Samuel, to be paid in the fullness of time.[6]

Unfortunately, time turned out to be all too full. Samuel was not able to release the three hundred pounds from his estate until November of that year, and as 1623 dawned, the prospects in New England had grown dimmer. Weston had fled under cover of night, and Gooch's patent had yet to materialize. Wessagusset, meanwhile, had fallen on hard times, and those who sailed on the authority of the council invariably disembarked at Plimouth, where the authorities were sure to give Katharine no quarter if she showed her face.

With her new London contacts and her handsome dispensation, Katharine was in a better position than ever to provide for her children, however many had survived. But when, and where—and how?

Katharine may have lacked some of the cardinal virtues, but fortitude was not one of them. If she could not achieve her aims by avoiding Plimouth, she might still by helping overthrow it.

Late in 1623 the *Charity* sailed up the Thames and dropped anchor in London. The vessel was no longer under Weston's command, having been seized by the Council for New England, and was expected to remain in town until two of its passengers, the peripatetic Saints Robert Cushman and Edward Winslow, back in England again, had completed their latest business.

One item ranking high on their list was to find a qualified pastor. The Saints had arrived in Plimouth without John Robinson, and it was becoming increasingly clear that he would never leave Holland. Although William Brewster had been able to stand in for Robinson at first, the colonists needed a permanent replacement.

For a woman tracking the *Charity* in the fervent hope of usurping Brewster in his role as a guardian, all this was interesting news indeed. And it became more so as the matter progressed.

The man the Merchant Adventurers chose—without much thought for the Saints' interests—was the Reverend John Lyford. As a graduate of Magdalen College, Oxford, Lyford was likely an acquaintance—if not an actual colleague—of Barnabe Gooch, who was presently angling for a land patent that conflicted with the Plimouth claim. In recent years Lyford had also fallen in with a minister named John Pemberton, whom the Saints openly despised as a "great opposite" of theirs. It would be hard to imagine a worse choice from the Separatist point of view. Nevertheless, Lyford it was.

For Katharine, of course, exactly the opposite was true—and not only because Lyford appeared to be working against the Separatists. The maiden name of Katharine's grandmother, whose portrait Holbein had painted, was also Pemberton. There were Pembertons all over England, true. But following the descent of the coat of arms inscribed on that portrait, one eventually would come upon a fifth cousin of Katharine's named John Pemberton who lived in London at the time when Lyford was appointed minister of Plimouth.[7]

The odds that these two John Pembertons were the same man are difficult to calculate. They are somewhat increased, however, by the fact that Katharine's relative was a first cousin to Roger Williams, the fiery preacher whose conflicts with the Massachusetts and Plimouth clergy in the following decade made him one of the greatest "opposites" the Puritans ever had.

In Lyford and his "Pemberton cell," Katharine may have stumbled onto a wing of her family that, like her, was engaged in a fierce battle against the Saints. In any event, by January 1624, when the *Charity* was preparing to set sail for New England, Lyford was already showing himself to be Katharine's ideal co-conspirator. At an opportune moment, he stole into Winslow's effects and, before anyone could discover him, removed a letter, copied it, and returned the original to its place. Then he retired to his room, where he began to write his own fevered comments in the margins.

We cannot, unfortunately, look over Lyford's shoulder to read along with him, but even over the chasm of time we can make out the writing on the envelope, which gave the author as an anonymous "Gentleman from England," for whom Winslow was acting as messenger, and the recipient as William Brewster, the foster father of Richard More.

AS FOR RICHARD, he knew nothing of these machinations back home. Since the *Fortune* had left, his life been taken up with much more elemental concerns: fetching water, gathering firewood, tending the garden, cleaning fish—a long list of chores punctuated by occasional interruptions, bewilderments, and fits of dread. He had learned about the Wessagusset colony when a man named Phineas Pratt came barreling into Plimouth one day, breathlessly announcing that he had been attacked by Indians. After that, and news of a massacre by Indians in Virginia, the adults erected a wall around the colony and began bringing their muskets into the meetinghouse for the Sabbath lecture.

The mood was getting dark at Plimouth, and the changing of the seasons brought little relief. One day Miles Standish, the military leader of the colony, had rounded up the ablest men and set off for Wessagusset, returning with the head of an Indian impaled on a pike, which he erected in town for all to see. The following summer saw Plimouth in the clutches of a drought, and Richard was often hungry.

One event that livened things up, if it did nothing to improve matters, was the surprise arrival of Thomas Weston in the colony. The passage over had done nothing to soften Weston's character. He made his entrance into Plimouth with a group of fishermen, having disguised himself as a blacksmith. This tactic failed miserably, of course, since many there remembered him all too well. Curious, perhaps, about the rotting head on display in town, he fitted out a boat and went off to learn how his Wessagusset venture was faring, only to be robbed by Indians and return to Plimouth dressed in beaver skins. It did not take long for him to wear out his welcome. A captain named Robert Gorges had also come to Plimouth (under the auspices of his powerful relative, Ferdinando Gorges) and quickly fell into an argument with Weston over the fate of a certain cannon. Gorges threatened to ship Weston back to England, but then there was a fire in the warehouse, and Weston used the moment to slip out of town—to Virginia, it was said.

So many arrivals, so many abrupt departures, and each as much of a mystery as the last. Where were they going, and when would the next one come? As is so often the case with boys, Richard's gaze often drifted out to sea, and without realizing it, he began to mingle his dreams with the horizon.

Then one day a speck appeared on that horizon, gradually growing larger and larger until it took on the shape of a ship, which anchored in the harbor. One of its shallops came ashore, and a middle-aged man stepped out, kissed the ground at his feet, and all but bear-hugged the colonists on hand to meet him. As Governor Bradford put it, Lyford "would have kissed their hands if they would have suffered him; yea, he wept & shed many tears, blessing God that brought him to see their faces."[8]

Bradford seems to have forgotten that he had reacted much the same way on arriving in the New World, but nonetheless, Lyford's histrionics had the desired effect. Asking to be admitted to the church after only two weeks, he made a florid confession, in which he disavowed his "former disorderly walking" and "the many corruptions which had been a burthen to his conscience." Satisfied that his corruptions consisted of little more than an adherence to the Anglican faith, the Saints brought him into the fold, and soon he was sharing the lectures with Brewster every Sabbath.

The arrival of Lyford gave Richard his closest view yet of the split running through the adult community: as Brewster strove to stay abreast of every shift in allegiance among the colonists, his charge looked on, watching the watchman.

For a while it seemed as if the Strangers would simply take over. Various roustabouts had attached themselves to the colony by then—some having spilled in from the flagging Wessagusset colony, and others, such as John Oldham, having arrived by ship. Within a short time, many were gravitating toward Lyford. Private meetings began to be held, and when passing a Saint in the street, these Strangers were sometimes seen to be "laughing into their sleeves."

Then it came out that Lyford had performed an Anglican baptism for one of the Strangers. The sign of the cross on an infant's forehead? In Plimouth? The Saints likened this breach to the iniquities of Ishmael, "who when he had slain Gedaliah, went out weeping, and met those that were coming to offer Incense in the house of the Lord, saying, Come to Gedaliah, when he meant to slay them."[9]

The Saints now counted Lyford as a dissembler and an enemy. But they decided not to move against him just yet. Better to give him more rope, and let him do the job himself.

After a time, the *Charity* returned to Plimouth from a fishing expedition, and Brewster began to get reports that Lyford was often at his desk late into the night, writing letters. Other informers spotted Lyford meeting with Strangers and speaking in whispers. Clearly, trouble was afoot.

It was William Bradford, the governor of Plimouth, who made the first move. When the *Charity*—already a vessel of much infamy—sailed for England one afternoon, Bradford waited until darkness had fallen and then set out in a shallop, overtaking the ship beyond the bay and out of sight of the colonists. The captain of the *Charity*, William Pierce, put up no protest, and in searching the ship, Bradford found more than twenty letters that Lyford had either written or copied and amended with his own comments, and several written by John Oldham. Bradford copied as many letters as he could, then returned the originals to the ship, except for a few that he kept as evidence while letting the copies continue on to England. Among these letters was the one Lyford had intercepted from Winslow on its way to William Brewster and then decorated with his own opinions.

Back ashore, Bradford had all the time in the world to look over Lyford's "slanders and false accusations, tending not only to their prejudice, but to their ruine & utter subversion." And so, one might add, did Brewster. Sitting in his chair one evening, he studied a copy of the letter addressed to him from a "Gentleman in England," this version marred by Lyford's contemptuous remarks, and looked up from time to time to see if anyone was watching him.

When the Lyford faction learned of Bradford's night visit, they "were somewhat blanke at it," but when no retaliation came, their confidence returned. Most likely, the governor was just passing along some last-minute information to the master of the *Charity*, to be sent along to England.

So the matter stood until one day in 1625, as fall turned to winter, when Oldham pulled a knife on Miles Standish and was put in chains for this transgression. Soon afterward, Lyford and his faithful began to separate themselves entirely from the Saints, to hold Sabbath meetings of their own, and generally "more publickly to act that which they had long been plotting."[10]

Clearly, the Saints could afford to wait no longer. The dissemblers would have to be unmasked.

By this time, Plimouth had swelled to a population of some 150 colonists, and every one of them was summoned to attend the court. Straightening his clothes and wiping the dirt from his face, Richard stood outside the town forthouse with the others until the signal moment when his guardian, Master Brewster, cordially opened the doors.[11] The crowd filed in and took their places, and waited for Bradford to rise.

For Richard, already caught up in the energies that swirled through the Brewster home, the trial was a golden opportunity. A Gentleman from England had written to Brewster and made everyone upset, but now everything, surely, would be explained to his satisfaction.

Bradford began by accusing Lyford and Oldham of plotting an insurrection, chastising Lyford especially for violating his ministry. Lyford stood stiffly and denied everything, demanding proof. Oldham, on the other hand, used the moment as a call to arms.

"Now show your courage!" he yelled, turning to his audience. "You have often complained to me so and so, now is the time if you will do anything, I will stand by you."[12]

Richard looked around. No one spoke, so he held his tongue as well.

Then Bradford delivered his coup de grâce: the letters the accused had written. After describing the circumstances under which these documents had been penned, he produced a sample that implored the Merchant Adventurers to send over as many

Strangers as possible, so as to dilute the ranks of the Saints. With the detachment of the victor, Bradford proceeded to have this letter read aloud before the crowd, while the confederates cringed.

"To the Reverend John Pemberton . . ."

To the colonists, this was a familiar name. If John Pemberton was involved, what was at hand could be nothing less than a revolution.

Richard, meanwhile, was caught in a swirl of conflicting discoveries. To have more Strangers like himself sent over—that, he knew, would be good, because he himself was the child of Strangers. But to hear the Gentleman from England insulted—could that be good, too? And if it wasn't, and Pemberton was actually bad, then wasn't having too many Strangers in Plimouth bad, too? And didn't that make Richard bad just for being there? Sometimes information arrives in such disconnected form that only shame can fill the gaps.

As the trial continued, it offered some object lessons in that emotion. Lyford, hearing his own words read back to him, broke into tears and confessed. "He feared he was a Reprobate," wrote one eyewitness, "his sins were so great . . . he was an unsavoury salt &c., and that he had so wronged them, as he could never make amends, confessing all he had written against them was false and naught, both for matter and manner."[13]

Oldham, having shown no remorse, was immediately banished—a harsh punishment in the days when English settlements were so few and far between. Lyford, on the other hand, was allowed to remain in Plimouth for six months, perhaps longer if he rehabilitated himself. Two months later, however, he was caught writing letters again.

This time, Lyford made it perfectly clear who his target was. He specifically singled out Richard's guardian for his invective, insisting that Plimouth had no ministry at all "but what may be performed by any of you." The colony defended Brewster vigorously in turn: "Our Reverend Elder hath laboured diligently in dispensing the word of God to us . . . and be it spoaken without ostentation, he is not inferrirour to Mr. Lyford (& some of his betters) either in gifts or lerning."[14] Still, Richard no longer had any doubts that the controversy rending the town centered on his protector. Was he, too, expected to side with his protector, then?

Lyford's wife complicated such questions by stepping forward to accuse her husband of siring a bastard child. She didn't even dare hire a maid, she lamented, for fear that he "would be medling with them." One strains to imagine the words Brewster found to explain to Richard what a bastard child was.

Meanwhile, the mutineers seemed not to have heard the news that they were unwanted. Lyford casually defied the order to leave town and was still there when Oldham returned uninvited. Standish was only too happy to lock Oldham up for a spell. Eventually, for lack of another solution, the trespasser was sent through "the gantlet"—two rows of soldiers who whacked him with their muskets as he passed between them—then thrown into a shallop and told to mend his manners. With this, the two ringleaders finally made themselves scarce around Plimouth.

There was one more drama to enact. In the spring of 1625, the Plimouth colonists sent a party to check on the progress of a fishing stage they had set up in Cape Ann, just above what became Boston Harbor, only to find Oldham, Lyford, and Roger Conant running the operation under the auspices of a rival group of investors. Again insults were hurled and threats made, and a brawl was narrowly averted. But for all intents and purposes, the mutiny was over.

Lyford, Oldham, and Conant soon found a more inviting harbor nearby and in 1626 made the fifteen-mile march westward, along with some stragglers at Cape Ann, to found the town of Salem. The Plimouth colonists, for their part, abandoned their fishing stage about the same time, after the man assigned to tend it proved incompetent.

Whatever the precise makeup of the Pemberton cell, there is

no sign that it posed a threat to Plimouth after 1626. The damage had been done, however. Despite the best efforts by the Saints, the Merchant Adventurers had been sufficiently influenced by Lyford to announce that they were disbanding, thus throwing Plimouth Colony into limbo.

The Lyford affair also appears to have exhausted Katharine More's resources, and with them, her prospects as a mother. There is some indication, in fact, that she may have died about this time. On June 11, 1625, Samuel More married Elizabeth Worsley, a distant relative of Lord Zouch. By English law, a divorced person was not allowed to remarry as long as his or her former spouse was living. Samuel, then, apparently believed that Katharine had died.

This conclusion was not so very far-fetched. An outbreak of the plague was sweeping through London that year, carrying off a large number of the population, with higher percentages among the disenfranchised. (The same years marked the passing of Katharine's uncle Mathew Smale, Barnabe Gooch, Lord Zouch—an entire array of characters from the More family drama.)

On the other hand, Samuel's legitimate descendants were questioned many decades later as to whether he had remarried too soon, and their defense proved less than airtight. To this one must add that Samuel received a general pardon in February 1626, of the kind that could be purchased in advance of all sorts of accusations. Contrary to his usual style, Samuel was acting quickly and worrying late.

It seems that Katharine had indeed lived on somewhere, at least for a time, far from Samuel's entitled circles, spending the remainder of her three hundred pounds, if there was a remainder, until plague, heartbreak, or plain old oblivion took her away.

The lost chances form a plaintive string: if Wessagusset had prospered, if Gooch had lived to receive his patent, if the Strangers had rallied around Oldham's call to mutiny—any of these outcomes might have brought Katharine and Richard closer together, and possibly into each other's presence. As it was, William Brewster stood at the end of the journey, holding firmly to his beliefs, never deigning to utter her name, his eyes cast heavenward even as the community around him teetered on the edge of collapse.

Richard, meanwhile, toiling away with an ocean separating him from home, was living out the results of that same series of failures, the wages of which, in his case, were disturbance and mystery. At the age of eleven, he was experienced far beyond his years, with a working knowledge of how to build a house and conduct a burial, yet he had no better idea of who he was than ever. He could remember dim, unformed images from the first half of his life—the Cree Hills on the horizon, the smell of the servant's house in which he lived, the cackles of Blakeway, and and the clatter of hooves that meant that Samuel was home again. But except for the abrupt cameo by Weston and the intense ambiguities that had sprung from the Lyford trial, the second half of his existence seemed to bear no connection to anything before it. Schooled at Brewster's knee, Richard was straining to read the will of God in the world around him and finding nothing but a veil, a disguise thrown over the work of mortals.

In 1626 the entrance of a new member into the Brewster household seemed to offer some hope of lifting that shroud.

5

To Sea

The Divil came from the worl' below
(Whisky Johnny!)
That is where bad whisky do grow
(Whisky for me Johnny!)
—Elizabethan sea shanty

NO ONE KNOWS what happened to Richard More between May 22, 1627, when he was living in the Brewster household, and the summer of 1635, when he resurfaced aboard the *Blessing* bound out of London for New England. Ironically, the moment our protagonist began to take an active role in his own destiny is precisely when he cannot be found. Once again we are left to look for clues, though this time we would be wise to focus our attention on spindrift rather than dust.

Children were entitled to appoint their own guardians in Plimouth, especially when an acting guardian had fulfilled his bargain. Brewster had promised to keep Richard for seven years, a term that coincided exactly with the articles of agreement for the entire enterprise. That Richard vanished from the record for another eight years suggests a second arrangement, possibly an apprenticeship, which expired shortly before he reappeared in 1635. There is a long list of possible guardians he could have chosen, but Richard's most plausible choice is a man named Isaac Allerton.

A large man with dark hair and eyes, a fair complexion, and a hot temper,[1] Isaac Allerton was a man of energy and ambition, a born trader, and, as it turned out, another in an increasingly long line of traitors to the Separatist cause. This last fact did not become apparent for some time, however, and certainly was not in the air when he enters our tale.

Of course, Richard already knew who Allerton was, and not only because the colony was so small. Allerton's children, Bartholomew and Remember, were among the very few *Mayflower* passengers close to his own age, and thus his likely companions upon their first meeting in Southampton. Since that time, Allerton had often been at the heart of the colony's affairs. He had been governor's assistant of Plimouth from 1621 to 1624, and thereafter he served on the council that decided many civil affairs in the colony.

Richard got an even closer view of this restless man beginning in 1626, when Allerton took a greater role in Plimouth's finances. With the collapse of the Merchant Adventurers and the seven-year agreement due to expire in the summer of 1627, action had to be taken—and soon—if not to find new investors for the gaunt freemen of Plimouth, then at least to find a way to pay the money owed.

At the same time, as Allerton dropped in on Brewster more often to discuss such things, he began to let his gaze rest a little longer than usual on the body of Richard's foster sister, the twenty-year-old Fear Brewster. A cynic might say that he was taking out a little insurance. In any event, the same year saw both his marriage to Brewster's daughter and his appointment to the task of straightening out Plimouth's accounts.

It would be going too far to place Richard aboard the ship Allerton took to London in 1626, but we cannot ignore the significance of the voyage. In reorganizing the Merchant Adventurers,

Allerton was headed directly into the company of the family that had disowned Richard. Indeed, Samuel More was living in London, making it a relatively straightforward matter for Allerton to meet with him and discuss the one hundred pounds that Christopher Martin had spent with such haste.

Did Samuel have any vested interest in such a meeting? Admittedly, he had never had a stake in the profits that Richard might yield at Plimouth—that money had always been earmarked for Richard himself. On the other hand, matters were not as simple as they had been in 1620. Samuel, after all, had arranged for *each* of Katharine's four children to receive fifty acres of land after seven years in the wilderness. Now that only Richard was left (and Samuel would have learned of the children's fate when he divested), the remaining hundred and fifty acres presented a quandary. If they were to be dismissed along with the lives of the children, one can imagine that Samuel expected a return of at least sixty pounds on his investment.

Allerton's stated goal, of course, was to reduce such debts, so his inclination would have been to propose the opposite—to call it even with Samuel, award Richard the full two hundred acres, and leave Katharine, the great undead herself, with nothing to complain about.

There was another benefit to this proposal. During the tumultuous first days of the More divorce, Samuel's father had promised to support Katharine's "spurious brood" until each of them reached the age of twenty-one. If Richard were to catch wind of this promise, he might well take a notion that he was due additional money and return to Shropshire to collect it. If, on the other hand, he were told of a handsome inheritance awaiting him in New England, he might be content to remain far away for the rest of his days. It was clearly in everyone's best interests to award the boy the extra land.

Samuel seemed to agree, at least to the extent that his name does not appear on the new list of adventurers. Likewise with

Samuel's relatives: the elder Richard More, Roger Harris, and Thomas Harris had long broken their ties with the older and more venerable Virginia Company.[2] By November 15, 1626, when the reorganization of the Merchant Adventurers was complete, the Linley Mores' interest in the New World was essentially history.

One is hard put to blame Samuel for washing his hands of the venture. Having remarried while Katharine was apparently still alive, he had already opened himself up to trouble. The specter of Katharine's son—revived by a man who was essentially the boy's brother-in-law—could only have been fresh cause for consternation.

Or, say, panic. Allerton first met with the Merchant Adventurers in November 1626. Eleven months later Samuel and his second wife, Elizabeth Worsley, had their first child together—a boy, baptized Richard More on October, 18, 1627.

It was not uncommon for a family in Stuart England to have two children with the same name, but generally only if the first child had died. Samuel, in effect, was observing this tradition in spirit. Whereas the new Richard More was legitimate and secure in his inheritance, the other might as well never have existed.

After all these years, the dreams of dead swans had not abated.

OF COURSE, the *Mayflower* Richard was very much alive, despite all ministrations of Providence to the contrary. In the summer of 1627, when Brewster's responsibilities to him were due to expire, he was in fact poised in every way to set out for new horizons. He had never really belonged among his accidental brothers and sisters, and the continuous stream of new Brewster arrivals had done nothing to enlarge his identity there. When Mary Brewster, William's wife, fell ill and died that year, Richard could mourn, but not with the dedication of the others in the household.

Unbound and unwanted alike, Richard had the world at his feet. The only question was where his feet should take him. The answer would depend a good deal on the news Allerton brought back from his negotiations in London. What signs from the Father, or the father, would his arrival betide?

Ambiguous ones, as it happened. Just as the original contract ran out, Allerton returned to Plimouth with a new deal to present. Using his limited bargaining chips, he had managed to create a party called the Purchasers, which included all self-supporting inhabitants of Plimouth, young or old, regardless of church affiliation. The Purchasers were to assume the colony's debt. In return, they would be entitled to twenty acres of land each—a decided improvement over Weston's original agreement, which denied the colonists even the houses they had built.

How this was explained to Richard one can only imagine, though we must admit to the scrupulous honesty of the Saints. Though still only a boy, Richard was considered a full partner in the Plimouth experiment, with an adult's stake in its success or failure. He was therefore technically qualified to be ranked among the Purchasers. On the other hand, twenty acres was not the complete two hundred due to Richard, and this smaller plot came with the stipulation that he would have to work for it—to support himself entirely, no less. Katharine More's hope for her children—the promised land—was still in force, but it remained very far away.

One document that has survived those Ancient Days is the Division of Cattle, which despite its title, served as a census of the humans living at Plimouth as of June 14, 1627. Most likely, the Division of Cattle was drawn up in conjunction with Allerton's new contract, as a formal statement acknowledging all those present and accounted for. Richard appears in Brewster's "lot," along with the Brewster family, the Prince family, Henri Samson, and Humility Cooper, suggesting that he had at least a nominal attachment to the colony at that date.

Given Richard's perplexing circumstances as a heavily endowed orphan, it makes sense that his future took some time to crystallize. It also makes sense to pinpoint 1628 as the year when his term under Allerton began. In that year Allerton returned from England yet again, having paid the adventurers their first annual installment of two hundred pounds and reduced other debts to four hundred pounds, sixty to Samuel More, representing the deaths of Richard's three siblings. (This left the total debt at two thousand pounds.) More important, Allerton returned with news of a land grant for the Plimouth colonists at Kennebec, which he had prized from the Council for New England. (Shades of the late Barnabe Gooch!)

FROM THE MOMENT the *Mayflower* arrived, the colonists had been sailing to Maine to fish, and over the years they had achieved some degree of permanence there. In 1626 a group of Plimouth men had gone up to the mouth of the Penobscot River, to the tiny settlement of Pentagoet,[3] and relieved Charles La Tour, a French trader who had grown up in the wilderness farther north,[4] of his duties at the fort erected there.

Pentagoet had given the Plimouth men their own point of departure for fishing expeditions, rather than the rougher outlying islands of Monhegan and Damarins Cove (known today as Damariscove). Additional land at Kennebec now augured a greater presence for Plimouth in the area, which in turn meant greater profits from fishing and trading. Once the grant was officially authorized, on January 12, 1629, the Plimouth colonists immediately began to build a fortified trading house some way up the Kennebec River, at Cushnoc,[5] with Edward Winslow heading the operation. There, the Saints would pin their hopes for financial restitution.

Richard's position now begins to come into view. He did not fit in easily with the Brewsters, and he was no longer required to stay among them. He was entitled to land, of which there was a new supply at Kennebec. He was expected to help pay off the colony's debts, a task being undertaken largely in Maine. Allerton had recently been in contact with Richard's father and had been central to the acquisition of the Maine settlements. All these factors pressed Richard irrevocably toward one decision: he would work under Allerton, for the usual seven years, developing the Maine business, and so earn his way toward a nice piece of land there, far from the suffocating atmosphere at Plimouth.

To this we may add one final supposition. By his twenty-fourth year, Richard was a full-fledged mariner, and before reaching a great age, he was addressed as Captain More. In early days of the colony, "captain" was a title of merit rather than rank, and only those who started sailing very young tended to achieve it. We may assume, then, that Richard took to the sea quite early. Condensing the image further: he apprenticed under Allerton as a shipboy, then as a sailor in his own right.

Some of Allerton's business continued to be in England, both as a negotiator and a trader, and Richard may have joined him on some of his transatlantic voyages. But with Samuel More loath to make any direct contact, he likely spent most of his time fishing on the American side of the ocean.

That was fair enough. Between Allerton's home in Plimouth and the wilds of Maine, Richard could abandon his troubles in the pitched struggle not to drown.

HAVING SPENT my summers on the Maine coast not far from Pentagoet almost from the time I was born, I was acquainted early with the area where Richard learned to sail. But only once have I encountered anything there that even remotely resembled the wilderness Richard knew.

When I was about thirteen or fourteen I began hanging out at night with the local boys. The center of town, where we congregated, was little more than an intersection of two roads, and there was really very little to do except drink cheap, warm beer. One time, however, we managed to knock over the pedestal that held the town sundial, an initiation rite that emboldened a local boy to invite me on an overnight expedition with him to an island in the bay.

A wooded piece of land about ten miles from end to end, Long Island cuts a stripe through the center of Blue Hill Bay, some two miles from the mainland. At that time, it was owned by a millionaire who had allowed nothing to be built on it beyond a hunting cabin or two. (Long Island has since become part of Acadia National Park and, as of this writing, remains undeveloped.) In essence, we were going to a shoreline that had hardly been touched since the days when the teenaged Richard first fished its waters.

Our own goal was to do some clamming, an activity best undertaken in the early-morning hours. A few days later, in the late afternoon, we crossed the bay in a rowboat fitted with an outboard motor, then circled around the southern tip of the island to the other side. I do not recall what we did after we pulled the boat ashore onto the sandy beach—probably because it involved more drinking. I do remember the unearthly quiet, however. It seemed to me as if we were speaking in a soundproof room that happened to be equipped with an open sky as far as the eye could see. And I certainly remember the following morning.

Clamming, at least the kind we practiced, has not progressed beyond the technology of Richard's day. Brandishing a clawlike tool called a clamming rake, we stood on the sand, waiting for the waves to recede. Whenever a bubble appeared in the riptide, the clam had betrayed its location and we dug. It was backbreaking work, and I hated it instantaneously. I gamely kept at it, however, until we saw a storm approaching. My friend, who knew his storms, said we would have to make for home without delay, so I promptly stepped into the boat—thus punching a hole in the bottom.

My companion could hardly believe it. "Who taught you to

stand in a boat?" he barked. But there was no way to undo what
had been done. He took us back across the bay, the motor full tilt,
while I bailed frantically. The storm arched over us, breaking just
as we made fast on the mainland.

As we parted, I attempted some pleasantries. He said, "Never
stand in a boat," and walked away.

I WOULD NOT have lasted long as a Maine fisherman even in my
own day, to say nothing of your century.

The sailors of your day had few of the outrageous luxuries that
I take for granted. Today we have lighthouses, self-propelled mo-
tors, maps that trace a coastline with stunning accuracy, and much
else besides. Richard had darkness, the wind and dead reckoning,
a navigational method that caused many a ship to be wrecked
when the longitude turned out to be wrong. On top of these difficulties were the usual dangers of storms and the usual hardships
of getting along with others while living together in a small space.
Only those with the sturdiest constitutions were able to survive
such a profession.

Of course, Richard's life had not been remotely easy before he
took to the sea. He had already lost his parents, buried his siblings, and watched an insurrection fail, all while adjusting to the
culture of his new foster parents. He did not need to learn bravery
from sailing. What he did not have yet, however, was the wider
view of the world that the sea afforded.

A ship putting in at New England, even those that flew the
king's flag, tended to be a floating cacophony of tongues and hab-
its and information from the length and breadth of the Atlantic
world. Any given sailor that Richard encountered might have
fresh news—and not of the sort that Brewster tended to impart—
from Ireland, France, even the Caribbean. These rugged souls represented the first "melting pot," an international culture that had
its own rudimentary laws,[6] its own customs, and its own patch-

work language, with a set of precise nautical terms, a wealth of profanities, and a variety of accents and dialects that were essentially placeless.

Nor did mariners have the unifying origin myth that the Saints did. Some might look to Neptune, others to Saint Dunstan (the patron saint of sailors), and others again to the various gods of their mother tongue for their archetypal sailor, but in any case, the iconography was makeshift, depending on the crew. Indeed, sailors were not really *from* anywhere, a fact that matched Richard's experience quite well, he having been conceived, after all, in a tunnel that did not exist.

As a shipboy, Richard's first task was to keep the watch, which meant watching the progress of the half glass. A day at sea began at eight o'clock at night by ordinary reckoning and continued up to the "dog watches" of the following day, with each half hour taking its own number. When the sand had run through, Richard rang a bell and a psalm was read—unless, of course, no respectable passengers were aboard. When he was due to be relieved of his watch, he gave a small stroke on the bell ten minutes before the hour.

Keeping the watch was a relatively comfortable job, but shipboys in the early years were also expected to lend a hand as soon as they could and to take part in every aspect of the work. This would have been especially true when sailing with Allerton, who improvised a great deal and cared little for hierarchy. At the age of thirteen or fourteen, then, Richard donned a tarpaulin hat, a thick-knit jersey, a leather apron, and a pair of heavy, tallow-covered, knee-length boots and began to learn the difference between a halyard and a sheet.

A fair amount can be said about the fisherman's life when Richard took it up. The fishing vessels coming out of New England had few of the amenities of the larger ships of the day. Their masts had no supporting stays, which meant that a gale could carry them away, and the ballast was sometimes no more than a collection of loose stones. Sometimes there was only a hold below. The typical crew in such a vessel might consist of no more than three men standing in the open rain for as long as it continued to fall.

The preferred direction outbound was invariably northeast—Down East, as it was called (then as now) because the easterly vessel sails downwind. The typical ship would hug the coast, as often as not, until it came to Cape Sable. From there, it might venture as far as Sable Island, otherwise known as the "graveyard of the Atlantic," but if the weather was fair, it might continue as far as the Grand Banks, off Newfoundland, where Vikings and Basques had plied the waters for centuries and the cod ran like the water itself in the murderous currents between the shoals.

Once out, Richard fished with his own handline—a line with two "snooged" hooks and a ten-pound lead—an exhausting procedure that left old-timers stooped and round-shouldered. Each time Richard caught a fish, he cut out its tongue and saved it for later accounting. When he was done for the day, he dressed, salted, and stowed his catch belowdecks. Then he sat down and took his meal—sea biscuits and pork fat, hardtack, and a halibut (not cod, which fetched too good a price back home)—in the fireplace on deck.

These fishing voyages were invariably dangerous. To maximize profit (or to make one at all), captains often loaded their ships until the deck was below sea level, gambling that the water in the bottommost fish would get pressed into the bilge from the weight of those above them and that the water would get pumped out before it mattered. But voyages could last as long as ten to twelve weeks, and everyone knew a storm might blow in and send the lot under.

Bringing in his catch, Richard would separate his fish, pressing the green corfish for its oil (the great New England whaling tradition, with its huge market in whale oil, being still a century away) and burying the finer fish in the ground, in a process called dunning, before digging them up and letting them dry in the open air until black. The fish were then ready to be stowed aboard again and shipped to the markets in England, Massachusetts, and, later, the entire eastern seaboard.

Most of the fishing was done in the winter, when the hauls were best, and between runs the fishermen usually camped out on either Damarins Cove or Monhegan. Richard called these islands home for several months of the year. In springtime, when the fishing slowed, the boats were hauled, their hulls scrubbed and tarred, and their rigging overhauled.

The Maine outposts themselves were just about as wild as wild could be. Only a few years before Richard went to sea, a captain at Damarins Cove had corralled his shipboy, William Couse, into his cabin, "wetted him in the fundament," and promised more where that came from. (Eventually, this captain was brought to trial and executed for the crime of buggery.)

Whether such acts were visited on the teenaged Richard will never be known, but certainly he was exposed to a life unlike anything taking place in Plimouth: the fishermen of Monhegan and Damarins Cove, it was well known all along the coast, drank like the damned and shared their wives as they did their boats. It was here, then, that Richard first learned what it meant to have his fill—discovered, as the waves lapped the shore and the stars came out, the elixirs that long ago had set Blakeway and his mother on fire.

And discovered, too, how history was recorded by sailors. The word *yarn* as a reference to storytelling stretches back into antiquity.[7] Yarns themselves, of course, have none of the linear evolution of literature. They have always been spun to the needs of the moment, elaborated into legend by repetition and mispronunciation, to be cast off when they have outlived their usefulness. Richard heard a great many of them as a boy—some true, some false, most a mixture of the two—and before long, his experiences with Allerton were giving him a length or two of his own to spin.

Since his appointment as the colony's accountant, Allerton had been a great boon to Plimouth, but things began to go wrong about the time the Kennebec grant was awarded. He had already demonstrated a worrisome habit of mixing his own goods with those of the colonists aboard ship, making it difficult to verify who owned what. To confuse matters further, he set up his own trading post at Kennebec to rival the official Plimouth counterpart. The trade at Kennebec was largely with the Indians, who received European goods in exchange for timber and, more important, beaver furs, which in addition to serving as a form of currency in New England were being shipped to London to satisfy a craze for fur hats.

But Allerton's superior trading practices were soon forcing the Plimouth colonists to buy from him, and to pay in heavily discounted beaver at that. This was incredibly galling to the Plimouth men, especially Edward Winslow, who had overseen the building of the Kennebec post and then opened the region to settlers from Plimouth. Indeed, from that moment on, Allerton and Winslow would be adversaries, facing off against each other in Maine, Plimouth, and London.

Richard's relationship with Winslow had also become strained some years earlier, at least in his own mind, when John Lyford stole into Winslow's luggage, pinched a letter addressed to Brewster from a certain Gentleman from England, and scrawled invectives in its margins. That relationship could only grow more uneasy again as Richard's protector continued to set himself against the colony's interests. (As evidence of his alliances, Richard later showed himself to be adept at slippery bookkeeping, a practice he no doubt learned in part during his time with Allerton.)

Not long after the Kennebec post was set up, Allerton was awarded land in Kingston, not far from Plimouth, from which he could conduct business more closely connected to the colony. There he built a house, twenty by twenty-two feet, in which Richard must have lived from time to time—although never with much sense of permanence. An earthfast structure, it had supporting poles that were sunk directly into the ground, as if to underscore the ability to leave on a moment's notice.

One can see why. Allerton seemed to think that Plimouth was useful only as a stage for introducing undesirable characters. On no particular authority, he brought over a pastor for the Plimouth church, who surprised the solemn churchgoers in his first few sermons by proving to be utterly insane. In his next trip home, Allerton added insult to injury by bringing Thomas Morton and installing him in his home as his clerk.

Morton's presence in Allerton's home gave Richard some of his best material for yarns to date. A few years earlier Morton had set up an idyll named Merrymount (not far from Wessagusset), inviting all comers to spout nonsense verse, dance around the maypole, and drink claret with him while he taunted Miles Standish with the nickname "Captain Shrimp." Who knows but that Morton recited again, for those gathered around the Allerton dinner table, some doggerel from his Merrymount jaunt?

> *Rise, Oedipus, and if thou canst, unfould*
> *What means Caribdis underneath the mould*
> *When Scilla sollitary on the ground*
> *(Sitting in forme of Niobe) was found.* . . . [8]

The Saints had already deported Morton twice for his transgressions, the second time going so far as to burn down his house. Understandably, when Allerton brought him back for a third round, the Plimouth authorities could only conclude that the purpose was "as it were to nose them" and accordingly sent Morton to England in chains once more.

While these acts may have served Richard as a kind of revenge by proxy, they did little for Allerton except mar his good name at Plimouth. Then again, little could be done about Allerton without marring the good name of his father-in-law, William Brewster—even Winslow had to relent on this point. In the first months of

1630, official business beckoned, and Allerton, as usual, was dispatched to London.[9]

Allerton returned aboard the *Lion* later that year, five hundred pounds poorer, with nothing to show for his efforts but recalcitrance and another batch of ne'er-do-wells. One of these was Roger Williams, later the founder of Rhode Island and pioneer of religious tolerance in America, who, in addition to terrifying the Saints with his theological beliefs, was Richard's closest relative ever to survive in the New World. (As a point of comparison, Katharine More was as closely related to her husband, Samuel, as she was to Williams; both were fifth cousins.)

Again the invisible machinery was working around Richard, calling him through its signs, and again these signs were telling him something he could not quite make out. There is no evidence that either Richard More or Roger Williams knew anything of their blood ties. If they stood shoulder to shoulder on the deck of the *Lion*, they did so as mutual acquaintances of Allerton, unaware that they had once been heirs to the same coat of arms.

They did have some time to miss this family connection, however. When the *Lion* arrived in Salem (which, four years after its inception, was beginning to thrive as part of the newly established Massachusetts Bay Colony), there were the familiar complaints that Allerton had mismanaged affairs: the ship had to be sent back to England for supplies. Williams's presence did nothing to alleviate the tension. Winslow made it a point to be present when he arrived and to reiterate the virtues of Separatism to a colony with still uncertain prospects. There would be no repeat of the Lyford mutiny in Salem!

Contentious as ever, Allerton finally returned to Plimouth with Williams in tow to break the news of his failure in London. Williams quickly fell into the predictable argument with Brewster and was asked to leave. Against their better judgment, the Salem authorities invited him to take their pulpit in 1631, and they felt the fireworks of their decision soon enough.

Allerton, for his part, was not far behind. In 1630 he had repeated his successful formula at Kennebec and set up his own trading post at Pentagoet, under the charge of a man named Edward Ashley. Perhaps the liveliest rogue yet in Allerton's gallery, Ashley preferred to affect the loincloth style of the Indians and was soon accused of being "unchaste" with them. Even worse, he was suspected of selling firearms to the natives. For this, he was replaced with his co-agent Thomas Willett and put under investigation.

On July 30, 1631, a Pentagoet local named William Phips, a gunsmith, gave a deposition in Plimouth that confirmed the colony's suspicions.[10] A small moment in the panorama of a continent perhaps, but Richard had cause to remember the name William Phips in later years, long after Ashley and Allerton were in their graves.

The immediate reality, however, was simply discouraging. Allerton had started out as a bulwark of the Saints' grand experiment, then slipped steadily into shady dealings, dubious business maneuvers, and finally, it seemed, willful malfeasance. Ashley proved to be the last straw on Plimouth's back; Allerton was fired and told to pack his bags.

After chewing over his options, Allerton settled provisionally on Marblehead, a rough-hewn peninsula across the harbor from Salem peopled by men with West Country accents. If that didn't work out, there were other possibilities up and down the coast. For a man of his pluck, there would always be something.

And so, naturally, it was time for Richard to go as well. He looked upon the land that had been his home for seven years, the grave of his brother and sisters, the scene of his unlikely flourishing—so many events indelibly branded into his mind. Was he saying good-bye to Plimouth forever?

Here we may lend Richard an artifact to support his late-night yarns. The story itself might have involved anything: a long-lost sweetheart, a friend, or merely a general strike at posterity. The artifact was found centuries later in a house beneath the ground just outside the spot where the Plimouth barricades had stood: a seal-top spoon (a type of metal spoon with a thin round handle) with Richard's initials carved into it.

RM

If nothing remained to remember Jasper, Ellen, or Mary by, at least there would be this small declaration that he, the surviving child, had once been there, at Plimouth Plantation, and lived through the worst of it.[11]

SAILING IN September 1631, the Allerton party made Salem Harbor in a matter of hours and claimed a spot on the windswept cliffs out at the edge of Marblehead Neck. There, among the small community of fishermen eking out a living and the few assorted Englishmen connected to the new colony of Massachusetts Bay, they built houses and fishing stages and commenced running a minor fishing trade.

The new man at Penobscot, Thomas Willett, was amenable to Allerton, and Richard could now resume his runs Down East un-hindered by the morally stringent Separatists. By 1633 Allerton had set up yet another trading post, this one as far down the coast from the Plimouth-owned settlements as possible, in a tiny port called Machias, and was running some six or seven fishing boats there and back. Once again, Richard eased into a harbor, unloaded his fish, and began stowing furs in the hold.

Unfortunately, the problem turned out to be larger than dif-ferences between Englishmen. With the signing of the Treaty of Saint-Germain-en-Laye in 1632, England had ceded most of the Maine coast to France, and France immediately began taking it

back. Charles La Tour, the irrepressible Frenchman who had originally built the fort at Pentagoet, was especially quick to seize the
day. When La Tour caught wind of Allerton's operation, he determined to take it by force.[12]

Arriving at Machias, La Tour met with resistance and in the
skirmish, he killed two of those defending the outpost. The remainder then gave way, and he pillaged the premises, bringing
prisoners and more than four hundred pounds' worth of booty
back north, to Port Royal. Allerton, shocked and possibly unsure
of his footing for the first time, asked for his men and goods back
and demanded to know La Tour's authority for the attack.

Richard may have been at Machias to face La Tour personally,
or he may have learned of the events there from a distance. At
the very least, he knew the men who were killed at Machias and,
no less, felt the force of La Tour's reply:

> I have taken them as lawful prize ;—my authority is from the
> king of France, who claims the coast from Cape Sable to Cape
> Cod ;—I wish the English to understand, if they trade eastward
> of Pemaquid, I shall seize them ;—my sword is all the commis-
> sion I shall show ;—when I want to help, I will produce my
> authority. Take your men and begone.[13]

Take your men and begone! That was a hard hangover to the
drunken tales of Allerton's misdeeds. Trading westward of Pe-
maquid meant retreating to territory under the sway of the Plimouth colonists, which Allerton could no longer do.

There would be no land in Maine for Richard. Nor, for that
matter, would there be any more business there for Allerton and
his fishing crew, and they became despondent accordingly. The
following year some of them got overly active in their mourning
and, accidentally perhaps, started a fire in the house of Allerton's
Marblehead neighbor. From there everything went completely

downhill. Allerton's wife, Fear, died. Several of his ships were wrecked. Eventually, the French even retook Pentagoet as well, forcing Thomas Willett onto a boat and into a devastating storm, which he only barely survived after "the bottom of his ship sank to the bottom of the sea."

Allerton's bad luck could not have come at a worse time; by May 1635 Massachusetts was going through a crisis of its own. The Council for New England had been dissolved, and several malcontents, correctly identifying a vacuum, were trying to void the colony's charter. The Massachusetts authorities were well aware that some of these people were Allerton's friends.[14] Clearly, it was time for Allerton and his motley crew to go.

Banished from the Bay as he had been from Plimouth, Allerton sold his Marblehead possessions in May and prepared to move to the burgeoning colony of New Haven to the south. Who could say? Maybe things would turn out better there once he reestablished his position.

This was easier said than done. After so many wrecks, Allerton needed a new fleet of ships and, after so many abrupt departures, new ports to send them to. Yet the best shipwrights still lived on the other side of the Atlantic, and the North American coast was becoming increasingly overrun by trading competitors.

Richard, meanwhile, was still beholden to Allerton for another few months—at least until he turned twenty-one in November. Perhaps, then, he could be more useful in Old England than he was in New.

One of Allerton's contacts in London was William Vassall.[15] Like Allerton, Vassall was a man of some standing who had been at loggerheads with the Massachusetts authorities and had left under a cloud of ill will. In an interesting confluence of events, the Vassalls had also been part owners of the *Mayflower*, which had since fallen to ruin and been junked. At the moment, William Vassall was in London on business. If Richard understood the concept of self-interest, he could always go calling on the man. After he got situated in town, of course. . . .

Richard's childhood, if one may call it that, was at an end. He had learned to sail, learned that one did not have to live like the Saints, and learned, too, that one could be ousted repeatedly, even after the primal expulsion. And so he set out, an able-bodied seaman, across the vast and furious ocean, toward the scene of the original crime.

6

Providence and Desire

Now the place for the best advancement of the Querents substance & preferment for him to Inhabit must needs be England because ye Sonn who is Lord of England is very strong the particular place in Englan is principally in or about London because Mercury the Lord of London is very strong.

—horoscope for an unknown member of the More family, born in the seventeenth century[1]

THE LONDON WATERFRONT was a huge leap from the creaky fishing stands of New England. In the 1630s it was the crossroads of the world, with sailors coming in from Russia, Smyrna, South America, Africa, even as far away as Indonesia, before shoving off with a black eye and a curse. The mariners' community extended from the Tower of London all the way out to Southend, an entire distended city of riggers and sailmakers, naval officers, sea-mad captains, privateers, haberdashers, tobacconists, smugglers, adventurers, failed and returning colonists, entrepreneurs of every stripe, haunted drifters, any of whom could have shared Richard's distinctive features and lineaments ... and women, some young, some not so young, some old enough that he had to look sharp or risk missing a stray sighting of his mother.

Where Richard lived while in England is not known, but his "grandfather," the elder Richard More, who long ago had grimly pledged to house him until the age of twenty-one, had owned six tenements in Stepney, just east of London proper, as recently as the 1620s. Quite possibly, Richard the younger availed himself of a room in one of these hovels[2] on Ratcliffe's Highway, amid the squabbling children and prostitutes and syphilitic-crazed sailors, in the last few months that the offer still stood.

WILLIAM VASSALL had property across the Thames in Rotherhithe, not far from where Richard had boarded the *Mayflower*. But if the scenery was familiar to Richard, his contact was not. Unlike the coarse sailors of Stepney and the severe people of Plimouth, Vassall was a man of the world, with business associates throughout Europe, even a servant who hailed from Genoa. Here was a man who understood the complexities of life, not just in business, as Allerton did, but in the halls of power as well.

Sadly, Vassall could not do much to help Richard get in touch with his family. The whole question of rights for New Englanders was quite tense at the moment. In fact, Vassall had come to London to protest religious intolerance in Massachusetts—more precisely, to militate for the rights of those who had not joined the church. In so doing, he had made an enemy of Edward Winslow, who had come to defend the very same practices.[3] Worse, while trying to colonize the Carolinas, Vassall's brother had fallen afoul of Samuel More's friend Edward Nicholas, who had risen in recent years to the position of secretary of state.[4] Now was certainly not the time to test the leniency of the good secretary.

Still, all was not lost. Ironically, the persecution of the Puritans was reaching such heights that even some of the aristocracy[5] were mobilizing for a mass exodus from the realm. As a result, there were several new territories where Richard might hope to stake out a place of his own.

One compelling effort at the moment was a venture headed by the earl of Warwick, a Puritan sympathizer with immense power to legitimize settlements in the New World.[6] Having been recently ousted from the Council for New England, the earl was concentrating his efforts on the Caribbean, where he had been sending ships to plunder the Spanish for some time. His current plan was to enlarge his settlement at Providence Island, a tiny dot of land just off the coast of South America. Vassall, for his part, was interested in settling in the Caribbean, too, and had become involved in the Providence project.

This venture, though nominally Puritan, was far different from its northern counterparts. Providence Island lay close to the Spanish Main, where plundering went on as a matter of course, and far from the control of extremist Puritan leaders. Those in charge of policing the colony were not far from being pirates themselves, carousing freely while their pastor idly made lists of the "catches" sung by the natives. As for practical justifications, a few years earlier, Allerton had shown an interest in an exotic staple crop being grown on the island—a sweet plant that showed every sign of becoming popular throughout the colonies.[7]

It looked as if there were profits to be made, and the call was on for settlers, especially those who could sail—provided they could proceed with discretion. Was Richard game?

One cannot underestimate the tension in the air at that time. With the king bearing down on the Puritans with all his regal power, it was necessary for many emigrants, especially those with views antithetical to those of the Crown, to operate in almost total secrecy.[8] The Providence Island Company, for its part, had been meeting in London, at Warwick House, while the occasional spy loitered on the street, waiting to discover something good. But although colonizers might keep some aspects of their plans under wraps, they often had difficulty concealing the identities of their passengers, and the king demanded an oath of fealty from anyone leaving his shores.

Thus, Richard found himself in a coach with Vassall's immediate family on June 17, 1635, wending their way through the crooked streets of London until they arrived at a nondescript building within the city walls. After a furtive glance up and down the street, they continued inside, where they queued up to sign the passenger list for the *Blessing*.[9]

William's ten-year-old son, John, appeared before the clerk first, followed by William himself. Richard then entered his signature, painstakingly learned at the footstool of William Brewster, directly below. The names of other Vassalls were then recorded as well, catch-as-catch-can in the milling crowd.[10] Out to the street they returned, in a purposeful gait, and were spirited away in the coach.

So far, so good. Richard returned to the bleak slums of Stepney and awaited his departure.

Unfortunately, the plan went sour before the *Blessing* ever set sail. In Providence, the advance colonists had become desperate, having failed to cultivate the land, and when rumors emerged of a new, unclaimed island in the Caribbean, they had bent their forces on seizing it. Only at the last minute was it discovered that this island, named Fonseca, suffered from the shortcoming of not existing. By then, precious resources had been squandered, leaving the Providence colonists racked by poverty and torrid weather. On July 7, when the Spanish launched a withering attack on the island, the plan to send the *Blessing* from London was canceled.

To the fictions that determined his destiny (let us not forget that Shropshire tunnel), Richard could now add an entire island. The need to leave England remained paramount, however, not only for Richard, who, when his legal grandfather's obligations ended in a few months, would have no place to live, but for any passenger intent on escaping England. And notional colonies would not do.

By that time, the Providence Island Company was increasingly shifting its meeting sites to more remote locations in Essex, half a day's ride to the east, the better to hammer out its plans unimpeded. Among these hideouts was Stondon Hall, the estate of the earl of Warwick's cousin Nathaniel Rich, in the village of Stondon Massey.[11]

As a nineteen-year-old sailor, Richard could take little part in the deliberations at Stondon Hall. Still, there were distractions to be had, particularly across the way at Stondon Place, home of the famous Renaissance composer William Byrd and, more recently, the home of Byrd's daughter-in-law, a woman by the name of Katharine More. Had Richard's mother married into a famous family and so escaped ruin? Alas, this Katharine More was someone else entirely.[12] A similar disappointment—or perhaps a relief—was awaiting Richard in nearby Braintree, where a destitute "widow More" was being kept in beer by the Puritan church wardens.

To all outward accounts, Richard's trip to England was beginning to look rather anticlimactic: no tropical home, no chance family reunion. Nevertheless, it was this small town in Essex that produced his next substitute father and got him a wife in the bargain.

STONDON HALL had been owned in the previous century by various members of the Hollingsworth family: Reinald, Lawrence, William, and, briefly, John.[13] These Hollingsworths had exerted great influence in Stondon Massey. For many years, a brass representation of Reinald Hollingsworth was on display in the local church. William Hollingsworth appointed the pastor at the same church as late as 1605. By then, however, the family's presence in the village was already waning. In 1610, after a protracted property dispute, Stondon Hall was sold to Nathaniel Rich, the earl's cousin and mastermind of the Providence Island venture.[14]

The Hollingsworth connection should hold our interest, because one of the passengers who ended up on the *Blessing* was a forty-year-old shipwright named Richard Hollingsworth. Although Richard Hollingsworth's parentage is unknown,[15] we would not be going too far astray by imagining that he became aware of the negotiations at Stondon Massey through family connections and subsequently cultivated a greater interest.

At the moment Hollingsworth became involved, a new destination had been established for the *Blessing*. Rather than Providence Island, it would sail for Boston, with a general eye toward settling the colony of Saybrook.[16] Located on the Connecticut coast, not far from present-day New Haven, Saybrook was the brainchild of two members of the Providence Island Company— Lord Brook and Lord Say and Sele. In a departure from the norm, its government was to be made up of aristocrats rather than the usual marginal subjects. For the moment, only an advance party had been sent there to build a fort and lay out the properties—no bushwhacking for the upper crust, thank you![17] But if conditions at Providence Island ultimately improved, Saybrook might well provide a good staging point for voyages south. And that meant plenty of work for a shipwright.

When a new passenger list was drawn up on July 17, 1635, Richard Hollingsworth sent the names of his family members to the clerk (rather than appearing in person), announcing their readiness to sail.[18] A peculiar family it was. At the age of forty, Hollingsworth was not only the father of four but guardian to a second family, also of four, all of them older than his natural children.

The eldest of this adoptive brood was the twenty-year-old Christian Hunter. Aside from her apparent relation as a sister to the three other Hunters under Hollingsworth's care—William, Thomas, and Elizabeth—Christian's past also remains a complete mystery. Like Richard More, she was a dispossessed soul, and almost his age.[19] Other than that, we can only infer the eternal truths of romance—the spectacular nuance of glance, the beauty in the eye of the beholder, the mysterious resemblances to oceanic currents. . . .

Again the city of London receded from view, again the bowsprit lay to the east. But this time Richard was sailing with wiser prospects for land, and rather than losing his mother, he was gaining the affections of a lover.

And what did Richard have to recommend himself to Christian's guardian? Perhaps only a submerged affinity: many years earlier, before there was a New England, even before Richard Hollingsworth was born, it so happened that Katharine More's father, Jasper, the cranky bailiff of Shipton, had learned that a certain John Hollingsworth had been thrown in jail in London without apparent cause, and had demanded his release.[20] The More and Hollingsworth families had been friends in the distant past.

How strong the bonds of extended families can be across time and space is a question best left to others. For our purposes, it is the result that matters: by the time the ship reached American shores, Richard had all but joined the Hollingsworth family and was working for Richard Hollingsworth, shipwright, as a laborer and "retainer."

The news in Boston, as usual, dampened any high hopes the voyage had created. Saybrook was not yet ready for settlers and would not be for some time. In fact, with its shortage of supplies and men, the advance guard was finding it difficult even to build a fort. Even worse, the local Indians were intent on driving out the English, causing gossips to predict a war in the making.

The master of the *Blessing*, John Leceister, did not fare much better. Steering onward to Providence Island, he joined a privateering mission against the Spanish. Not only did this mission fail, but it resulted in a prolonged captivity for the entire crew when the Spanish bested them.

Faced with these discouraging developments, many of the Saybrook colonists gravitated to Salem and nearby Marblehead, where they waited for conditions to the south to improve.[21] And so, following the market, this is where the Hollingsworth family ended up, too, with the new addition of Richard as an employee.

From Marblehead he left, to Marblehead he returned.

No sooner had Hollingsworth set up his shipyard at Marble-head than the work began to come in. In 1636 Hugh Peter, an eminent political figure (and another would-be Saybrook settler), was traveling door-to-door, exhorting Massachusetts colonists to build their own ships, in the interest of establishing a world-class fishing industry. Hollingsworth was, by his very arrival, the most accomplished shipwright in the region, and therefore worthy of special attention. Thus, Richard—in his capacity as a laborer and retainer for Hollingsworth at that time—almost certainly had a hand in building the *Desire*, New England's first large ship.

WHETHER FATE decides our course or the imagination persists through the generations, I cannot say, but it is a fact that in addition to going clamming on the same remote Maine islands where Richard drank, I briefly held a job as a shipbuilder at the same age he did, at a location only half an hour north of Marble-head.

The atmosphere inside the factory where I worked was a study in hellishness—loud, ugly, and mean-spirited. Most of the employees revealed their passions on their bodies. One had a mountain range of scars on his chest from a bar fight. Another, the most approachable man from my middle-class standpoint, had an oval pupil in one eye where a knife had picked it. No one had any aspirations beyond their misery, except for me and the born-again Christian, who wore a perpetual grin as the disaster of his circumstances unfolded around him.

The technology was far different than it was for Richard, of course. We built fishing boats, thirty-five and forty-two feet long, out of fiberglass, a material that you in your innocent, wooden era would certainly ascribe to witchery. In exchange for this material's light weight and durability, the worker must breathe extremely poisonous fumes all day long and worse, submit to a total-body itch that is as strong upon waking as it is upon going to sleep. The shipbuilder of today is a cursed man who literally cannot bear being in his own skin.

Not so for a shipwright such as Richard Hollingsworth, or his laborer Richard More. Building ships was a dangerous business for them, to be sure, but it was also a respected one, especially in those earliest days, before your time, when the colony could live or die on the strength of its vessels.

The shipwright's career generally began with five or six years as an apprentice and then ten years as a journeyman, culminating in the title of master shipwright. But a master still needed about ten additional years of experience before he could attempt a ship of three hundred tons such as the *Desire*. This was because a larger ship demanded that everything be larger. Timber was chosen for its resemblance to the ship's various parts and was cut whole whenever possible in order to minimize leakage. A long hull required planks that reached stem to stern: a tall mast had to come from a tall tree. (When joining had to be done, the shipwright held the joints together with special pegs called fished parts.) This oversize timber also had to be stored in a shelter large enough to keep it dry, then laid out on the ground like a massive puzzle.

That most of the trees on Salem Neck were clear-cut during the first years of its settlement suggests that it was the source of the wood for the *Desire*. Richard, who moved to Salem Neck a few years later, first became acquainted with its terrain at this time as he walked the uneven ground in search of the tree that resembled a bowsprit or a gunwale, then hauled it across the harbor to the open cliffs of Marblehead. He may also have spent his time pulling the old trimmings from the *Warwick*, a ruined ship belonging to the earl that had seen better days roving the Caribbean, and fitting them onto the new vessel. Each of these items told a story of the privateers who had handled them: three falcons and a falconet (light pieces of ordnance), a lanthorn poop, a small crow of iron, a pump bolt and a wooden brake, a small anchor stock, a pistol barrel and three small tackle hooks, a cooper funnel, two sponge staves, a rammer and a ladle, eleven falcon shot, a small bell, and a small anchor.[22]

The completion of the *Desire* was considered a big event around Salem—persuasive evidence that the colony was beginning to stand on its own. And so it was. When the vessel was completed, in the summer of 1636, it was immediately stocked with one hundred men and shipped off to Block Island, where, so it was said, the Pequots had killed a man. Or rather, not just any man, but John Oldham, John Lyford's partner in crime during the early years of Plimouth.

Richard, who remembered Oldham as the man who had vainly rallied the Strangers to overthrow the Saints, could not have failed to register this darkening of the atmosphere. No fighting occurred on this expedition, largely because the nature of Oldham's death could not be easily determined. Still, suspicions of murder lay heavy in the air, and the English vented their anxieties elsewhere by murdering fourteen Niantic Indians and as many dogs as they could, and by taking several Pequot children hostage. The Pequots retaliated by capturing some English colonists and torturing them.

In essence, the Pequot War, much predicted and by 1637 a fact, consisted of only two battles: the fort fight and the swamp fight. The first of these was hardly a fight at all. On May 26 English forces cornered their enemy in a wooden fort on the Connecticut coast, then entered the building by surprise and burned it to the ground. The number of deaths, and the proportion of women and children dead, began to be debated almost from the day of the event, but the severity of the action is not open to question.

After the swamp fight, which a combined force from Plimouth and Connecticut won on July 28, the English chased down the Pequot stragglers, either killing them or taking them captive. Seventeen of these prisoners—fifteen boys and two girls—were taken by Captain William Pierce (the very man who had allowed Bradford to intercept Lyford's letters during the Plimouth mutiny), clapped in chains, and marched aboard the *Desire*. From there, they were taken to Providence Island, to be sold into slavery.[23]

In February 1638 Captain Pierce brought the *Desire* into New England with a cargo of Africans, procured in exchange for the Pequot prisoners. Some of these captives were sold to local colonists. Others were deemed too violent to keep and were returned to tropical climes. Whatever their fate, the first black slaves had been disgorged in New England, and the ship that disgorged them had been built in part by Richard More, from the wood he had helped pick out on Salem Neck.

Richard knew the principal characters in this slaving transaction, as they were sea captains with central positions in the failing remains of the Providence Island colony. What he could not have known was the effect of their actions—that slavery, heretofore a temporary circumstance that could befall almost anyone in any part of the world, would, within his lifetime, become a permanent condition in North America for anyone of African descent.

SEX AND VIOLENCE running ever together, the Block Island incident was soon joined by another disturbing development. In 1634 a woman named Anne Hutchinson had landed in Boston and begun to preach a variety of religion that tested the patience of the authorities to the limit. It was Hutchinson's misfortune to arrive at a time when the charter of Massachusetts was in jeopardy (its validity being under review just then in London). As proved to be the case more than once later on, New Englanders tended to respond poorly to the threat of dissolution. Virginia might fall under royal supervision and be none the poorer for it, but Massachusetts would eat its own first.

Hutchinson's creed came to be known as antinomianism, which, strictly speaking, means "against the law." As a general practice, however, the authorities tarred her with the all-purpose label of familism.

Founded by the Dutchman Hendrik Niclaes in the sixteenth century, familism sometimes went by the name "the Family of Love." Its central tenet held that mankind had become sinless since the Crucifixion; thus, any human impulse should be deemed pure. Familists freely practiced adultery (with one early adherent going so far as to marry his own daughter) and sometimes held property in common. The most pernicious aspect of the sect, however, was the tendency of its members to infiltrate normal society, attending church and holding positions of prominence. Caught, familists would renounce their ways, then simply continue to observe them on the sly.

In their insistence on stripping disguise from the human form, your forefathers thus arrived at the razor's edge where disguise meets the human soul. What, after all, was the practical difference between a spy in the house of the Lord and a man who fell to temptation and tried to repent?

By 1636 the Antinomian Controversy, fueled by the fumes of familism, was raging through the colony of Massachusetts. Hutchinson was holding forth before large audiences in her Cambridge home, while bands of hecklers roamed the countryside, dropping in on local preachers and taunting them. As in every social phenomenon, the progression was less than neat. A Captain John Underhill, for one, took all this as license to commune with God by smoking tobacco and to counsel married women behind locked doors in the love thereby discovered.

Still, neither the Hutchinsonians nor the free interpreters posed the greatest threat. The greatest threat lay in the impressionable minds of the young. Massachusetts governor John Winthrop put the fear succinctly when he wrote "that many [who] now adhere to these Familisticall opinions, are truly godly . . . yet the next generation, which shall be trained up under such doctrines, will be in great danger to prove plain Familists."[24]

All of which placed a rootless young man like Richard at great risk of contagion. Indeed, familism revisited the outlines of his childhood with startling accuracy. His mother and Jacob Blakeway romping through Larden Hall, Samuel appearing with rebukes, Katharine agreeing to desist and then continuing as before—didn't that cover the basic positions in the familist conflict fairly well? For that matter, hadn't Katharine, with a defiance worthy of Anne Hutchinson herself, once quipped that her vows to Jacob were "all one before God"?

In 1636, as summer turned to autumn, Richard, like many others, watched the prospects at Saybrook dwindle away. The likelihood of civil war in England was intensifying, and the colony's leading lights—aristocrats all—were too preoccupied with domestic troubles to think about relocating to the New World. Still, Richard could not simply live off the good graces of the Hollingsworths forever. He needed to find a place of his own to live—and to get it in a way that did not cast suspicion on his immortal soul.

By this time, William Brewster had moved to Duxbury, a coastal town within the bounds of Plimouth Colony, a few miles north of Plimouth proper. Richard was immediately entitled to twenty acres of land, thanks to the ministrations of Allerton (with more to be rewarded at some future date, as a fulfillment of his mother's original demands). Most likely Richard had come into this land in 1632, when Brewster received his allotment. What more logical place for him to go than to his own property, at least until things calmed down at Saybrook?

Admittedly, the idea posed certain problems. Solitary dwellers were ostracized by the Saints in normal times and would be especially so at a moment when the familist crisis was reaching fever pitch. Brewster would never approve of Richard's arriving alone to settle his land. Add to that the growing signs of war with the Pequots, which, like all wars, stirred up a confusion of mortality and lust, and the course of action was clear enough.

Richard More and Christian Hunter arrived in Plimouth sometime before September 1636, when they posted their intention to marry—their marriage banns—on the meetinghouse door. A month later they were wed in the same meetinghouse, probably by William Brewster himself.[25]

Imagine the thoughts that raced through Brewster's mind as he conducted this ceremony. He was aware, at least to some degree, of his charge's past, of the home torn apart because of a marriage arranged for the sake of land. It could not have inspired confidence to see his former ward repeating that scenario so closely. Was the boy uttering his vows cynically, simply to legitimize his presence in Duxbury until he could cash in on his property? And if so, was he doomed to repeat his mother's sins?

Such reasoning would not have been a stretch, since William Brewster had had every opportunity to suspect Katharine More of familism when her story was originally explained to him back in Southampton. On the other hand, what was the alternative, except to let the boy live unwed on land abutting his own? Was it, to put a fine point on it, God's design that Katharine More had secured property for her disinherited son? Like any sincere Puritan, Brewster must have pondered the impurities in himself as he pronounced the couple man and wife.

It did not take long for his doubts to be confirmed. Richard and Christian did not follow the pattern so often seen among your New England families, even those with seagoing fathers, of producing a child within the first year of marriage. On the contrary, fully four years would pass before Christian gave birth.

It is possible that Richard and Christian had trouble conceiving, but I personally do not believe it. Christian was quite capable of issuing children once she got started—she would have no fewer than seven of them—and Richard managed to spread his seed more easily than perhaps even he would have liked. The problem, in my estimation, was not one of fertility. Rather, the Mores did not immediately have children primarily because their marriage was one of convenience—a marriage for appearance's sake and, by extension, for land, much like the marriage of Samuel and Katharine More some twenty-five years earlier. And, of course, with

Richard gone so often, even the warmth of convenience had little time to work its charms on their life behind closed doors. But most of all, the problem was that, within a short time after their marriage, there was already somebody else.

7

A Familist Affair

Marvilous it may be to see and consider how some kind
of wickednes did grow and breake forth here, in a land
wher the same was so much witnesed against, and so narrowly looked unto.

—William Bradford

K NOWLEDGE CAN BE GAINED and lost many times. The
record of Richard's bigamous marriage lay fallow until the
late twentieth century, when Robert M. Sherman unearthed a set of obscure documents detailing the activities of American colonists in England. These revealed that "Richard Moore of
Salem, mariner" married Elizabeth Woolnough of Limehouse on
October 23, 1645, in St. Dunstan's Church in the parish of Stepney.[1]
From there, the trail led to the Stepney parish register, which shows
the baptism of Elizabeth Woolnough, daughter of Benjamin Woolnough, on December 21, 1623, and the baptism of her daughter by
Richard More on March 2, 1646. Beyond that, the combined research of modern *Mayflower* scholars screeches to a halt.

How do these pieces of information connect? Under what circumstances did Richard and Elizabeth meet—and when? Was
Richard coerced into marrying Elizabeth when she discovered she
was with child—or was the story more complicated than that?

Of course, Richard's bigamy may have been well known during his own lifetime; it may even have been the source of the "common fame" that encouraged you to stand witness in the church against him. But today one may search the archives the world over and find no theory, not even a rehearsal of one. It is more than a matter of sketchy records. The task has simply never been undertaken, for the keepers of the Ancient Legend have not particularly cared to find out.

This is surprising, because bigamy in its full-fledged form—that is, a consciously undertaken, symmetrical pair of marriages, as opposed to cases in which a spouse was believed dead or refused to cross the ocean—was an unusual occurrence in the English-speaking world. In the first half of the seventeenth century, very few instances appear in English court records, and only three or four in Middlesex County, in which Stepney is located.

In New England the story was much the same. The most famous bigamist there, quite apart from legal charges, was Stephen Bachiler. A minister much maligned as a familist, Bachiler was dogged his entire life by accusations of infidelity and, finally, when he moved back to England, of having two wives at once. This charge was never proved, however, only suspected.

Indeed, it might be more accurate to say that few bigamists were caught. On the other hand, Richard was surely aware of the price paid by Benedick Goffe of Middlesex, who in 1610, "being married to a certain Barbara Goffe, married a certain Dorothy Ellis, the aforesaid Goffe being still alive. Confessing to the indictment, Benedick Goffe was sentenced to be hanged."[2] The penalty for bigamy, in every corner of the English realm, was death.

What could have caused Richard to risk such a fate and what steps did he take to avoid it?

Admittedly, the leads are few and far between. Elizabeth's surname had enough variants—Woolnough, Wolnaugh, Walnugh, Woolner, Woolmer, even the occasional Wulnoth—to tax the patience of anyone. There is, however, plausible evidence that Richard and Elizabeth met and conceived their daughter some seven or eight years before their marriage. This evidence, gleaned from rubble that time has strewn, illuminates a story that began almost at random but ultimately cast a shadow that reached all the way to his grave.[3]

THE MARINER'S EXISTENCE removed Richard from most of the events that taxed the landlubber's soul. He did not have to bother with petty disputes over fence lines or penalties for falling asleep during the Sabbath lecture. So what if the life of a sailor was hard? Once out, he was as free from social constraints as a man could be.

Given a typical run, Richard would make first for the Grand Banks, where the fishing was best, then take his haul on to England, where he could exchange his catch for other goods much in demand back home. There is reason to believe that in October 1637 his specific destination on the sceptered isle was Portsmouth. As the Pequot War caught fire in New England, a man named More appeared in Portsmouth aboard the *Saul*, coming in from Newfoundland with seven tons of train oil (that substance squeezed from corfish to light the lamps of millions).

Portsmouth was only a few miles from Southampton, a town Richard may have remembered from his traumatic days before the *Mayflower* voyage.[4] Now he walked the same cobbled streets, taller but no less vulnerable to the reverberations of his foot-steps—his loss reflected back at him in the simple fact of the eerily familiar steeples and doorways.

This is the first plausible moment when Richard and Elizabeth Woolnough could have crossed paths. Benjamin Woolnough had been doing business in Portsmouth earlier that year as a wine merchant.[5] By the time Richard arrived, however, Benjamin had departed as master of the ship *Elizabeth*, alias the *Old Leammon*, bound for Virginia.[6]

Richard's relationships with women might best be described as confused, so it is perhaps not so strange to imagine him warming to the thirteen-year-old and temporarily unattended Elizabeth. It would not have been the first time that a twenty-three-year-old man had done such a thing—or that a barely teenaged girl had looked back, either.

What a contrast that was to the experience of Elizabeth's father just then. On October 13, 1637, Benjamin Woolnough was some 150 leagues off the coast of Virginia when his ship was overtaken by a fleet of eleven Spanish vessels. Benjamin, his crew, and his ship were taken back to Cadiz, and from there to Madrid, where they were held hostage for a ransom of four thousand pounds sterling. England and Spain being at peace, this was an act of piracy. The Spanish, justifying their actions by claiming that Virginia was outside of England proper, responded to the appeals of the English ambassador with the utmost delay,[7] and Benjamin languished in an Iberian jail.

A child of the waterfront, just now at the zenith of her beauty, easy prey—or was it exquisite relief? Between the clatter on the wharves and one rum too many, Richard and Elizabeth found themselves in close quarters, in a tavern or along a quay or, reasonably speaking, nowhere at all, someplace far from the leaden pressures of New England. And then things, in that magical and perfectly natural way, began to get a little unclear. . . .

BUT WHAT TAKES PLACE AS FOG is sometimes best left in fog. Richard's land in Duxbury lay between Eagle's Nest Pond and the shore—a twenty-acre lot that, to a colonist of a different mind, would have represented the culmination of a dream. But Richard was not the settling kind. In contrast to Brewster's full-framed house next door, with its complete complement of servants, he built the most temporary sort of abode for Christian to live in, most likely an earthfast structure of the type Allerton had built in Kingston. After that, he was mostly gone to sea, in search of the fish that represented his future.

As fall turned to winter, Richard returned to Duxbury, with a new plan to announce to his wife. They were moving—not to Providence Island or Saybrook, which had all but failed as a colony, or even to any other place in Plimouth, but to Salem, where Richard Hollingsworth had set up a new shipyard.

On November 1, 1637, Richard sold his "twenty acres of land thereunto belonging and all the fence around the same"[8] to Abraham Blush for the sum of twenty-one pounds, to be paid in money or beaver, in three installments. Richard and Christian left Duxbury sometime after November 16, when he received his second payment, in the amount of ten pounds. Most likely they packed their belongings aboard a small boat, sailing being faster and easier than riding.

In the usual New England custom, upon their arrival in Salem, Richard was subjected to a "warning out" period, during which a newcomer was required to state his religious affiliation and general intentions. Normally, one was considered warned out after a term of three months. With the antinomian crisis, this grace period had been tightened down to three weeks, in hopes of keeping heretics out. In any event, Richard must have used William Brewster's credentials to his advantage, because he was admitted into Salem on January 1, 1638, without having taken the mandatory step of joining the Salem church.

Not long after arriving, Richard became involved in the motley crew that had taken root on Salem Neck. Predominantly mariners and their families, these people had little in common with the churchgoers in town and, in fact, were already searching for a more tolerant social climate elsewhere along the coast. A fair number of them had emigrated from Suffolk, England, among them the Sallowes, the Yonges, and a sailor named Robert Lemmon. Richard got to know all these people. He knew Robert Lemmon best. When someone accused Lemmon of trespassing, Richard responded by killing the accuser's pig. Years later, when Lemmon died, it was Richard who proved, and possibly wrote, the man's will.

These new faces in Richard's life were all very interesting, because as Suffolk people, they hailed from a county with the highest concentration of Woolnoughs anywhere in the world. More interesting again, Benjamin Woolnough's ship, the *Elizabeth*, sometimes went by the alias of the *Old Leamman*—an alternate spelling of Lemmon. In moving to Salem Neck, Richard was staying close to his dreams. One might even say he had fallen in love.

Unfortunately, it was a little late to be practicing his courting techniques. The following October Richard was again in Portsmouth, selling corfish from aboard the *Sarah*. By this time, Benjamin Woolnough had been released from captivity but had returned to Madrid to seek financial compensation for the loss of his ship, leaving his daughter alone again. Here was another opportunity for illicit love—and another opportunity for Richard to spilt his life along two forks that could never be put together again.

Richard apparently had some inkling that he had impregnated Elizabeth by this time because, once back in Salem, he began to undertake a series of bizarre preparations that seemed designed to bridge the gap between his unstable past and his increasingly disturbing prospects as a father.

On November 18, 1639, Richard appeared in the county court to receive the right to set up his own fishing stand beside his house, far out on the neck, at Winter Harbor. Beside him in court, oddly, stood a woman known as "the widow More," who received a grant for a farm in the same area of the neck.

No relation to Richard, Anne More, or Moore, had originally come to Salem from Southold, Suffolk, with her husband, Thomas. Still, one of her daughters had married Richard's friend Robert Lemmon, and Richard could easily have endowed her with some vestige of symbolic power. If he had failed to find his mother in London or in Stondon Massey, or anywhere else, he could cobble together a fantasy family all the same.[9]

That same year the reappearance of a familiar face from Richard's past seemed to confirm as much. When Thomas Weston surfaced in Marblehead in 1639, he had been on the run from the Crown for a decade, engaging in his usual smuggling activities, and perhaps in something worse. With such a man, it was always hard to separate fact from fiction, but one thing was certain. Weston so feared for the safety of his seven-year-old daughter, Elizabeth, that he was looking for someone to care for her in his stead. This was not the type of arrangement, so common among New Englanders, whereby parents found a temporary guardian during a relocation, but rather a permanent handoff performed under a cloud of danger.

Weston eventually found haven for his daughter with Richard's childhood friend Remember Allerton and her husband, Moses Maverick, who were living in Marblehead by then and expecting a child of their own. Richard, who recalled this event decades hence in a detailed deposition in 1684, was intimately acquainted with the details of the transfer, if not actively involved.

It must have felt peculiar, to say the least, for Richard to help hide the child of the man who had taken him away from his parents. Looking down into the eyes of Weston's daughter, he could hardly have avoided the thought of himself at a younger age. But did he perhaps also foresee the day when he would have to do the same for his own daughter?

History is but a chain of confessions derailing the destinies of its inhabitants, from parent to child, ad infinitum. . . .

WHATEVER DARK CURRENTS it stirred in his heart, Weston's reappearance turned out to be well timed for Richard's purse.

In November 1638 Richard had received the final payment of ten pounds from Abraham Blush for his land,[10] which he apparently used to buy a small ketch, the name of which is not known. He now had a fishing stand as well, and though it was little more than a warehouse protruding into the water on stilts, it gave him a base of operations for any voyages he might take. At the age of twenty-five, Richard was ready to sail on his own account.

And Weston was ready to send some business his way. Before arriving in Marblehead, Weston had begun negotiations for an estate in Maryland and was, in fact, leaving just then to consolidate his tobacco trade down in that colony.[11]

Richard did not need to be told the benefits of the tobacco business. Cod could be caught by any crew willing to try, but tobacco could be grown only where the climate was right, and it was fetching top prices in London. Since 1622 the imports into England had increased from 60,000 to 1.5 million pounds of tobacco a year. With one pound of tobacco fetching three pounds of beef, a hogshead holding some thirty-three pounds of tobacco, and a ketch the size of Richard's bearing about forty hogsheads, the logic spoke for itself. There was a future in tobacco, all right, if one could only seize it.

There were only a few minor things to take care of. In setting up his fishing stand, Richard had discovered that drinking water was "scarce out on the Neck," so he proceeded to dig a well on Salem Common, a tract of public land near the Hollingsworth shipyard. This involved some concerted digging and a bit of masonry work—nothing complicated for a man who'd been forging new settlements for two decades.

Then, late in the summer of 1640, Richard set out in his own small ketch—with his thirteen-year-old brother-in-law, Willy Hollingsworth, along as a shipboy—and headed for St. Mary's City, Maryland.

AT THAT TIME the only road between New England and Maryland—apart from Indian trails—was the sea, and the two colonies had developed largely as strangers to each other. The differences started to show even before Richard sighted the landing at St. Mary's City. As he rounded the tip of Virginia's Eastern Shore, the air grew balmy and the waters began to run with crab, diamondback terrapin, and canvasback ducks.

On land, the contrasts were even more apparent. Among the wooden houses, there were buildings made of brick—a material that had only come into wide usage in England after most New Englanders had emigrated. The people were certainly different, too. Settled by the Catholic aristocrat Lord Baltimore in 1634, Maryland was not weighted down by cumbersome ideals. Its inhabitants openly cultivated their fondness for horse racing and gambling, and a good many were illiterate. Even some of the court officials could not read.

But above all, the contours of Maryland—in mind and matter alike—were shaped by tobacco. Having attained the status of currency, the weed was being cultivated on every bit of arable land that could be found, then rolled in hogsheads through the fields (thus creating the famous "tobacco roads") down to the docks. As Richard walked up the landing, the waterfront was thick with indentured servants, many of them kidnapped from England, hoisting the treasured sweet-scented tobacco onto ships bound for England, and the coarser oronoco in vessels making for the Continent.

The undertaking would have been concluded quickly enough: Weston was sending a shipment of tobacco (from what planter, only God knows—and only God protected) aboard the *Blessing*, a ship Richard knew well from his passage on it five years earlier. In the midst of the negotiations, one must assume, Richard found a way to stake a modest interest in the cargo, and so gained his first foothold in the tobacco business. (It was undoubtedly from

Weston, as much as from Allerton, that Richard learned the virtues of keeping his name off the books.)

Then it was off to sea, where Richard found himself a member of a crew again, hauling the familiar halyards and furling the familiar jibs of the *Blessing*. The voyage itself was apparently uneventful except for the annoyance of a passenger named Thomas Gerrard, who incessantly asked the crew for soap.[12] Richard, like most people, took a bath only once a year; Gerrard's use amounted to a new bar almost every day!

Richard had sterner things to think about than getting paid back for soap once he arrived in London. After his long struggle with the Spanish government, Benjamin Woolough had moved with his daughter and her toddler back to the London area—specifically, to Ratcliffe, a parish bordering Stepney.

Within the space of a year and a half, Benjamin had been kidnapped, held prisoner in a foreign land, then sent away without a penny, only to discover that his daughter had become a mother in his absence. Few fathers would be happy about that, and fewer still pleased to see the man who had made him a grandfather. Whatever Richard expected to find in London, he was no longer eager to find it in the Woolnough household.

After buying a respectable shipment of English-made goods, then, Richard doubled back on his journey, returning to Maryland, loading up his own nameless ketch, and making for Salem just as the winter was catching its teeth on the steeples. They must have looked good just then, compared with the rickety roofs of Stepney.

BY NOW Richard has far outpaced me in interesting adventures, and I will be happy to let him hold center stage for the remainder of our tale, but I do want to record one more time when the circumstances of our lives touched strangely before I slip into the background: I found myself one fall day retracing part of the route that Richard had taken from Maryland to Salem.

In November 1999 my sailing friend, Chick Bills, descendant of the *Mayflower* pilot, bought a fifty-foot sailboat and was planning to transport it from Maryland to New York, a voyage of three days. Chick invited several sailors along as crew and a few lubbers such as myself, for what I imagine was meant to be comic relief. Naturally, I took him up on the offer.

Unlike Richard, of course, we had those outrageous luxuries: a motor, which we could use in lieu of the sails, and such niceties as batteries, radar, and well-charted maps. We also had access to the C & D Canal, which makes a straight-edge cut at the top of Maryland, between the Chesapeake and Delaware Rivers.

One might suppose that Richard would have appreciated the C & D Canal, and indeed he would have. In fact, a Marylander named Augustine Herman, whom Richard knew through the Maryland courts, proposed this very canal in the mid-seventeenth century. The plan did not go forward until 1829, but the irony was not lost on me when Chick explained how convenient it made his life. By cutting across to Delaware Bay, instead of rounding the entire peninsula of Maryland, we were able to shorten our voyage by an entire day.

We were not entirely immune to the age-old dangers, however. We arrived at the mouth of the canal late at night, the water like glass, and proceeded in slowly, giving wide berth to the tankers coming from the other direction. Then, out of nowhere, a wall of fog appeared dead ahead. A minute later we were engulfed in it. The lights on shore were no more than thirty feet to either side, but we could see only one of them at any given time—not enough to navigate. It would have been a simple act of physics for a tanker to have plowed right into us, neither of us seeing the other. I remember craning my neck to identify a peculiar shadow above us: only when we were directly under it could we see that it was a bridge.

Fortunately, just as the fog was joined by nightfall, we came upon a small pump dock where we could tie up until morning, and in the end no harm was done. But I got some idea of the speed and silence with which disaster can move on the seas, in this or any other century.

Such moments were offset by the long stretches on the open water, during which I experienced some inkling of the music of the sailor's life. To the east, a massive blue table stretched toward nowhere and ended abruptly. To the west, the land was simply irrelevant—a place where crazy people lived in the firm belief that their world was a fixed objective reality. At night, when I closed my eyes, the sea spoke its secret truth in vast and brilliant swirls.

When the voyage was over and we were sitting below, celebrating, one of the sailors began to tell stories of his love life back home. He and his wife, he explained, liked threesomes. Once they had chained their son's ex-girlfriend to a bed and given her a whipping. Another time, a woman brought into the proceedings had hit upon the novel idea of putting a funnel in her mouth.

By now, our storyteller was on his feet with the excitement of it all. "I told her, 'Get your ass in the air, honey: I'm going for the hoop!' "

That scene took place on the same ocean that Richard once coursed, and doubtless he and his crew recounted similar exploits as they lounged belowdecks in Salem Harbor, drinking their last drafts of rum before going home. *Ah, that Elizabeth: she was fantastic. I wonder what'll ever become of her. . . .*

But then it was back to those fixed objective realities. In Salem, a blacksmith named Thomas Tuck had been specifically waiting for Richard to return: one of Tuck's cows had fallen into the well that Richard had dug and broken its neck, and now the man was seeking compensation. Richard Hollingsworth, meanwhile, was set in the stocks hand and foot for the nefarious crime of traveling on the Sabbath.

Against this backdrop of petty accusations, the plan to colonize Providence Island fell conclusively apart, with a voyage undertaken in May 1641 that ended with an attack by the Spanish, killing one of the captains and would-be settlers.

The prospects of colonization were everywhere dwindling. No Providence Island, no Saybrook, nowhere but Salem to live—and some rather unpleasant impediments to continuing his love affair in England. Richard accordingly started putting some effort into his marriage to Christian, and they began to have children.

Not that he was very organized about it. Up until then, Richard had never bothered to join the Salem church—and why should he, when he was hardly ever there? By early 1642, however, his time had run out. He joined the church in February, simultaneously becoming a freeman, a civil designation that allowed him to vote. A week later he trundled his first two sons, Samuel and Thomas More, into the Salem meetinghouse and had them baptized.

It is interesting that Richard chose to name his firstborn son Samuel. Of course, to the extent that the elder Samuel More symbolized legitimacy, his name was a natural choice for a member of Richard's legitimate family. One might extrapolate that Richard still mistook Samuel More as his biological father, and Katharine as the cause of his exile.

Then again, legitimacy is often in the greatest demand where it is lacking, and in this Richard was coming up against a curious doubling effect. Samuel, after all, had rushed to have children when the legitimacy of *his* marriage was thrown into doubt, then called his first child by that marriage Richard, as if to identify the dilemma rather than the soul. And now here was the original, illegitimate Richard, doing very much the same thing. Perhaps Richard was not so much concerned with honorary titles as he was engaged in a form of mimicry.

If so, he soon had reasons never to want to mimic the elder Samuel More again.

8

The Double Life of Richard More

October 20, 1645. Richard More, of Salem in New England, mariner, married Elizabeth Woolno of Lymehouse at St. Dunstans Church, Stepney, England.

—George Sherwood,
American Colonists in English Records

IN 1642, when the English Civil War began, Samuel More had no doubts about which side he was on. Some years earlier Samuel had befriended Sir Robert Harley, an influential figure in Parliament, going so far as to attend several of Harley's "private days," in which those present prayed for key Puritan leaders in both England and New England. In 1643 Samuel was at Harley's estate, Brampton Castle, when it was besieged by the king's forces for almost seven weeks. Harley's wife died from the stress of captivity, and Samuel was appointed temporary guardian of Harley's children. He was released from Brampton just in time to see his father, the elder Richard More, die of old age. And no sooner had he assumed the role of heir to Larden and Linley Halls than he was appointed the commander of a force at Hopton Castle.[1]

Samuel had become a settled family man since his days as a secretary to Lord Zouch (now many years dead), with five children by his second wife, Elizabeth, and the comfortable estate of a gentleman. By no means was he a soldier, as his behavior soon attested. Nevertheless, the version of the story that reached the public made him into something of a local hero.

"As memory serves me," Samuel wrote afterward in a journal devoted to the episode, "I went to Hopton Castle—18th of Febry which was ye Sab: day at night."[2] Two weeks later the enemy troops arrived before the castle on horseback, scaled the walls on ladders, and were repulsed. Samuel's soldiers killed three Cavaliers, and the king's men sent an emissary to tell Samuel that they had captured his son—almost certainly the "other" Richard More, who had replaced his New England counterpart at Linley Hall. However, Samuel knew that they were lying and rebuffed the emissary's demand for surrender.

According to the contemporary conventions of warfare, one could surrender within a certain period of time after the demand to do so and be "given quarter"—be allowed to abandon one's post without harm. If one waited too long after the demand, there would be no quarter given.

Samuel, interpreting these rules of engagement by his own lights, decided to wait the Cavaliers out, even though he was monstrously outmanned. Having amassed a mere thirty-one men, he tried to hold off more than five hundred soldiers. For a time, the tactic seem to work: "we repuls'd them," he wrote of the next skirmish, "& took six musketts 10 pikes & clubs wch they call'd round heads boards." Another week passed in relative quiet, until the king's men again offered Samuel the option to surrender. "Myself wou'd leave it to them that trusted me," came Samuel's reply, "& if I might live with a safe conscience at home I shou'd be glad of, so that was not hearken'd to & I parted with them."

The following Saturday a larger engagement ensued, the king's men shooting with culverin and demiculverin, firing ninety-six shots at the castle wall and breaching it. Samuel's men laid boughs of trees to block the enemy's entry and, after hand-to-hand combat, killed two hundred Cavaliers. Again the two sides fell quiet, this time for two weeks, except for a moment when the king's soldiers set fire to the castle's brick tower. But in fact the king's men had been using the lull to dig a tunnel under the castle. It was then that Samuel saw that all was lost and asked to be given quarter, only to be told that there were "no conditions but to yield to the Colonels mercy."

Samuel's men ran to a barricaded room, where they heard the enemy digging underneath them. Knowing that they were about to be blown up, he surrendered at last, with no quarter given. In strictly statistical terms, the feat was tremendous: he had successfully defended Hopton Castle with a few soldiers against hundreds for more than a month!

WHILE SAMUEL MORE rose to minor celebrity in England, Richard was busy building up his business as a sea captain and merchant. Most likely he was not sailing to London during the early 1640s. Many colonial mariners were wary of the war being played out at sea and chose Bristol as their preferred port, or simply stayed in the Americas. At the end of May 1643, a "Virginia merchant by the name of Moore" trading on the Delaware River sold three thousand pounds of tobacco to a Hendrick Huygen of New Sweden—yet another in the series of spectral sightings of the elusive Richard. On July 8 of that year, Richard was granted, as a fisherman, half an acre abutting his house out on the neck—evidence that he was expanding his operations.

But news of Samuel's exploits probably reached Richard's ears nonetheless. Like everyone else in New England, Richard was paying rapt attention to events as they unfolded, especially as victory came within the grasp of the Parliamentarians. Indeed, in the summer of 1645, when many New Englanders were going off to join the Puritan cause—or at least to prosper from it—Richard himself crossed the Atlantic and was walking the streets of London by October.

England was much altered since Richard had been there last. Five years earlier Puritans were still being hounded out of the country. Now the Parliamentarian forces were in the ascendant and, in their confidence, had splintered into a dizzying array of sects and factions. There were Ranters, Levellers, Diggers—a welter of visionaries and malcontents, each with their own social program to advance. At the same time, there were soldiers waiting beyond patience to be paid. If the recent Parliamentarian victories were cause for jubilation, they also allowed a strain of discontent to surface.[3]

The atmosphere on the London waterfront, then, was one of both high spirits and frustration, a tumble of the soldiers' crude joy and "unhappy revolts" waiting to happen. It was also a place where news tended to coalesce, and where Richard could catch up on events with a more immediate bearing on his own life—for example, a more complete report of his own father's feats in battle. Samuel's appointment, in May of that year, to oversee Montgomery Castle was especially promising: what honors did the family name broadcast throughout the land these days?

The most convenient source of family news would have been Robert Moore, Samuel More's younger brother and a mariner just then living in Stepney.[4] Samuel had recommended Robert for a captaincy in the 1620s, on the grounds that he had served well in the battle at Cadiz.[5] Robert apparently did not receive the promotion, because later in life he requested a lesser promotion for meritorious duty in an engagement against the Dutch.

Certainly Robert Moore was of a cruder cut than his gentleman brother. When Richard showed his face in London, Robert was serving as a vestryman—one of those appointed to handle the affairs of the church—at St. Dunstan's.[6] Known as the Church of the High Seas, St. Dunstan's was ostensibly Presbyterian, but this was merely a word. People were apt to throw their garbage on the church lawn, oblivious to the women of ill repute who congregated there. In the middle of a wedding held at St. Dunstan's in 1642, the groom took time out from his vows to molest the curate.[7] In 1647 William Culham, the sexton of Stepney parish, owned a house that contained a tavern called the Sign of the Rose. This tavern was famous for serving raw meat and displaying four women "set in the stokes" until their husbands came to fetch them.

Let us situate Richard and Robert at this charming inn, sharing a cup of wine as their colleagues have their fill of the captives. Let us also give Robert the honors, between winces at being addressed as "uncle," of filling Richard in about what had really happened at Hopton Castle.

Taken prisoner by a Lieutenant Aldersea, Samuel More had been marched away, thinking—so he claimed—that his remaining twenty-eight soldiers had followed behind him. They had not. Samuel's life had been saved because of his friendship with Edward Nicholas, who had once been a fellow secretary under Lord Zouch and was now in the enemy—that is to say, the king's— camp. The other soldiers at Hopton Castle did not know Nicholas, so they met a different end. Their captors tied them up, stripped them naked, and tortured them one at a time, castrating them, stuffing their penises in their mouths, and then clubbing them to death while their fellow soldiers looked on in horror.

Held prisoner for a time and treated with the utmost civility, Samuel was eventually exchanged for a Royalist prisoner—a relative who, as the exchange request shows, was the more highly valued of the two. Then he went home to Linley, which had been plundered in his absence, to be greeted as a war hero. In May 1645 he was given charge of Montgomery Castle, where he was currently in command.

So this was Richard's reward for honoring his presumptive father with a grandson: to learn that he was at best an idiot and at worst a craven deal maker who had deserted his men. Exactly as he had abandoned Richard himself—by waiting too long to act, then using his connections in high places to disentangle himself.

Richard had retained only the vaguest memories of his original family, and this vagueness had allowed him to imagine the facts as he pleased. With this latest news, however, his creativity had been dealt a punishing blow. He could no longer pretend any dignity in the name of Samuel More. And to think he had named a son after the man!

But there were worse things to come. For example, Benjamin Woolnough had discovered that Richard was in town, and was determined to bring him to accounts.

RICHARD WAS A BAD SEED, you would probably say, doomed from the start to follow in his mother's footsteps, as surely as winter follows the fall. And, true enough, if he had reconstructed his mother's plight by marrying Christian Hunter for land, he had done so again by rebelling into the arms of Elizabeth Woolnough. Yet Richard, though worse than his mother in one respect, was ultimately more honorable than his legal father in another.

Probably it was only a matter of time before Benjamin Woolnough caught up with Richard: as sea captains, both were inevitably drawn to the maritime parishes of Stepney, Limehouse, and Ratcliffe, and they were bound to have associates in common. As it was, Benjamin's ire seems to have been reawakened by the coincidence of two events: the resurfacing of the court case regarding the ship *Elizabeth*, for which the king of Spain had still not offered any compensation, and the reappearance in London of Richard More, who had taken his living Elizabeth in a comparable fashion.

There is no question that society was on Benjamin's side. The church, Anglican or Puritan, would not baptize a child born to unwed parents, being content to leave the likes of the younger Elizabeth prey to the jaws of damnation. The law, meanwhile, took the view that a single mother could not support herself and tended to press for marriage. If the deadbeat father resisted this idea too long, the punishment was either jail or a large fine.

Presented with the seed of his loins, Richard could have stone-walled, as his mother had, or taken the moment to flee, as his biological father, Jacob Blakeway, did. Admittedly, the times allowed for libertine responses. Around London, there was talk of communal living, land for the poor, even institutionalized free love. What's more, there was, in this brief interlude between the monarchy and the Protectorate, no clear government to whom the people were answerable. In a moment when two Englands existed at once, who could say what was required and what was not?

On the other hand, Benjamin Woolnough had been in contact with some people whom Richard would not want to meet, no matter which side claimed the ultimate victory. One of the adventurers in the *Elizabeth*, who had lost a handsome twelve thousand pounds sterling when the ship was seized, was none other than Sir Henry Marten—the man who had authorized Jacob Blakeway's pardon. As the court case progressed through diplomatic channels, its particulars had also come to the attention of Edward Nicholas, whose good name had recently saved Samuel More's neck.

Not at all an easy decision: running away meant upholding the law, while staying meant upholding his integrity, regardless of the consequences.

As the bride and groom walked up the pathway to St. Dunstan's that October Sunday, the mariner's red flag flew as always from the tower, and the Stepney bells rang out its age-old part in the nursery tune "Oranges and Lemons": When I grow rich, said the church bells of Shoreditch / And when will that be? asked the church bells of Stepney / I'm sure I don't know, said the church bells of Bow . . .

Sidestepping the piles of debris, the couple passed beneath the archway, graven on the left with the image of a ship, square-rigged and tossed by waves, on the right with forceps and a satyr, known betimes as Robin Goodfellow, symbol of fertility, at others as the Devil. Then, while prostitutes plied their trade outside the thick stone walls and vestryman Robert Moore looked on with a certain rough humor, the preacher pronounced Richard and Elizabeth man and wife, and the fact was recorded in the parish register for all to see. Bent on complete satisfaction, Benjamin made certain that it was just not any Richard More who spoke the vows, "but Richard More of Salem in New England, mariner."

Elizabeth More, the daughter of Richard and Elizabeth More, was baptized in the same church, under similarly garish circumstances, on March 2, 1646. Sometime around this event, Benjamin Woolnough passed away—exhausted perhaps from his parental duties.

In his own strange way, Richard had solved a problem that had stumped all of his parents, legal or otherwise: how to reconcile desire with responsibility. Of course, this solution came at a heavy price. Having cooled Benjamin Woolnough's fury, Richard now had do everything possible to keep the New England authorities from discovering his marriage to Elizabeth Woolnough, and the English government in the dark about his marriage to Christian Hunter. To maintain this firewall, he had to be exceedingly circumspect around anyone who traveled between London and Salem—even the sailors with whom he trusted his life. And in 1646 the list of such people in London was already a little too long for comfort. For starters, the *other* Richard More, legitimate son of the conquering hero, had recently arrived in London as well.

The English Richard was experiencing a very different life from his American counterpart. Having served for a year as a lieutenant in the Parliamentarian army under Lord St. John, he was admitted to Grey's Inn (in essence a law school) in 1646. In that same year he was appointed to serve on the Compounding Committee, a body authorized to handle the repatriation of land to Parliamentarians on the eve of the king's imminent defeat.[8]

That this impostor should be able to gad about London handing out land awards was bad enough, but rumor had it that Edward Winslow—the *Mayflower* passenger who had been the guardian of Richard's sister Ellen—was coming to London that fall to serve alongside the English Richard More on the Compounding Committee.

Edward Winslow was exactly the type of person Richard had to avoid like the plague. He knew people in Richard's circles on both sides of the Atlantic. He was still involved in settling Plimouth's longstanding debts.[9] As if the agent of Providence were actually cackling from on high, he had also come to London in part to defend Massachusetts against charges brought before Parliament by William Vassall—he of the *Blessing* voyage in 1635.[10] If Winslow should ever get wind of Elizabeth More née Woolnough, it would be bad news for Richard for sure.

This possibility was made eminently more probable in April 1646, when Elizabeth was called to appear before the High Court of Admiralty. Though her presence was desired largely for her contribution to the endless case against the Spanish Crown for taking the ship *Elizabeth,* Richard could expect nothing remotely good from her intersection with upper diplomatic circles of the English realm.

His response was, basically, to fall to pieces. Sometime during the first week of April, he went out and got completely plastered with a group of people that seems to have included his daughter and a local prostitute. Eventually, the party got out of hand, and on April 6 Richard was summoned to appear before the king's provisional Session for Peace, "to answer for being taken in the company of a lewd suspitious woman and a common feildwalker, and for assaultinge a childe about eight yeares of age, whose parents are unknown."[11]

This is hardly a complimentary view of Richard. One might charitably suppose that the young Elizabeth was about to explain her parentage to an unsuspecting watchman and got a cuffing for her efforts. The common "feildwalker," however, is less easy to discount: an employee from the Sign of the Rose perhaps, relaxing a little after a night on the stocks?

Whoever it was, the whole situation was a mess. Richard could not afford to appear in court for wandering about with a "lewd suspitious woman" without risking the wrong end of the hangman's rope. He was, to put it bluntly, the wrong Richard More— not the one who could sit back and soak up the pleasures of the gentry, but the one who had to leave town, preferably quickly.

On April 7, 1646, the day after Richard failed to show up in the King's Session for Peace, his English wife stood before a judge in the High Court of Admiralty and, erring on the side of caution, identified herself as "Elizabeth, wife of Richard Moore of Stepney."[12] By that time, Richard was already headed for home, rehearsing how he would meet the gaze of his Salem wife as she endured the birth pangs of *their* latest child, Joshua.[13]

Everywhere the central events of his childhood were doubling, trebling, spinning out of control . . . the wages of a lust for land, paid by a man who had chosen the sea.

9

The Bell

I go, and it is done. The bell invites me.
Hear it not, Duncan, for it is a knell
That summons thee to heaven, or to hell.

—*Macbeth*, II: 1

UNDERSTANDABLY, a relative quiet descended on Richard's Salem household after the vanquishing of King Charles I. Between 1646 and 1652, Richard appears in the records almost entirely in the capacity of father, as the number of his legitimate children grew to a total of seven. The first two sons, Samuel and Thomas, were followed by Caleb, then Joshua,[1] whose birth had brought Richard rushing home from London. After them came Richard Jr. and, at long last, two daughters: Susanna and Christian.

On October 3, 1649, when Christian, his wife, was pregnant with Susanna, Richard bought a house in Salem Town and an additional ten acres in the fields toward Boston, to accommodate their swelling brood. The move into this house, located on three-quarters of an acre on the South River,[2] brought the More family into closer contact with the landbound community and required them to keep up appearances somewhat. In this spirit, Christian

More received her full communion into the church on September 1, 1650.[3]

Meanwhile, Richard worked as hard as ever, perhaps harder, now that he had all those new mouths to feed. As before, he steered clear of England as best he could and spent his time plying the North American waters. In 1650 he made a voyage to Virginia and brought back tobacco on the account of Miles Ward, a Salem resident; one may assume that he was often setting his bearings for Maryland as well.

Then, not long after the birth of Christian, his seventh and final Salem child, events conspired to send him back to England, where fate was ready to throw him another bone.

Falling in step, with a mock unison of land and sea, as the peals rang out in the air, mingling with the story of the New World itself . . .

THERE ARE SEVERAL plausible explanations for how Richard landed in London in the spring of 1654. In 1652 England and Holland had gone to war just as the English were experiencing a severe timber shortage, making the repair of their warships difficult. The most urgent need was for tar, to seal the hulls, and masts, to replace those that had broken—both of which could be found in abundance in New England.[4]

Possibly Richard was called upon to satisfy this need in 1653. If so, it put him in a precarious position, because the man in London spearheading the tar-and-mast project was Edward Winslow. Time had not softened Winslow. Quite the opposite, in fact. In 1651 he had savagely accused an attorney, whose only visible crime was to represent a defendant before the Compounding Committee, of holding "dangerous opinions" and of going to bed with two women at once, before throwing him into jail.[5] For a bigamist such as Richard, any dealings with Winslow were best kept to a minimum.

Meanwhile, Richard had also revived his own transatlantic dealings. In September 1654 he was in Maryland, petitioning a certain Captain William Batten on behalf of a Boston investor for unpaid bills on tobacco that had been shipped to a Londoner named Ninion Butcher. This suggests some parallel business in England for Richard, as either the conveyor of the tobacco or a merchant in his own right. And, indeed, two days after agreeing to pay Richard "on one of the next ships out," Batten admitted to the court to being behind on his payments for tobacco delivered to another London merchant, named Joshua Woolnough.

Although Joshua Woolnough's exact relation to Elizabeth Woolno is unknown, this coincidence of events, combined with the relative scarcity of Woolnoughs in London at the time, militate strongly in favor of a family connection.

Joshua Woolnough was a fairly well-to-do member of the middle class. The son of Henry Woolnough of Alborough, Norfolk, he began an apprenticeship to a merchant tailor in London in 1622. By 1638 he had a shop and a residence on Gracechurch Street, then known as Gracious Street, an upscale address in the parish of All Hallows Lombard. During the 1650s Joshua supplied canvas to English warships and, as is evident, got involved in the tobacco trade on the London end, with Richard bringing in the hogsheads from Maryland. These business ventures were successful enough for Joshua to own, briefly, a piece of history.

The piece in question was Hampton Court, a royal palace just south of London, in Surrey, done up in style by Henry VIII and subsequently occupied by every king up to Charles I, who had been held there prior to his beheading in 1649. Since that fateful day, Hampton Court had been vacant.

Here was a scene dropped in from another world—the silent tennis grounds, the abandoned stables, the tilting yard empty of jousters, Anne Boleyn's gatehouse, an astronomical clock marking the ages for no one, an oak tree planted at the time of the Norman invasion (and still alive today, I might add)—all made more ghostly again by the untended hedges growing out like a beard on a dead man.

Joshua Woolnough's involvement came on November 13, 1653, when he bought a portion of the grounds called Old Bushy Park for a mere 1,528 pounds from a man who had recently purchased the entire property from the state. Old Bushy Park was a large expanse of land east of the palace, containing "lodges, stables . . . and houses"6 and, incredibly, extensive hunting grounds that had been a favorite of James I for giving chase to stags. Those were the very same stags, it must be said, that the king had procured from Lord Zouch, at times with the help of his secretary, Samuel More.

Almost as soon as Joshua Woolnough bought this sumptuous stretch of land, squatters began to encroach on it, setting up fences of their own and living in the lodges spread around the woods. One is tempted to imagine Joshua's relatives—the elder and younger Elizabeth More, for example—among this crowd, defiling the outrageous fortune according to their own modest means. One is also reminded, by the sheer force of the parallel, of a scene from Richard's childhood: that of Katharine More and Jacob Blakeway taking Larden Hall to pieces while Samuel was gone. Was it all a dream—just plain too good to be true?

Alas, no sooner had Joshua Woolnough made his down payment than Oliver Cromwell, soon to be Lord Protector of England, decided that Hampton Court would be a nice place to live, and the state began proceedings to buy it. To his credit, Joshua held out for a while, finally settling on February 9, 1654, for a payment of three hundred pounds. Others found ways to prolong the exchange even longer; that August, Cromwell's people were still rooting out stragglers on the grounds. But ultimately there was no getting around the wishes of the ruler of the English-speaking world, and by the time Richard arrived in the spring of 1654, the fairy tale had evaporated as quickly as it had come.

THE BRIEF MOMENT when the trappings of royalty lay within Richard's sight explains a great deal about his subsequent actions. In particular, it reveals the place a certain bell occupied in his heart—why he came to own it and why it mattered so much to him long after it was gone and he was old and gray.

Up until the age of forty, Richard had basically been taking life catch-as-catch-can. Thrown into a community far from his first home, he had improvised as best he could: going to sea with Allerton, finding a wife in the Hollingsworth crowd, chancing on another wife in London, and always getting his business where the money was. As with many sailors, he followed the wind, whether it sent him into triumph or trouble. Gradually, his past had begun to revisit him with variations on a theme, but these variations had been invariably negative. Joshua Woolnough's fleeting tenancy at Hampton Court was different, because it seemed to invest Richard's London family with a touch of divine intervention. Rare is the human who can resist ascribing such a moment to destiny—and rare, too, the human who can ward off the disappointment of seeing it slip away.

Richard was given a consolation prize, however. As the war against the Dutch wound to a close, many soldiers and sailors were again becoming disgruntled, just as they had during the Civil War. Cromwell knew well the virtues of keeping his Roundheads occupied and, accordingly, devised an expansionist military campaign called the Western Design. When the particulars were drawn up in the spring of 1654, Richard received a commission as one of the captains in a four-vessel fleet, with the tacit understanding that some percentage of the prizes would never make it to Hampton Court.

Richard already knew some of the principal characters in this operation. The takeover was to be led by Robert Sedgwick, a prominent Boston man, and his son-in-law John Leverett, who had recently brought an otherwise insignificant case in a Salem court, for which Richard had served as a juror.

The target was not entirely alien, either. The fleet was commissioned to sail on New Amsterdam, where Richard's old master, Isaac Allerton, had been doing a bang-up business in recent years. In fact, Richard had some ideas about doing some trading there himself.

This was less of a conflict of interest than it appears. As captain of the supply ship for the mission, Richard soon learned that Cromwell had given the fleet secret orders to attack the French in Canada instead. The talk of New Amsterdam was just window-dressing—perhaps to excite the blood of the seventy Roundheads recruited for the mission (they having private vengeances to honor) or perhaps simply to throw the French off guard. It was not a bad proposition, all in all. If Richard would never wander the splendiferous gardens of kings, he could at least avail himself of some booty and, in the process, repay a cruelty he remembered all too well from his shipboy years. In sailing on the French colony of Acadia, he would be attacking its governor, Charles La Tour, the very man who had flashed his sword at Machias way back when. Richard was not so different from the Roundheads; he had his own private vengeances to honor!

The Sedgwick fleet—consisting of the *Augustine*, the *Church*, the *Hope*, and Richard's humble ketch, now armed with guns—met with heavy headwinds when it sailed out of London that May.[7] Before long, Sedgwick's ship proved leaky and was forced to return to England for repairs, delaying his arrival in New England. Leverett's progress was slowed by something quite different. On the way over, he encountered a Dutch ship and, believing the two countries still at war, took the vessel as a prize.

At that point, it may have been Richard who sailed on ahead and warned Allerton of a possible imminent attack—or rather, informed him that any reports of an attack were not to be taken seriously. In any event, Allerton was tipped off, and the New Amsterdam authorities, tipped off in turn, organized a tepid defense.

The rest was simply a matter of waiting for the New England Puritan leaders to go through their usual naïvetés. By the time the entire Sedgwick fleet was anchored in Boston, in June 1654, England and Holland had signed a peace treaty, which technically made Leverett a pirate for having plundered a friendly vessel. Leverett was thus removed from the mission and put on trial. (In the end, he was deemed "useful," despite his infraction, and went on to become a governor of the colony.) Meanwhile, various authorities convened in New Haven and labored over what to do about the New England soldiers they had recruited for the cause, and the captains gently steered the discussion toward the French.

Richard had little time to take part in these deliberations, however. In the early months of 1654, while he had been wiping the dust of Hampton Court from his shoes, his father-in-law Richard Hollingsworth had died, at the age of fifty-nine. With the administrators of the Hollingsworth estate appointed in March, the claims were scheduled to be heard in the last week of June. That was mere days after Richard arrived back in Salem, and the creditors had already gathered in anticipation of their just reward.

Not that they had much to hope for: Richard Hollingsworth, despite his output of "prodigious ships" over the previous two decades, had died almost penniless. Other than the usual pots and pans, there was a ketch on the stocks, still unfinished, and another vessel worth a measly seven pounds, but that was about it.

As a result, Richard was forced to compete for his due, even though he was family. Another seaman, Edward Prescott,[8] petitioned the administrators for 120 pounds for building the ship on the stocks. Two days later[9] Richard received an acknowledgment for an unspecified award. As the estate was insolvent and the ketch on the stocks unfinished, it seems that a novel form of payment was arranged: both Prescott and Richard were given shares in the *Swan,* a ship that one of the administrators had recently brought from England.

The *Swan* was a vessel with an interesting past. Built in 1641 for Charles I and subsequently taken by Cromwell's forces, it was a frigate of about a hundred tons, designed for easy maneuverability in battle, with short decks fore and aft, both about the same height, and a longer, lower deck amidships. It had seen heavy use during the recent war against the Dutch, being forced into port several times for repairs. It had seen several captains as well. The most recent of them was Thomas Wilkes, or Wickes, a Shropshire man whose politics had prompted Cromwell, at war's end, to have him deported. There was apparently some basis for the expulsion: centuries later, a portion of the *Swan,* lost in a battle off the Irish Sea, was recovered. Found among the salvage was a Royalist crest.

So it was that a traitor to the Protectorate ended up in Salem as an administrator to Richard Hollingsworth's estate. The ship that Wilkes had "borrowed" to make the crossing needed to disappear, naturally, and here was a way to effect exactly that. Richard, who may well have supplied the tar that now held it together, could hardly be discouraged by the award of a minority share in the frigate. Whereas his ketch could hold only about forty hogsheads of tobacco, the *Swan* could probably carry ten times as much.

Nor, one imagines, was the symbolism of the moment lost on him. He still had to sail his own ketch while the *Swan* earned him money elsewhere, but for all intents and purposes the emblem on the More coat of arms—that "Sable a swan beaked and legged Or"—had just become a wild goose.[10]

BY THE BEGINNING of July, the New England authorities had muddled through their own, larger property disputes, and the

Sedgwick fleet sailed on the fourth, under the flag of the Protectorate, through the icy Down East waters that Richard knew so well. On July 14, when they reached St. John's, a small French settlement tucked into the coastline of Acadia, the takeover proved to be child's play. La Tour had been busy feuding with a rival Frenchman and was completely unprepared for an attack from the outside. After a three-day siege, the French soldiers were given quarter and permitted to "march out of ye fort with Collers flying and with Drums." Then they were put aboard a ship—one of their own, it seems—and transported home to France.

As captain of the supply ship, Richard rode anchor in the harbor while the others commenced plundering the town of its cannon and brandy and furs. Thomas Lathrop, a Salem man from the earliest days, had been told he would receive a bell and asked if he could have the one in the fort tower at St. John's, but he was advised by Sedgwick to wait until they arrived at the second outpost.

Two weeks later the fleet sailed for Port Royal, where the French surrendered after some of the Roundheads, eager to see action at last, mauled them badly. The largest take at Port Royal was the ship *Chateaufort* and its sumptuous cargo, but there was indeed another bell, weighing about two hundred pounds and worth some three hundred English pounds. With the help of a few men, Sedgwick threw it down from the friary into the courtyard, where Lathrop and some other men carried it to the vessel waiting in the harbor: Richard's ketch.

Bells were especially prized possessions in North America in the seventeenth century, for the simple reason that there were very few ironworks in which they could be made. The bell that ended up on Richard's deck, in fact, was among the very first in the New World. It had been brought to Acadia sometime not long after 1632, when Isaac de Razilly arrived with three hundred men and three Capuchin monks, who had subsequently built a chapel, monastery, and school at Lequille, near Port Royal.[11]

As a religious object, this bell was also imbued with symbolic power. De Razilly's expedition having embarked from the town of Auray and the port of Saint Goustan, patron saint of sailors, the bell most likely was cast in that area of Brittany. A famous chapel had been built in the same diocese in the 1620s, after a farmer visited by visions of Saint Anne, mother of the Virgin Mary, received permission from the bishop to erect a shrine in her honor. Sainte-Anne d'Auray later became a major pilgrimage site and may have been one by the time of the Sedgwick expedition. French bells tended to be feminine; this one was therefore likely to have been dedicated to Saint Anne—the perfect mother of the perfect woman.

That was all too popish for Sedgwick's men, to be sure; the Puritans had abolished the baptizing of bells, to say nothing of dedicating them to women. Nevertheless, a bell was still considered the mouth of God, and this one had been marked for a new meetinghouse in the northern part of Salem, which was soon to become a town called Beverly. Boarding the supply ship, Lathrop told Richard as much and pressed into his hand a letter addressed to Mrs. Lathrop, detailing the capture of the bell. Richard agreed to carry out Lathrop's wishes to the letter—or so it was later claimed.

From Port Royal, the expedition went on to Pentagoet, scene of Richard's apprentice fisherman days, and reduced it to English obedience on September 2, 1654. Though there was little booty to be had at Pentagoet, its capture was symbolic enough in itself for Richard, who had seen it taken by La Tour two decades earlier.

Besides, there was plenty of plunder from the two other settlements. By the time the mission was over, the fleet had loaded up ten thousand English pounds worth of goods: brandy, French wine, salt (with "som Lining"), beaver, moose, other furs, plate (a general term for any goods made of precious metals), and forty-four pieces of ordnance, including cannon, small stock fowlers and "busses," ammunition . . . and those two bells.[12]

Richard's instructions on returning home to Salem were clear: he was to deliver the letter to Mrs. Lathrop and the bell to several men living in Beverly. Then again, how to reconcile this course with what he knew of events back in England? One might venture that, for Richard, the bell symbolized the reversal of a train of humiliations—beginning with Cromwell's recent occupation of the royal hunting grounds and leading inexorably back through a maze of collapsed deals to the loss of his most imperfect of mothers.

Certainly, having deposited the bell in his front yard in Salem, Richard was slow to uproot it again. That September, when several Beverly men came to his house looking for their prize, he asked them for "an order from the General" as proof of ownership.

The Beverly men had no such thing—not in writing, anyway—and when they admitted as much, Richard told them to be gone until they could produce one. At a loss for any other immediate response, they promptly left.

Begone! Now there was a word with staying power.

RICHARD'S SEIZURE of the Port Royal bell marked a moment of great confidence in his life. Not only had he avenged the French, but he had taken matters into his own hands with his own countrymen, looting from the looters, as it were, and then defied them as well. In the headiness of success, he seems even to have briefly forgotten that he had something to hide.

After rebuffing the would-be bell owners of Beverly, Richard immediately turned around and sailed for Maryland, where he received partial payment of the debt owed to Joshua Woolnough. Then he returned to Salem. By mid-November he was en route to London with the Sedgwick fleet and the vast majority of the Acadian booty that remained.

This particular voyage was more treacherous for Richard than many. The *Augustine,* one of the three ships that sailed alongside him, had been loaded with masts for English ships, by request of the ever worrisome Edward Winslow. Worse, by this time Winslow had himself become involved in the Western Design, having been appointed one of the commissioners in an assault on the Spanish-held Hispaniola. In this endeavor, he was joined by Robert Moore, witness to Richard's bigamous wedding, who had petitioned to sail in the campaign aboard the *Mary.*

It was a most unpropitious time, to say the least, for Richard to be discovered carrying money belonging to a Woolnough. After all, even with Cromwell in power, the sentence for bigamy was still death.

As it happened, fate was still blowing Richard's way. In London, recruits for the attack had been rounded up by beat of drums, ships had been fitted out, and sentiments raised, and both Winslow and Robert Moore were gone by late December, just before Richard made fast on a Wapping dock.[13] That left only the English Richard More to worry about, and he was soon effectively neutralized as well. Though Richard's counterpart had moved up in the world in recent years—having married the daughter of Sir Isaac Pennington, erstwhile Lord Mayor of London[14]—his comfort was disturbed in March 1655 when he was accused of sedition and brought in for questioning by Cromwell's spymaster, John Thurloe. Probably nothing lay behind the fears. Cromwell had become increasingly touchy about even the minutest sign of disloyalty, and by 1655 most of the sects that once could have challenged him had dwindled away.[15] Nevertheless, the English Richard could no longer go about pointing fingers as easily as before.

Having narrowly averted discovery, or at best the fear of it, Richard thus settled down to the more prosaic difficulty of getting paid. Massachusetts did not get around to remunerating him for the Acadia mission until January 20, 1655,[16] by which time he was in London and unable to collect. Cromwell's treasurers were not much better. In the end, winter would come and go and even the spring would be looking old before payment was released to Sedgwick.[17]

Then again, Richard had held on to various items from the Acadian expedition in addition to the bell, and these made do in the interim. Able to visit his London family with uncustomary ease, he was also in a position to make up, if only in some small way, for the lost windfall of Hampton Court. Certainly, at sixteen the younger Elizabeth was old enough to appreciate the virtues of furs and brandy brought in from the wilds of Canada.

Ah, that Cromwell—maybe he was all right after all. . . .

THAT SUMMER, the news from the Caribbean, terrible as it was, seemed to confirm that Richard had put the worst behind him. A disaster from start to finish, the expedition had reached Barbados and picked up thousands of additional recruits, most of them untrained and ungovernable idlers looking for easy plunder. This rambunctious population soon fell victim to a wide range of diseases aboard ship, including dysentery and yellow fever, and was in no shape to take the heavily fortified Hispaniola. Sailing on to Jamaica, where the Spanish forces were considerably weaker, the fleet managed at least this victory, but not before Edward Winslow succumbed to the raging epidemic.

Here a certain poetic justice cannot be overlooked. While Richard dallied with his secret wife, Winslow, who had taken his eldest sister away from him, who had stood in the path of everyone since, from Lyford to Allerton to Vassall, who had banded together with his replacement at Linley Hall and thundered against libertines from his chair on the Committee for Compounding, lay slumped over the rails, puking his guts to extinction.

With Winslow's death, on May 7, 1655, Richard could for the first time reasonably hope that his secret life in England was safe from the ears of his fellow Salemites. He could also afford to join

Sedgwick, who had finally been paid, on a voyage to the Caribbean with provisions for the English soldiers. It would have been a hard-hearted man who refused to do so, because the soldiers were dying like flies.

If Richard did sail to Jamaica, though, he did not feel the loyalty that Sedgwick did. Seeing that the top command had deserted, Sedgwick stayed on as the de facto governor of the new colony. Richard, for his part, had other needs calling him, not the least of which was the state of his New England family.

But Richard could not juggle all his affairs in the English realm with equal skill. Returning to Salem late that summer, he made his way from the waterfront to his house, where wife and family were waiting, and was immediately met with a glaring absence. The bell he had looted from the plunderers of a thief, worth a cool three hundred pounds, had been removed from his front yard. By whom was a riddle that would take him twenty-three years to solve.

WITH HIS LEGAL PROCEEDS from the Western Design, Richard was able to expand his property in town, buying a house and an acre of land on September 13, 1655, catercorner to the waterfront property he had bought a few years earlier.[18] But he was not around much to enjoy it. Instead, he began to spend time away from *both* of his wives, mostly in the balmier climes of Maryland.

With Cromwell's ascendancy to Lord Protector, the Protestants had taken control of Maryland—and done nothing whatsoever to improve it. On the contrary, something evil was afoot in the colony, the likes of which never broke forth in New England.

In February 1656 Richard was at the house of Joseph Wickes[19] in Patuxent, Maryland, discussing their plans to go together to the Dutch-held Manhattan, known as Manhattoes or Manahatans but their conversation was rendered almost impossible by the presence of Wickes's new servant, Anne Gould. Since her arrival in the house, Gould had complained of numerous pains. As Wickes eventually discovered, she had contracted the "French pox," when her former master had raped her. So advanced was her syphilis when Richard saw her that she could barely walk for the pain in her bones.

That was a typical Maryland scene of the time. Another acquaintance of Richard's, Captain Robert Henfield, had recently brought a group of Irish boys to the colony to sell them into servitude. Henfield's idea of a good time was to beat these boys savagely with his cane while threatening to give them all fifteen-year terms instead of the usual seven.

Richard had only so much patience for this sort of behavior—when it interfered with business. Already he was having trouble with Edward Prescott, co-owner of the *Swan*: Prescott's partner in a separate venture had run the *Sea Horse* aground, resulting in a large loss of tobacco.

That was bound to set Richard back one way or another. Meanwhile, he was still trying to get Captain William Batten to make good on a payment of 1,950 pounds of tobacco from five years earlier and on a similar payment to Joshua Woolnough in London. By September 1657 Batten had failed to satisfy these debts, yet in that same month he found it within himself to give a bond of 150 sterling to one John Saffin as a pledge against a delivery of seven thousand pounds of tobacco.[20]

Richard could stand it no longer. Calling to mind that Batten had recently taken a local woman, Mary Dod, "in the sight of six or eight men or thereabouts with her coats up to her middle," he began casting aspersions about the man and his cohorts, until he landed on John Saffin, using untraceable but undoubtedly colorful imagery.

John Saffin was not someone one wanted for an enemy. A lawyer by trade and by temperament, he knew how to handle bad-mouthing. In 1653 Thomas Hyland had brought a case against him in Scituate, Massachusetts, which ended up with Thomas Hyland

Jr. fearing for his life.[21] In Richard's case, Saffin similarly went for the jugular. Thus we see in the Plimouth court records:

> 13 October 1657: Wheras Mr John Saffin Arrested Mr Richard More of Salem in an action of Defamation to the Damage of five hundred pounds for that the said More had uttered and Reported that the said Saffin his carriage and behavior in Verginnia was very Scandalous and of evill Report in Divers respects; the which suit was to bee tryed at a County court held att Boston the twenty seaventh of October 1657 but by the earnest Request of the said More and som frinds in his behalfe the matter was Refered to the Arbetration of those whose names are underwritten; whose Determination: therof is heer underneath Inserted and by Authorities ordered to bee Recorded as followeth viz:
>
> Wee underwritten being Chosen to end a difference between Mr John Saffin and Mr Richard More whoe by exchaung of money are bound in five hundred pounds to stand to our award; and having heard and seen what was aledged on both sides doe award and Determine that mr More hath uttered and spoken many groundles Reports from which Mr John Saffin is for ought wee can see legally free and ought to bee soe accounted and that mr More shall acknowlidge before us hee Did speake unadvisedly and shall Desire Mr John Saffin to forgive him; and shall further promise not to Intermeddle about any thing of this Nature for time to come witnesse our hands this 23 of the 8th month 1657
>
> William Paddy James Olliver Josias Winslow John Winslow[22]

The award sought—five hundred pounds—amounted to the entire estate of the average colonist. For Richard it represented a hundred hogsheads of tobacco—essentially, his take for an entire voyage of the *Swan*.

The most curious aspect of this case, however, is not the venality of the plaintiff but the circumspect behavior of the defendant. Richard must have dearly wanted to avoid cross-examination in court. Otherwise, why choose to settle and then still pay the same amount, complete with a hangdog apology and promises never to "intermeddle" in Saffin's affairs again? Why not march into court and insist that Saffin was indeed a scoundrel and knave for whatever he had done? Richard had deposed as boldly before, and would do so again.

Then, too, what exactly was Josiah Winslow doing as one of the arbitrators? As the son of the recently deceased Edward Winslow, Josiah was perhaps the New Englander most likely to have caught wind of Richard's bigamy. He was also the New Englander in the best position to punish or reward Richard in the future, because he had become involved in a number of land purchases from the Indians, for which Richard, as one of the First Comers, was expected to receive a share.

The entire case smacks of blackmail, exacted by someone who had caught wind of Richard's secret—given away a little too easily, admittedly, by Richard's close proximity to cases involving Joshua Woolnough—and then led him straight to the lion's den.

Richard was not free of his past. And it was beginning to look as if he never would be.

10

The Quaker Crisis

Then to the stout sea-captains, the sheriff, turning, said,
"Which of ye, worthy seamen, will take this Quaker maid?
In the isle of fair Barbados, or on Virginia's shore,
You may sell her at a higher price than Indian girl or
    Moor."

— John Greenleaf Whittier, "Cassandra Southwick"

IN JUNE 1658 Richard was called to a town meeting at the Ship Tavern in Salem to discuss the latest news. Town constables had recently raided the house of Nicholas Phelps and discovered a Quaker meeting in progress. Nineteen of the attendees had been arrested and were in jail, awaiting trial the following week.

Among the many questions raised at the Ship Tavern was the matter of jurors. It made sense, some thought, for the mariners to be involved. After all, they were the ones who would be deporting the Quakers when it was all over.

Captain David Corwithin agreed to serve . . . what about Captain More? He knew a lot about these things, didn't he?

In some ways the Quaker crisis was a reprise of the Antinomian Controversy of the 1630s. As usual, theology was not the real issue at stake, because no one was studying it. In London a man calling himself a Quaker had recently entered Parliament with a gun, saying that his inner light had commanded him to kill everyone there. The Massachusetts authorities, for their part, tarred the new sect with the familiar generalizations about free morals until it took little imagination to turn a believer into a "Quaking slut."

The second crisis was more confrontational than the first, however, and the punishments far more violent. It had erupted two years earlier, in July 1656, when Captain George Corwin declared the presence of two Quakers aboard his vessel, the Swallow, lying in Boston Harbor. These heretics had been promptly arrested, inspected for marks of witchcraft, and then sent back to the ship in a summary deportation.

Ironically, this expulsion only encouraged more Quakers to arrive in their stead, and soon Massachusetts was writhing with them. On October 14, 1656, the authorities passed a law imposing a hundred-pound fine on any captain who brought a Quaker into the colony. There were also whippings for any Quakers found on land, and even stiffer penalties for anyone found harboring a Quaker. And still they poured in, intent on suicide, it seemed.

Richard knew a thing or two about these morality storms, of course. When Anne Hutchinson had preached in her home in the mid-1630s, he had found safety in his marriage to Christian Hunter and, as a result, secured a patch of land in Duxbury. By now, however, his circumstances had become, shall we say, more complicated, and he could not afford to arouse suspicions.

Nor could it have helped that Richard was so well connected to the Quaker community. One of the accused, Samuel Gaskill, was the son of a man who had worked alongside Richard in and around Hollingsworth's shipyard. Another defendant, Anthony Needham, had actually been present when Richard took possession of the bell in Acadia.

In effect, then, Richard's appointment to the tribunal became a test of his character. He would have to hang tough and look happy about it, or risk questions about various Quaking sluts of his own acquaintance. At the same time, he would have to tread lightly on the likes of Anthony Needham, who might begin to remember a little too much about the destination of certain plunder last seen aboard his ketch.

Then again, since his defamation case, Richard More had become nothing if not wily,

On June 29, 1658, Richard arrived at the Salem courthouse to fulfill his duties as a juror. Before doing so, however, he stood and requested that the court acknowledge a debt owed him by Edward Prescott, co-owner of the *Swan*. This debt, nestled no doubt in some tangle of bad Maryland tobacco, was obviously beyond the jurisdiction the Salem court, but Richard's declaration had its tactical benefits nonetheless.

As everyone knew from the rumors, Prescott had recently run afoul of the law. Bound for Maryland out of England as master of the *Sarah Artch*, he had got no farther than the Hebrides when his crew suspected a passenger named Elizabeth Richardson of being not just a Quaker but an actual witch. Whether they feared a fine for conveying her or superstition got the best of them, the result was the same. Fashioning a hangman's noose, they slipped it around her neck and dropped her from the yardarm.[1]

Richard's decision to sue Prescott just as the Quaker trial opened was a case of exquisite timing. Not only had he cornered a debtor during a period when he sorely needed money, he also showed that he could be tough on lawbreakers, while at the same time giving the impression of his readiness to defend Quakers in life and limb. For a man in Richard's position, one could hardly ask for a better finesse.

THE QUAKER TRIAL amounted to a set piece in the Puritan experiment. When the trial began, the accused—Lawrence and Cassandra Southwick, Josiah Southwick, Joshua Buffum, Samuel Gaskill, and Samuel Shattuck—filed into the Ship Tavern without taking off their hats. This act of defiance set the tone for everything that followed. There was no prevaricating, no subtleties for Richard to parse from his juror's seat.

Several defendants openly professed to being "such as are called Quakers." In the midst of the trial, when one of the defendants complained that the maximum penalty for his offense was nothing more than a fine, one of the magistrates broke in, saying, "As I have told you before, you and we are not able well to live together; and, at present, the power is in our hands, and therefore the strongest must fend off."[2] And so it went.

We do not know the sentiments of the individual jurors who sat at Salem's Ship Tavern, but in this case it hardly mattered. Jurors were authorized only to judge the law and the facts or, if there was insufficient evidence, to find strong grounds of suspicion. These particular defendants had already saved Richard the trouble by professing their guilt outright. As a result, they were summarily committed to a Boston jail on July 16, 1658, and given over to the judgment of the General Court.

When the prisoners were released later that summer, some of them persisted with enough clamor to be brought before the next county court session, held on September 28, 1658. Richard, though no longer a juror, nevertheless appeared at this session, in an effort to bring his case against Prescott to a more satisfying conclusion. The records summarize the case in cryptic terms:

Richard Moore v. Edward Prescott. Debt. Verdict for plaintiff at last Salem court but no judgment was entered because it was out of that court's jurisdiction. Judgment now granted.[3]

If the nature of the debt is unclear, we can at least hazard a guess at the payment.[4] In February 1659 we find Richard in Maryland, with his brothers-in-law Richard Hollingsworth Jr. and William Hollingsworth, securing a warrant for the arrest of William Batten—predictably, for nonpayment of that same outstanding debt from a few years before. This was only a few months before

Prescott was cornered in Maryland for the separate infraction of having hanged Elizabeth Richardson.[5] We may infer, then, that Richard now relieved Prescott of his share in the *Swan*.

Certainly Richard lost no time in spreading his wings. While in Maryland he and the Hollingsworths petitioned the court to lighten the local duty "of ten shillins per hogshead layd vpon all Tob: [tobacco] exported to the Manahatans or other Dutch Plantacon."[6] Weighed down with tobacco, he sailed first to Manhattan and then home to Salem, where, with the proceeds of his trading, he bought a wharf and a warehouse not far from his waterfront home. Before the year was out,[7] he mortgaged the warehouse to Henry Shrimpton, an up-and-coming Boston merchant. This sale further galvanized Richard's distribution network, allowing him to unload goods from his ship to his wharf, and from there into Shrimpton's warehouse. Conversely, when Shrimpton had goods to ship out, Richard was the first logical choice for the job.

If Quakers were going to be hounded out of the colony, Richard was at least going to get something out of it. He seemed to be succeeding, too, even to the point of getting out of debt, because one of the people to whom he had owed money began working on his behalf.

WHEN RICHARD had been a boy in Plimouth, he had encountered the great sachem Massasoit, leader of the Wampanoag and ally of the Saints, at the autumnal feast that has since become the holiday of Thanksgiving. By the late 1650s Massasoit was an old man, and his son Wamsutta was preparing to take over the mantle of tribal leader. Though relations between the English and Wampanoag were still relatively stable (the Pequot War having been fought against other tribes), economic hardship had increasingly forced Wamsutta to sell off Indian lands.

On April 2, 1659, Wamsutta sold one such piece of land, located between Plimouth and Rhode Island, to "the twenty-six" of the Ancient Freemen of Plimouth, one of whom was Richard More. The man who had negotiated the sale was Josiah Winslow, son of Edward and one of Richard's creditors for his defamation against John Saffin.

Richard's award was not entirely prestigious. Some of this land, which came to be known as Freetown, was awarded to "those who had been servants" in Plimouth Colony. On the other hand, the Freetown lots were located precisely where Barnabe Gooch, intercessor for the interests of Katharine More, had intended to settle almost forty years earlier. As the long-delayed fulfillment of a mother's promise to *all* of her children, the windfall in Freetown had special resonance—and not least because it came into Richard's possession at a time when, in far-off England, the other Richard More was still doling out land to aristocrats through the Committee for Compounding.[8]

Richard never lived on his Freetown lot—though at about two-thirds of a mile long and four miles wide, it was big enough—preferring instead to use it as an outpost for trading with the Wampanoags. That he would strike up a commercial relationship with Indians at that moment is telling. His brother-in-law Willy Hollingsworth was embarking on a similar business in Delaware, and the following year he would run into difficulties as the English, Dutch, and Native Americans clashed in the area. Meanwhile, in London, Joshua Woolnough had joined the Society for the Propagation of the Gospel in New England—an organization dedicated to converting Indians to Christianity. Conversion had its religious purposes, but it was also the perquisite of trade: Englishmen were not supposed to do business with heathens.

Richard's coordinating his business practices with Joshua Woolnough suggests that he was still keeping a close eye on his London family, if not still visiting them. Considering the political climate in New England, this was risky behavior indeed, no matter how wily a seasoned sailor could be.

While Richard had been busy with personal matters, the

Quaker crisis had been getting altogether more volatile. One of
the visitors at the meeting at the Phelps house (who had been sent
straight to Boston rather than coming before Richard and the other
Salem jurors) had been whipped 117 times and was left for dead,
his flesh "beaten black and as unto jelly, and under his arms the
bruised flesh and blood hung down, clotted as it were into bags;
and it was so beaten into one mass, that the signs of one particular
blow could not be seen."[9] And still the Quakers seemed to ask for
more. Deborah Wilson, for one, challenged Salem in a way that it
had never been challenged before: by appearing in the street entirely naked.

And truth be told, Richard seemed unfazed as well. At a February session, the Massachusetts General Court sentenced two
Quaker children—Daniel and Provided Southwick—to be taken
to Virginia or Barbados and sold into slavery. Edward Butler, the
colony's treasurer, accordingly sought a ship master who would
transport the Southwick children to their doom.

The mariners would have none of it. "One master of a ship to
whom he applied," writes John Gough in his *History of the People
Called Quakers*,[10]

> in order to evade a compliance, pretended they would spoil the
> ship's company. Butler replied, no, you do not fear that, for they
> are poor harmless creatures that will not hurt anybody. The mas-
> ter rejoined, will you then offer to make slaves of such harmless
> creatures? and declined the invidious office of transporting
> them, as well as the rest . . .

The response from the captains, which brought the plan to de-
port the children to a dead halt by June 1659, was apparently
unanimous. Nevertheless, I think we can catch a glimpse of Richard among this crowd. After all, as one who had recently dealt
closely with Edward Prescott the witch-hanger, he had a concrete
understanding of how a Quaker could "spoil the ship's company."

Did Richard give a damn about the children, or was he merely showing a strain of the famous New England pragmatism? Certainly, if he cared, he did not demonstrate it later that month, when he transported the Reverend John Higginson from Boston to Salem. For this courtesy, Richard received forty shillings from the town coffers. Then Higginson, as the new minister of Salem, pushed anti-Quaker sentiment to new heights.[11] Mrs. Nicholas Phelps, wife of the Quaker whose house had originally been raided, lived to excoriate Higginson for sending "abroad his wolves and his bloodhounds amongst the sheep and lambs."[12] Indeed, Higginson's appointment as the minister of Salem contributed to a new round of persecution, which culminated in the hanging of Mary Dyer on June 1, 1660, for the crime of sedition.

Richard would not take Quakers out of the colony but was willing to bring Quaker hunters in—a delicate balancing act in which he appeared not to give a damn, when in fact he was still deftly looking out for his own.

TO THE LANDBOUND, the Quaker hysteria appeared to be a local event, but sailors like Richard knew it to be part of a larger crisis that, at least in its final stages, encompassed England as well.

Oliver Cromwell had died in 1658, leaving his ineffectual son Richard Cromwell to inherit the role of Lord Protector. Seeing his position with some lucidity, the younger Cromwell abdicated his title on April 22, 1659. Charles II, however, did not assume the throne until May 29, 1660. In the interim, the usual chaos that attends transitions of power ensued, and those who had thundered for the head of the king suddenly had to fear for their own. If the Puritans continued to blot out every last sign of transgression in Massachusetts after 1658, it was largely because they feared that they were about to be the only Puritans left.

This put Richard, a man with families on both sides of the Atlantic, in a particularly convoluted bind—in one of his wives' homes, he had to appear to be Puritan, while in the other he was supposed to be anything but. The problem was made more complicated again by the fall from grace of Joshua Woolnough. In the 1650s Joshua had achieved some prominence in London affairs. In addition to his membership in the Society for the Propagation of the Gospel in New England, he was given a seat on the Council for Foreign Plantations, which Charles II had formed to oversee events in the colonies in advance of his return to the throne. Joshua did not last long in the post, however, as it was soon remembered that he had once been a bit too keen on owning a piece of Hampton Court.

Such was the state of events when Richard made his customary triangle run. Arriving in Maryland in February 1660, he again raised the matter of Captain William Batten's nonpayment. On March 21 Batten finally agreed to pay 1,950 pounds of tobacco, which promptly went onto Richard's ship and thence onward to England.

Any hopes Richard may have had for a simple turnaround in London were quickly dashed. The political changeover was already well under way. Samuel More had suffered setbacks and a loss of reputation that would be restored only after his death two years later. Hugh Peter, the onetime shipbuilding advocate in Salem, was in prison, his head destined for a spike on Tower Bridge. Joshua Woolnough, meanwhile, had been labeled a "fanatic"—a designation that did not bode much better.

Understandably, a good many English Puritans made their way to America when the Restoration rolled around. Was that the case of Richard's London family—or at least of his daughter, who at twenty-three still had a long life ahead of her?

There is no evidence that Richard's London wife ever set foot in America. The best that can be said is that a woman his daughter's age named Elizabeth More, of unknown parentage, appeared in Salem for a brief moment in 1660 before marrying a local shipwright named Richard Clarke. Soon afterward the Clarkes moved out of Salem, to Long Island, where they could grow old, far from the jaws of the Puritan "wolves."

If this Elizabeth More was the bigamous Richard's daughter, he could at least console himself that he knew where she had gone and that she was in good hands. Of course, he could not acknowledge either her marriage or her departure. In 1661, when he sold his house on the neck, he could not explain to his buyer why he no longer needed it. As it had been for him and his own mother, the entire separation took place without ritual or recognition—it took place, in fact, in anxious whispers, followed by silence.

What a complexity of sorrow and pride and terror the captain nursed in that solitary heart: having used the Quaker crisis to gain a ship, he had refused to ship Quakers out of the colony, imported one of their worst persecutors, and then let his own child slip away unremarked—all against a larger backdrop of stolen bells, blackmail, and ancient land awards. On the surface, his lot was improving, but what of the many dark currents that ran beneath? Who, in peering deeply into them, could possibly chart a course?

IN 1660, when Charles II was restored to the throne, the meaning to New Englanders was unmistakable: the Protectorate had failed, and with its passing had gone the Puritan dream. Henceforth, Massachusetts would be a far-flung colony on the margins of the English consciousness, rather than the wellspring of a godly English government.

This was your time, an era not of miracles and visions but of uncertainty and hesitation—the lot of those who come late to the enterprise of forging a world. By 1660 many of the First Comers had died (making Richard doubly special, as both an early survivor and a late one), and as the Ancient Beginning vanished from living memory, it became both larger and smaller in the public awareness, to be alternately ignored and protected, but in any event vibrating less and less with its original force. This was your legacy then: to come of age under a demoralizing star, blinking dimly and hardly a guide at all.

The Puritan attitude toward Quakers did not evaporate overnight, but Massachusetts could no longer operate with impunity. To mollify the new king (and to distract him from its more contentious claims for autonomy in legislative matters), the General Court quickly agreed to a new set of Navigation Acts that reiterated the worst aspects of those originally drawn up by Cromwell: a sea captain was permitted to carry goods from England to the colonies but not between the colonies, and certainly not to the colonies of other nations.

In effect, the Staple Act of 1660 and the others that followed it in quick succession forced New England into the very position it had so often denounced: one of systematic duplicity. Whereas once the Puritan had behaved with total transparency, he now hid his intentions beneath a disguise. This was especially true for mariners, who were forced to do most of the smuggling that the colony now required.

And so Richard, who had all but smuggled his daughter in and out of Salem, extended his expertise to economic matters. On June 27, 1661, one William Shackerly complained to a Salem court that his crew had taken the *Hopewell* on a voyage to Monhegan without his permission and damaged it en route, making it unfit for a voyage to Newfoundland. Richard, along with Robert Lemon and William Hollingsworth, was commissioned to inspect the ship and deliver his findings to Captain William Hathorne within a month's time.

This was a standard procedure whereby a seaworthy vessel would be condemned under false pretenses, then "inspected" in order to unload its cargo without paying customs duties. That Shackerly was not being completely honest is clear from his willingness to repeat the same accusations several years later in New Amsterdam, again calling on Richard to board his ship and concoct fanciful damages.[13]

In addition to acting as an accomplice to smugglers, Richard continued working on his own account. On December 13, 1664, he brought a cargo of tobacco into New York (which the English had taken from the Dutch earlier that year) and, while his ship was still anchored in the harbor, was arrested on what could only be called specious charges. His buyer, a man named Liefletheit, having failed to pay a creditor of his own, was absurdly demanding that his debt be paid with the tobacco aboard Richard's ship. Richard employed his usual strategy of asking for the paperwork (and one gets the sense there was none), but he was kept in jail nonetheless until the debt was discharged.[14]

Clearly, sailing was becoming a dubious business, in which the normal contentions were made worse by politics. Yet for as difficult as business became, Richard did not lose sight of the larger picture. Perhaps he was moved to action by the ghosts around him—the ghosts of stories untold—or perhaps it was more the memory of his own dispossession that spurred him on. Whatever the cause, as he plied the Atlantic, he found the time to complement his smuggling with acts of rescue. Before the 1660s were out, he became the guardian to William Henfield, son of a captain who had died at sea (the very same who had cackled as he beat Irish boys in Maryland), and to the children of Captain Robert Starr, who, like Richard, had married into the Hollingsworth family. More magnanimously, in 1662 Richard bought a girl named Mary Brite out of a London ship that had anchored in Virginia.

At the time, both Maryland and Virginia were experiencing a series of servant uprisings—a side effect of the recent influx of Quakers from Massachusetts who were not taking their bondage lying down. Richard knew well what that was all about and did not instill servility in his new servant. On the contrary, for as long as Mary Brite lived in his house, he would encourage her to be headstrong and outspoken.

Surely that would help make up for his past shortcomings— the silence and the absences—would it not?

PERHAPS. By the mid-1660s Richard was able to play the rescuer over a large sweep of the known world, with multiple lines reaching into the distant past, but it was a role that was increasingly elegaic wherever he went.

In 1665 Robert Lemon passed away, leaving Richard to prove his old friend's almost incomprehensible scrawl of a will in court.[15] Not long thereafter, Richard received word that John Vassall, the son of William Vassall, who had stood with him aboard the *Blessing* in the 1630s, was heading a new colony south of Virginia, at Cape Fear.

The news from Cape Fear was not good. Vassall had nearly died on his arrival, when his ship was beaten by the waves and dashed to pieces. A certain Captain Starnyard, expected to arrive with provisions, had gone mad and jumped overboard instead. The colony, at that point no more than a handful of adventurous settlers, was surviving on almost nothing. Whether spurred on by feelings of mercy or by simple business sense, or both, Richard decided to sail to Cape Fear with much-needed provisions.

Paid with a promissory note "by 673 pounds of good Muschovadee sugar,"[16] Richard then made for Jamaica, where he was detained for some time because the English were at war with the Dutch—again—and the waters around the island were being heavily monitored. While waylaid, Richard had time to hear a few yarns about a certain Henry Morgan who had gone out on a privateering mission and retaken Providence Island from the Spanish—a welcome change, but one that came twenty-five years too late for Richard to entertain anything but a rueful nostalgia for the place.

Once he was free to leave Jamaica, Richard collected his Muscovado sugar and again set sail. By early 1667 he was making a tobacco deal in Chesake, Virginia, where Thomas Weston had once operated in secret. The tobacco safely stored in his hold, he then turned to and set out for home, where he stayed long enough to sell some land before heading off for London.

Richard sailed up the Thames sometime in 1667, not long after the twin blows of the Great Plague, which had hit his familiar Stepney harder than any other outparish, and the Great Fire of 1666, which had finished the job. Stopping at his usual watering holes (if they indeed still stood), Richard learned that Joshua Woolnough had died of the plague the year before, only months before his house on Gracechurch Street was devoured by flames.

Meanwhile, the English Richard More had taken a mistress, Dorcas Owen, without exhibiting any pressing need to conceal the fact. Richard's namesake, openly cavorting with another woman![17] That, apparently, was the difference between Old England and New, and the difference between one More family and another.

In November Richard brought the *Swan* back into Salem[18]—the last of the ships from London before winter set in. He had stories to tell, and stories to keep to himself. We may imagine, for example, that he had both the time and the inclination to regale his sons with the yarn of how the Spanish were sacked at Providence Island. He might also have passed along hair-raising tales he had heard of the plague, with details fresher than anything that *God's Terrible Voice in the City of London*, recently published in New England by Thomas Vincent, could ever hope to offer. But once again his greater rites of passage remained within: Under no circumstances could he unburden his heart on the fate of his own Other Woman, the one he had been forced to leave behind.

Richard went to sea one more time, in 1668, on a voyage to Virginia, but the wages of seafaring were beginning to take their toll, and he would never again set foot in London. Whether dead or missing, or simply fading prosaically into the hardships of old age, his London wife, like his own mother before her, existed thereafter only as a memory.

IN THE NEXT FEW YEARS, Richard increasingly turned his sights to property matters, as if trying to find the magic equation that would release the meaning of solid land. Having acquired various properties in Mattapoisett, near New Bedford, he sold some of them in 1668, apparently in order to buy land in Swansea, a fledgling settlement right across the river from his lot in Freetown. In Salem he got hold of half an acre in a lawsuit and proceeded to sell it off as fast as he could.

Gradually, his wife Christian also began to take part in his property transactions, as if to rein him in. In 1671, when he sold property in Marblehead,[19] she added her name to one of his business transactions for the first time. She made her presence felt again on August 30, 1673, when he sold his purchasing rights at his Swansea land to Samuel Shrimpton (Henry Shrimpton's son) "with the consent of his wife."

Meanwhile, Richard's interest in easing the plight of mariners continued unabated. In 1668 he and Willy Hollingsworth added their names to a complaint meant to ease the plight of New Englanders suffering under the Navigation Acts.[20] In 1669 he deposed on customs laws for vessels entering Maryland. And so it continued into his old age. As landbound as Richard ever became, he never stopped defending the interests of sailors or the merchants who relied on them.

Yet smuggling remained on a level distinct from other sorts of secrets, and as Richard spent more time at home, he discovered that no amount of loyalty to his fellow mariners could keep him completely safe.

In 1670 or 1671 Richard found himself in the company of two old sea captains—Joseph Gardner and Thomas Lathrop, the man from whom Richard had prized the Port Royal bell. At the time, a new meetinghouse was being built for Salem,[21] and a discussion arose between the three men as to the bell that would go in it.[22]

Gardner suggested to Lathrop that Salem and Beverly switch bells, because the Salem meetinghouse was large and its bell small, while the Beverly meetinghouse was small and its bell large.

Lathrop replied that the bell was fine where it was and that it had been given to him for the Beverly meetinghouse. This, of course, was true, but it only opened an old wound. In fact this was Richard's first clue as to what had become of the bell after its disappearance from his front yard a decade and a half earlier.

"The bell was given to you," said Richard, jumping in with his favorite defense, "but I might have kept it because I brought it home and never received a bill of lading or was paid for freighting it."

To which Lathrop, seizing his chance, slyly replied, "You might have kept other things besides the bell, and I had no bill of lading for them, either."

That seemed to bring the matter up short.

"Come, come," answered Richard, "let us drink up our wine and say no more of it. I suppose we shall never trouble you for none of them."

Why, after a lapse of sixteen years, would a passing reminder of stolen goods frighten Richard into silence? Again the specter of a secret hung in the air. Or rather, a secret and a loss: what *had* become of "those other things," those brandies, those furs . . . those *days?*

The bell stayed where it was, and Lathrop's information, whatever it was, did not pass his lips.

11

Battles Large and Small

No more I'll go to sea,
Beat down the Bay of Fundy,
Forever more I'll stay on shore,
I'll go to sea no more.

—Traditional sea shanty

A T THE AGE OF SIXTY, Richard walked down to the Salem courthouse and applied for a license to open a tavern in his house on the waterfront. The selectmen granted his request, taking time to observe that the old man had seen hard times—and possibly that he had deserved them:

"Considering how that by the Providence of God Captain More is brought very low, they judge it meet to grant him liberty for the keeping of a public house of entertainment, and selling of beer, wine and cider."[1]

Richard's switch to a career as a tavernkeeper marked his permanent retirement from sailing. His sons Thomas and Caleb had both learned to handle a ship, and Richard Jr. was sailing as far away as Barbados. They could be trusted to take up where he left off. Having spent his life on salt water, Richard would now sell strong water.

He would also find life among landlubbers to be an unending

chain of interlocking arguments, the likes of which he had never seen at sea. In truth, Massachusetts was beginning to come apart at the seams. The preachers were compelled to work harder than ever to convey the gravitas of the original experiment, and they were succeeding less than before, and in the vacuum left by the departed state of grace, what was left, really, except for the land, hedged in more and more each day and unable to yield enough for the sustenance of the body? What was left but to bicker over fences and settle old scores?

Of course, the most debatable borders coincided with the largest behavioral differences, which put neighboring Indian tribes in a particularly bad position. The Wampanoag had enjoyed a long peace with the English, barring a few tense moments in the 1640s. But with the passing of the decades, New Englanders had been steadily growing in number, and as they increasingly sought new territory, the Wampanoag increasingly found themselves on the defensive.

Conditions worsened in 1662, when Wamsutta, who had sold land to Richard and the other Ancient Freemen, became embroiled in hostilities with Plimouth Colony. After a series of misunderstandings, Josiah Winslow—Richard's old creditor, now a military captain—had taken Wamsutta into custody at gunpoint and marched him off to Duxbury. When during his stay Wamsutta suddenly fell ill and died, suspicions that he had been poisoned were quick to surface—and perhaps not without reason.

Such was the inheritance of Metacomet, who succeeded his elder brother, Wamsutta, as sachem for the Wampanoag. For the purposes of dealing with the colonists, Metacomet took the name King Philip, but ultimately no gesture of respect was enough. By the 1670s the Wampanoag had been pushed onto a small peninsula called Mount Hope, surrounded on all sides by Rhode Island and Plimouth settlements. Since time immemorial, they had moved freely over much of southern New England; now their way was barred.

In 1673 Richard sold the last of his land in these settlements and ceded his purchasing rights to Samuel Shrimpton at Swansea. These sales would seem to absolve him of any part in the growing hostilities. On the other hand, he had an ongoing business relationship with Samuel Shrimpton in Salem, and his sons most likely continued to use Swansea as a port of call. Richard thus does deserve some share of the blame for contributing to the largest and bloodiest armed conflict ever to take place in New England.

Who could have predicted such a turn of events half a century earlier, when Richard, a scrappy child, was sharing in the feast of that first autumn with King Philip's venerable father? Or that the promise of land, so justified in one context, would prove to be so tragic in another?

THE WAR BROKE OUT on a Sunday in June 1675, in Swansea itself. Knowing that the English would be at church, King Philip's men began to roam their traditional grounds at will, walking into houses and taking what they pleased. One colonist, exempt from the lecture because he was standing guard, came upon them and was killed. Retaliation followed, then retaliation upon retaliation, and before long the conflict mushroomed into the war everyone had expected.

By far the largest escalation came from the English side. In August 1675 a force of a thousand men was mustered from Massachusetts, Plimouth, and Connecticut, headed by Josiah Winslow. The target of the invasion was a group of Narragansetts—drawn into the war along with many of the New England tribes—who had retreated to a large fort near Rhode Island.

Indian custom demanded that warriors declare their intent to attack beforehand, but the English had no such custom and proceeded by stealth with their invasion. Their designated meeting point was on the western edge of Narragansett Bay, at Wickford. From there the combined forces moved inland. From captured

Narragansetts they learned that the fort was in fact a fortified city, about five square acres, built in the middle of a swamp, housing some thousand men, women, and children.

With the help of some sympathetic Indians, the colonists were able to learn the best method of approaching the fort. But by the time they were ready to attack, conditions had deteriorated. It was then December, and the weather unusually cold. Worse, provisions had run low. The Plimouth soldiers were especially hard put, not having "one biscuit left" before the battle.

All of this news got back to Salem one way or another. Joseph Dudley, the chaplain from Boston, wrote several plaintive letters to the Massachusetts governor, John Leverett, describing the preparations for battle and the urgent need for provisions. (This was the same Leverett who had been involved in the Acadia expedition with Richard twenty years earlier.) Richard's family seems to have been active in couriering as well: a Mr. Moore was trafficking between Wickford and Boston, reporting on the status of the so-called praying Indians—natives sympathetic to the English side.[2]

With these and other reports, Richard's tavern was filled with talk of the impending battle. What would become of their trade in Swansea? What was the latest news? How far would King Philip go? More to the point, how far were *they* willing to go?

Though he was already past the age of sixty, Richard was ready enough. By early June 1675 he had drawn up a will[3]—excluding his sons Thomas and Samuel, who planned to participate in the war themselves—and delivered his ship, the *Swan*, for service.[4] In doing so, he entered into a web of associations that echoed his past even as it brought new and disturbing harbingers for the future.

One regular in Richard's tavern was his brother-in-law Humphry Woodberry. Humphry was one of the very first settlers of Salem, having come while still a boy in the party that included that long-ago mutineer John Lyford. He had since married the elder Christian More's sister, Elizabeth Hunter, and they had produced a family of their own, including a son, William Woodberry. The Mores and the Woodberrys were close enough to share vessels, and over a pot of beer this is what they decided to do. By June 28, 1675, William Woodberry, Richard's nephew, had declared himself master of the *Swan*.[5] Thomas More, Richard's son and now a mariner in his own right, joined the crew as well, and together they readied the vessel for action.

Thomas had done well for himself in recent years. He had lived in Salem until 1670 or not long after, when he moved to Boston and bought a house near the second meetinghouse. When the war broke out, he had offered his services as a sea captain and by the time of the Great Swamp Fight had already seen action as far north as Kennebec.[6]

Tutored at his father's knee, Thomas knew how to handle himself in an emergency. Particularly shrewd was his decision to embark on this mission with the help of Andrew Belcher. A ruthless profiteer, Belcher would soon become one of the most powerful figures in New England by buying shares in as many vessels as possible and then freighting them with anything that was in demand, up to and including slaves. Admittedly, Belcher's reputation was already sufficiently established in 1675 to lend an unbecoming air to the rescue mission. On the other hand, he could be counted on to deliver the goods.

Even with Belcher's pragmatic influence, the *Swan* did not find its rescue easy going. Sailing with the *Primrose* and another vessel owned by Richard Goodale, it met with harsh weather rounding Cape Cod. By the middle of December, Thomas More and William Woodberry were standing on deck, looking out at a sea of ice. The *Swan* was frozen in place.

By this time Dudley was writing to Leverett of the desperate conditions at Wickford and bemoaning the fact that neither "Goodale nor Moor arrived we fear want of shot."[7]

When the *Swan* finally did arrive, Thomas beheld a panorama of soldiers in dire straits, many of them dying as he watched. As in the Pequot War of the previous generation, the first tactic had been to set the fort on fire, and again the effect had been atrocious: of the six-hundred-odd Narragansett casualties, many met their end in flames. The colonists, however, suffered almost as badly. Entering the fort, they had met with heavy resistance, and no small amount of friendly fire, until a quarter of their number was either dead or wounded, and the remainder on the verge of collapse after the long freezing march back to Wickford.

In this way Thomas was able to relate to his father back in Salem that Captain Joseph Gardner, the old salt who had recently learned of Richard's propensity for making plunder disappear, had been accidentally "shot mortally through the head" from behind by a fellow New Englander while advancing on the fort. Thus, another potential informant met the hand of Providence!

But there were other things that Thomas could not see before he returned home to receive his modest fee of ten pounds. We would do well, for example, to rest our gaze for a moment on Joseph Dudley and his fellow chaplain from Connecticut, Nicholas Noyes, as they stood over the fallen and prayed for their souls.

These two churchmen, at the moment so inconspicuous, would both come to play significant roles in Richard's life within a few years. And who knows but that at Wickford they quietly wondered what had really kept the *Swan* from arriving on time.[8]

THOUGH THE ENGLISH SIDE eventually won King Philip's War, it did so at great cost, in lives and morale alike. The Great Experiment, so infallible when it began, now seemed more lost than ever, and even the church authorities began to sense it.

In the More household, the signs were as foreboding as anywhere else. On March 18, 1676, Christian, Richard's wife of thirty-nine years, died at the age of sixty, leaving nothing to posterity but her gravestone in the Old Burying Ground. The following November a fire began in Thomas More's house in Boston[9] and quickly spread until much of the neighborhood lay in cinders. Seeing a black cat emerge unharmed from the flames, the preachers confirmed their belief that great sins were upon the land.

Then Samuel, Richard's eldest son, took matters over the edge entirely. Samuel had served among the troops that marched on Narragansett, though the record tells us little more than that. Perhaps his tour exposed him to the atrocities of war. In any case, there is no doubt that he emerged from the conflict a hardened man.

At first, his behavior looked like the normal family weakness. In 1676 he was fined for incontinency with his "wife" Joanah—specifically, for having sex before marriage, a revelation that must have interested his lawful wife, Sarah. (The More apples were still falling close to the tree!) But with his mother's death, Samuel took a turn into outright savagery.

On December 9, 1676, Samuel, fellow war veteran Blaze Vinton, and Thomas Lenard overtook Jonathan Stacy on a Salem road, stealing his hat as they passed. Farther on, the three horsemen came upon one Leonard Bellringer, who was laying his nets by a bridge. Samuel stooped down with his stick, snagged Bellringer's lines, and threw them in the river.

"You dog," snarled Samuel, "fetch them out or else I will put you in or throw you into the river."

Bellringer dutifully retrieved his lines. Then the three men beat him anyway, instructing him never to sit on a bridge when gentlemen passed.

This accomplished, the brigands next accosted William Lattimore, Richard Simmons, and John Trevit on their way back from Boston on the King's Highway. After hurling a barrage of insults, Lenard challenged the men to a "contest of horses." Then Lenard and Samuel followed Lattimore, "plucked" him from his horse, and robbed him of a gold ring, two shillings in silver, a gold ribbon, and four yards of silver "twist."

Simmons, meanwhile, had been pulled from his horse as well,

and then chased and forced against a tree, where he was struck with as many as a hundred blows. From there, he was dragged to a nearby house and pummeled further, until John Bassay came along and restrained Simmons's attacker. Samuel and his fellow rogues subsequently took Lattimore to the house of one Theophilius Bailey, where they beat him in like kind as he called them bastards, rogues, and fools and tried to fight back.

For these acts, Samuel was hauled into court in March 1677. There being no disputing the facts of the case, he was sentenced to pay five nobles to William Lattimore and twenty shillings to Richard Simmons, sentenced to have the letter *B* branded on his forehead, and bound to good behavior, with his father Richard posting his bond.[10]

Whether this final sentence was ever meted out is unknown, although Samuel disappeared, never to be seen in Salem again after his day in court. One might offer that the father took his son aside and advised him to keep his hat pulled low thereafter—to disguise himself against the piercing eyes of history. Certainly, the name Samuel had never done the More family proud.

And still the troubles poured in. That same year, for unknown reasons, Richard also posted bond for a hardened sailor named Joseph Gillam, who had imprisoned his ship's doctor in Lisbon for complaining about his lack of pay.

At about the same time, Willy Hollingsworth, once Richard's cabin boy, went off to sea and never came back. William's wife, Elinor Hollingsworth, mourned briefly, then took over the family business of running the Blue Anchor Tavern, a lively ordinary next to Richard's property in the South Field. Elinor was a woman of considerable pluck and quickly began doing well for herself. For this she was accused in 1679 of practicing witchcraft.

Although the Gloucester man who brought the case against Elinor, William Dicer, ultimately had nothing to back up the charge, his meddling nevertheless did little to ease matters for Richard. Soon afterward, Robert Starr, Richard's old sailor friend, met his death at the hands of "murderous heathens" and, as the two men had agreed, Starr's three children became Richard's responsibility—more mouths to feed in the midst of general collapse.

Then Richard's third son, Caleb, died, unmarried and childless, at the age of thirty-five. Richard fenced in Caleb's grave, along with the grave of his own wife, in the burying ground right behind his house, leaving the cause of Caleb's death a mystery to the generations that followed.

The human spirit generally answers death with life, and there were attempts in this direction even as darkness seemed to be claiming victory. Samuel had sired at least one child with the help of his various wives. Richard Jr., now a veteran of voyages as far as the Caribbean, managed to have a legitimate son by his wife, Sarah, on June 1, 1679. And Richard's two daughters had at least found spouses. In 1675 Susanna wed Samuel Dutch, a local mariner. The following year Christian married Joshua Conant, scion of the original Salem patriarch.

Richard himself did not wait long after the death of his wife Christian to seek companionship. In 1674, while he was first opening his house to the roustabouts of Salem, Richard Jr. had commanded the *Friendship* to points unknown outside New England. On his return, the younger Richard had brought with him several passengers, including Samuel and Jane Crumpton. The Crumptons moved to Salem, and Samuel had been preparing to set up as a saddler when the war broke out. Crumpton met his end promptly, in the massacre at Bloody Brook, leaving Jane with almost nothing, not even an established circle of friends to console her. Through one turn or another, she ended up at Richard's tavern and by 1678 had ensconced herself there as his wife and barkeep.[11]

ACCORDING to the ubiquitous practice in New England, Richard's tavern, or ordinary, was based in his own home, in the larger ground-floor room called the hall. Typical fare included beer, wine, and hard cider, with entertainment extending to shuffle-board and cards. Though some tavernkeepers bought their alcohol locally or brewed it themselves, Richard preferred his beer imported: in 1677 his name appears as a merchant for "two tonnes [tuns] of strong beer" to be shipped by way of Virginia.[12]

(Though Jane's marriage to Richard may not have taken place for another year, she was already prepared for the role. In the same shipment, she is given as the importer of "2 doz. men's woollen hose; 12 lbs. shoes; a doz. castor [beaver-skin] hats; ¾ cwt. wro. iron; 1 small minikin baye."[13] Shoes by the pound!)

There were many social expectations surrounding taverns. Moderate drinking was universal, but excessive drunkenness was not permitted, as it was seen as a deformer of character: one Salem man was fined by the court for being "disguised with drink."

Who drank what was also carefully prescribed. Beyond the sale of alcohol to Indians, a grave breach of the law, the tavernkeeper had to know the hometown of any English customer before he set his drink down. In September 1674, when Richard succeeded in getting his original tavern license renewed, it had been on the condition that he sell wine to "strangers only." This was an old word around New England, and one Richard knew intimately: in its capitalized form, it had originally referred to non-Saints at Plimouth, including himself.

Gradually, however, the meaning of the word had changed. According to laws drawn up in Massachusetts in the 1640s, a traveler coming within the bounds of a town was considered a "stranger" until he made his religious views known. This sense of the term had persisted with the passage of the years, although its bite had grown progressively weaker until theoretically it referred to transients of any kind, and, in the case of tavern customers, mainly to mariners.

These sailors, who constituted the bulk of Richard's clientele, could be expected to fall easily to blows. Thomas Chubb was hardly atypical when he stood up in Richard's tavern and vehemently denied having borrowed someone's boat without permission. Nor was it unusual that his accuser responded by beating him to within an inch of his life. Such incidents belonged to the fringe world that sailors have always occupied.

But with the breakdown of Puritan morals after the war, church members also began to haunt the Salem taverns more often, and more taverns began to spring up in turn. This development prompted the Reverend John Higginson, recent persecutor of Quakers, to decry the excess of drinking holes around town.

> Being credibly informed that there are at this time belonging to Salem about 14 Ordinaries & publick drinking Howses, some of them licensed others of them unlicensed [here he lists all fourteen taverns, Richard's among them] . . . I find it to be my duty at this juncture of time to present this information to ye Honoured County Court . . . not seeing how such a multitude of drinking houses can possibly stand with ye law made in 75, for a Reformation of excessive drinking under ye title of provoking evils, when it is well known yt till within these few years 2 ordinaries werre judged sufficient for Salem, & ye divers of these haue set up since ye making of ye law in 75; & most of them are known to be frequented by the town dwellers. . . . Therefore it is humbly propounded to ye serious consideration of the Honoured County Court . . . whether there may not be a pulling down of all such publick howses as are found upon mature deliberation not to be absolutely necessary for ye entertainment of travailers & strangers.[14]

No one took the preacher's apprehensions very seriously. One month after Higginson lodged his complaint, Richard had his license renewed for the third time. And, truth be told, Higginson lived to run a tavern of his own in Salem without suffering any visible pangs of conscience.

Nevertheless, Higginson did voice some degree of prophecy in his complaint. As the Salem taverns became more popular, they became focal points for the gathering fractiousness, which before long would combust into something far more terrifying. And though Elinor Hollingsworth had been among the first in Richard's crowd to feel the vibrations directly, it was the regulars at Richard's tavern who were ultimately marked for greater trials.

One man who often dropped in on Richard for a pot of beer was Thomas Oliver. A widower whose first wife had been tried (and acquitted) for witchcraft, Oliver had since married a woman named Bridget. One day in June 1678, Oliver appeared in Richard's tavern with a piece of paper in hand. On it was a petition, with a long list of signatures, protesting the sale of portions of the Salem Common, an area of the neck that had long been open for public use. Richard looked over the document and signed it, the second-to-last man to do so, in a relaxed and confident hand.

Petitions were highly irregular in that day and age—which is to say that no such thing had been waved in the streets of Salem before. Oliver was a dissident before his time and the response, predictable. Although the court agreed not to punish the signatories, it being their first offense, the sentencing of Thomas and Bridget Oliver to public penance that year was probably related to their forays into the realm of political protest.

Thomas Oliver died in 1679 and so did not live to see his widow, Bridget, accused of witchcraft the following year. It was the first time she had been singled out for this crime, but it would not be the last.

A little more than a month after Oliver's petition was dashed, two men sat conferring at one of Richard's tables, quite unaware that they, too, were witches. One of them, Giles Corey, had first entered the More household as a suitor to Mary Brite, the woman Richard had bought out of a ship in Virginia in 1662, and had taken her hand in marriage by April 1673. Corey was known as a disagreeable man and could be worse than that: rumor had it that he had beaten a servant to death, despite his wife Mary's efforts to dissuade him. More recently, Corey had been accused of setting fire to the roof of his neighbor John Proctor's house. The two had argued for a while, and now they had come to Richard's tavern to make their peace with the usual disregard for the local liquor laws. As he later testified, Richard observed that they "showed great love for each other" and split the price of the wine they drank.

In the end, Corey and Proctor were able to settle their differences with the help of Jane (Crumpton) More, who testified that Proctor's "boy" (another unlucky servant!) had accidentally started the fire with a lamp. But the disagreement had underground roots and emerged again in more tangled form that August, in a case arbitrated within the walls of Richard's tavern.

This time, it was Mary (Brite) Corey whose behavior was in question. A strong woman who did not mince words, Mary was accused of swearing, drinking too much, and whipping her servant. At first, the case proceeded with some decorum. Richard's daughter vouched for Mary's upstanding character while she had lived with the More family, as did others.

Then, as often happens when people are drinking, the matter splintered into multiple disputes. One John Parker was charged with being too drunk to stand. A sailor who simply happened to be on hand testified as to Mary's good character and found himself abruptly accused of drinking the punch aboard Phillip English's privateer.

Phillip English was an up-and-coming Salem merchant and, as the recent husband of Mary Hollingsworth, a nephew of sorts to Richard. Like Corey and Proctor, he was also a man destined to fall into the grip of an unforeseen hysteria before the century was out.

Aside from what they foreshadowed, these incidents offer glimpses into the day-to-day rhythms at Richard's tavern. It was a relaxed place where neighbors could make amends quietly and where Jane More could freely serve wine to church members, even though the license expressly prohibited it. It was also a place where hard feelings could erupt without warning and where family members, sometimes on hand only by accident, could find themselves acting as unofficial judges.

One gets the sense, too, from ephemeral appearances of various people described each in his turn as "Captain More's man," of comings and goings, of the milling quality so common in large, loose-knit communities. Certainly, in this regard, we will want to take note of a black woman about the house, visible only at the odd moments when she cleared the tables or emerged from the kitchen in the back to freshen the stock of tobacco.

Whether Judeth was slave or servant is impossible to say definitively, not only because the record describes her simply as Richard's "neager" but also because the distinction in New England at the time was slight. Neither condition was racially defined, and neither was necessarily permanent. Some slaves were bound to a term of seven years, just as servants were. By the same token, a servant could be forced to serve an extra term if his master decided to starve him just when freedom lay in sight. Nevertheless, we are relatively safe in asserting that Judeth was a slave and that she had probably been procured by Richard More Jr. on one of his recent voyages to Barbados.[15]

As a black in Massachusetts, Judeth was able to attend church, though she would have been required to sit in the back of the meetinghouse and receive Communion last. She was entitled to marry, though she would remain property and could not assume her husband's surname. Some of her culture was imported—her dress tended toward the colorful, and her folklore toward African tales—but she and her fellow slaves also celebrated an event called Election Day: after electing their own "governor," they rode in their masters' carts to an evening of dancing, singing, and toasting.

How much Judeth took part in any of this is untraceable, but she has not been completely lost to time. In 1678, while the whites of New England bickered, Judeth made her stake in history by falling in love with David Geffard, described in the record as Mr. Pilgrim's "neager man." Not owning any property themselves, these lovers had to conduct their romance as best they could, which generally meant that David would come over to Richard's front yard and try to find Judeth. Even then, of course, there were few places where they could carry their feelings to their natural conclusion, and ultimately they were discovered in the act. Brought to court in November 1678 for "fornicating," they were sentenced to be whipped (the penalty for Judeth was "five stripes," for David ten) or pay a fine.

Many masters would have angled for a harsher punishment. Dr. Richard Knott of Marblehead, whom Richard knew by name if not by face,[16] had imprisoned his servant on a far lesser charge and then gone so far as to terrorize the man through his cell window.[17]

Richard did not resort to any such tactics on this occasion. He merely paid the fine, remarking that he had asked David several times not to come into his yard. Still, it is worth pointing out that at least one *Mayflower* passenger—quite apart from the glorious myth of the Ancient Beginning—held complete power over a black human being, to do with her as he wished.

INDEED, Richard seems to have wrapped himself in the mantle of a more general sort of power by this time. Though all manner of transgressions took place within his earshot, he behaved as if he were impervious to any accusations against himself. Whereas others fell prey to petty infractions, Richard appeared almost exclusively in his familiar role of rescuer. And when he did choose to settle an old score, he did so with an almost brazen abandon.

In 1677 Richard had encountered some men from Beverly, and after some brief conversation, accused them of stealing the bell from his yard in 1654. They denied it—honestly it seems—but it was not long before Richard was able to learn the true identity of the thief.

How dense is the webwork of vengeance—as dense, possibly, even as the ways of the Lord: a bell dedicated to the virgin grandmother of Jesus Christ had been stolen first in glory, then in pride, and finally in spite by Thomas Tuck, the man whose cow had fallen into the well that Richard had dug on the Salem Common way back in 1640.

Incensed and feeling vengeance within his grasp, Richard brought Tuck and his conspirator, William Dodge, to court in November 1679—a quarter century after the fact—for the "illegal removal of a bell from his property." His goal was not actually to get the bell back, but merely to recoup the original cost of shipping it from Port Royal, which amounted to a paltry two pounds and change. This was no gripe over money. It was the principle of the thing that mattered, and that, of course, made it personal.

The last time Richard had been faced with a court case that involved more than posting a bond or paying a small fine, he had been hobbled by the threat of blackmail regarding his bigamy. Now, however, no highly placed accusers could be expected to threaten his well-being. Captains Lathrop and Gardner had fallen, each in their way, during King Philip's War. John Saffin was preoccupied with his own affairs down in the Old Colony, as was the aged and failing Josiah Winslow.

Nevertheless, it is interesting to note that a crucial deposition came from Anthony Needham. Still smarting from the whipping he had received after the Quaker trial of 1658, Needham gave an eyewitness account that firmly established Richard's lack of any claim to the bell.

More nerve-racking again perhaps was the testimony of George Stanley. Casually describing the meeting between Richard, Lathrop, and Gardner in which the relative size of bells was debated, Stanley went right up to the edge of revelation and then stopped short: "Captain Lawthrop answered Captain More that hee might have kept such and such things naming severall things as well as the bell for I had no more bill of lading to show for them said hee than for the Bell."

This was a way of telling everyone in court, of course, that Richard was little short of a pirate, and one imagines it dimmed his appetite for setting the record straight.

Indeed, although Richard walked away from the courthouse that November day having won his long-awaited victory, it would not take the imagination of a Puritan to wonder if the bell were somehow still benighted. Even as it continued to peal in the Beverly meetinghouse, the Beverly town border was being redrawn, with all the frictions that such divisions ever create. Women were attacking their neighbors, men were threatening surveyors—the Lord in his providence was exacting his due.

And in fact, open hostilities were no longer the only problem. Beneath the insults hurled in Richard's tavern, and others like it across Massachusetts, another, more sinister means of redress was taking root. Much of the coming tension would center on a figure who was still back in the courthouse, folding up his papers after hearing the final testimony in Richard's case.[18] This man was Joseph Dudley, now risen from military chaplain to assistant of the court, and Richard had not heard the last of him.

12

Under Watchful Eyes

Welcome, Sir, welcome from the easterne Shore,
With a commission stronger than before
To play the horse-leach; robb us of our Fleeces,
To rend our land, and teare it all to pieces . . .

> —from an anonymous poem composed on the occasion
> of Edward Randolph's return to Boston in 1681

N O MATTER how violently they argued, New Englanders
agreed on one point: breaching the Navigation Acts,
which required colonists to trade exclusively with England, was the right and proper thing to do. To this end, they
continued to allow their mariners to smuggle at will, to the point
that it became completely routine, even though it meant ignoring
their own strongly held religious beliefs about disguise and duplicity.

Richard was implicated in this contradiction as much as anyone, and had been since the 1660s, if not earlier. In addition to
his sham inspections of ships for captains such as William
Shackerly, he had long moved goods from his wharf into Samuel Shrimpton's warehouse in Salem, many of which, we must
assume, had never benefited from the marvelous properties of
English soil. Richard's habit of requesting nonexistent bills of

lading is another giveaway. Whenever he could work "off the books," he could transport cargo as he liked and London be none the wiser.

The beginning of the end of this arrangement occurred on December 7, 1679, when an ambitious and fearless Englishman named Edward Randolph shook hands with Edmund Andros, the governor of New York, and launched his career as the surveyor general of the English colonies of North America.

Randolph and Andros were Royalists through and through, and anything but mild about it. Seeing that the smuggling business had become an issue of international economic significance, they were determined to bring the Americans to heel. For this they would earn a hatred so undying that New England colonists would be cursing their names 150 years later. And one of their first targets was the family of Richard More.

The story begins in early 1679, when, as the master of the *Jacob and Mary*, Richard More Jr. accepted a number of Quakers aboard ship in England and carried them to the New World as an advance guard for William Penn's fledgling colony. No witch-hanger, the younger Richard faithfully delivered his passengers to the appointed site near Burlington, just below the falls of the Delaware River,[1] in August or September. One or two ports of call later, he was riding anchor in New York Harbor, with plans to shove off for Barbados before the year was out.[2]

While the younger Richard waited, his crew grew impatient and rowdy, and their behavior came to the attention of the New York governor Andros on Christmas Eve. Sitting in his gubernatorial chambers at the tip of Manhattan, Andros was informed that some sailors were shooting their guns in the harbor after the last bell, in violation of the law. Andros promptly dispatched the twenty-five-year-old John Collier to investigate.

A man of uncertain origin,[3] John Collier seems to have been peculiar-looking, as his appearance is emphasized on several occasions. One account describes him as "a short thick and and full faced man, of brown colored hair, and ordinarily wares a light colored worsted chamblet loose coat."[4]

Collier and Richard Jr. were already acquainted by reputation when they encountered each other in New York. In 1676 Andros had sent Collier to southern New Jersey, across the Delaware from Penn's colony, in part to keep the Quakers out, even as Richard was bringing them in. Collier was not a very capable marshal. When he was recalled to New York, his notes were found in disarray. He was also accused of setting himself up as a judge on his own authority. Nevertheless, Andros saw something in him—loyalty, perhaps—and appointed him sheriff of New York, which is what got him out of bed on Christmas Day 1679.

Collier awoke, put on a disguise, and went out to the harbor, where he learned that the ship in question was the *Jacob and Mary*, commanded by Richard More Jr. As he arrived at the waterfront, Collier saw a small boat coming to meet him.

The men aboard this boat knew who Collier was, and showed no fear for the knowing. After making the boat fast, a certain Mr. Pinhorne stepped onto the dock and began ridiculing Collier for meeting them in disguise. Lifting the sheriff by the breeches, Pinhorne cackled, "Do you see what a color this is?" The men then encircled him, shouting and laughing in kind. So it went until the mayor of New York appeared nearby, and Collier, "apprehending greater Abuses," used the opportunity to escape.

The *Jacob and Mary* remained in port for another few days, until Andros gave it a pass to sail for Barbados. What Richard Jr. trafficked in there is uncertain, but he certainly had no bill of lading for his cargo when he returned to Marblehead by way of France.

Which was precisely as Edward Randolph had expected.

Randolph had left New York about the time of Collier's humiliation and headed for New England, intent on catching honey where it was thickest. After a hurried trip to New Hampshire to settle a crisis, he returned to Boston, where he was met by a jeering crowd.

Randolph's unpopularity did not deter him from employing a "waiter"—meaning a customs official—to board "Capt Moores Sloope of Salem" on April 3, 1680.[5] It is quite possible that this man was John Collier, intent on repaying Richard Jr. for his drubbing, as he had been sighted around Salem about this time.[6] On the other hand, it may have been William Dicer, a surveyor general of His Majesty's customs sometime before 1685, whose wife had accused Elinor Hollingsworth of being a "blackmouthed witch and a thief."

Whoever it was, the waiter spent six arduous days rummaging through the hold until he had unearthed everything he could possibly find. Then Randolph boarded the ship, waving the governor's warrant, and, while Richard More Jr. seethed in silence, marked the "broad arrow" on the mast with a piece of chalk, and seized the vessel for the Crown.

Once Randolph had impounded the ship and its cargo, court action was initiated by the informer who detected the violation. If the court found evidence of smuggling, the ship would be condemned to be sold, and the proceeds divided evenly between the king, the colony, and the informer. Randolph had seen to it that the position of informer was open to anyone, a tempting proposition in an era when the proceeds routinely amounted to hundreds of pounds. Even when ship owners were able to settle out of court for a smaller sum, a man could land himself a tidy nest egg for the negligible effort of betraying his neighbor.

With this kind of help, Randolph was able over the next two years to seize thirty-six ships, including vessels owned by Richard's business associates Samuel Shrimpton and Andrew Belcher.[7] Nevertheless, Randolph was hard put to make any headway, because many of the Massachusetts magistrates refused to recognize his commission, and when they did, their juries often did not. Of the thirty-six cases Randolph brought, all but two ended in acquittals.

For the moment, this recalcitrant attitude afforded Richard

More Jr. a reprieve on his goods aboard the *Jacob and Mary*. But Randolph was not one to be put off. In order to gain a foothold in the Massachusetts power structure, Randolph played on its divided interests. The more pragmatic government officials worried that too much noise from New England would awaken the king from his torpor and remind him of his royal prerogatives. The Massachusetts merchants, favoring business by any means, did not especially want to rock the boat, either. As a result, a vast duplicitous game came into play, with Randolph trying to co-opt influential colonists even as they alternately appeased or humored him, depending on their level of desperation.

Of course, this meant that New Englanders had all but institutionalized the very characteristics they had so often denounced. They had become dissemblers on a mass scale, appearing to follow one course while in reality taking another, until no clear motive could be discerned. Samuel Shrimpton, Richard's first choice in Salem merchants, was a textbook case in point: he initially tried to evade Randolph, then became a member of one of his committees, and finally opposed him in the most vehement manner possible.

Richard, meanwhile, seems to have understood the lay of the land. Having let his tavern license expire, he continued to serve customers until called to appear before the Essex Quarterly Court in June 1682. The fine was waived despite testimony that Jane More had been seen selling beer. This same court did him one better on October 16 of that year, appointing him a surveyor of damaged goods aboard vessels lying in Salem Harbor.

Richard's quite unofficial job was to board inbound ships and declare their cargo unfit for sale. These goods could then be unloaded into the various warehouses along the waterfront—including Samuel Shrimpton's—and sold without the encumbrance of taxes.

By the end of 1682, Randolph had despaired of getting any convictions, and prepared his return to England to secure more sweeping powers of authority. As for John Collier, his services no longer being required in Massachusetts, he made his way back to New York and resumed work under Governor Andros in the admiralty courts, deliberating on piracy cases.[8]

During this same period, Richard's son Thomas More made his presence felt in New York's admiralty courts by doing something just as interesting: sailing home with a hold full of Spanish doubloons.[9] And in so doing, he awakened the interest of a man who would become the Mores' most powerful ally.

IN LATE 1682 or early 1683, Frederick Phillips, a New York merchant, member of the governor's council and profligate bankroller of pirates, commissioned John Cornelissen to assume command of the *Delaware Merchant* for the salvage of a Spanish wreck near the "Bohemiah Islands" in the Caribbean.

Cornelissen sailed from New York on January 16, 1683, and arrived at the correct location on February 26 but found the spot coveted by French privateers and others. One deposition has it that Cornelissen was persuaded by the French to plunder the Spanish town of St. Augustine and subsequently went with them, taking several of his own men. Another account says that Cornelissen boarded another English ship in the area before the French left. Either way, the men of the *Delaware Merchant* eventually joined up with several other English ships in the area, including those commanded by Stephen Crego, Richard Rook, Nicholas Ingoldsby, and Richard's son Thomas More.[10]

Thomas had moved away from Boston by then: not long after one of his houses burned down in the fire of 1676, he sold a second house on the waterfront and apparently moved to New York. He still retained his ties to New England, however, as we shall see.

Cornelissen had brought with him "an Instrument" by which the men hoped to recover the sunken treasure. When this curiosity—probably a tub that could be lowered by chains—failed to perform, some of the men went to Florida for "divers." On March 17, 1683, the English mariners entered into articles of agreement, allotting one share to each man and a part share to the "boys" on any of the ships. The agreement included any Indians procured, presumably a reference to the divers. Whether or not the divers became slaves, they apparently did their job, because on March 26, Crego's crew of twenty-one men received their share: 574 pounds and 11 ounces of silver in plate.

Unfortunately for the crew of the *Delaware Merchant*, Frederick Phillips had his own deal with Cornelissen, and it fell to a New York admiralty court to apportion the booty. As Phillips sat on the governor's council, it is not surprising that the case was decided in his favor. Years later the Reverend John Higginson bemoaned that Phillips had amassed a fortune of more than 100,000 pounds over the previous twenty years through his piratical ventures in Madagascar.

Thomas More fared better than Cornelissen. After loading up his vessel with booty, he sailed not to New York but to Salem, where his father was on hand to appraise his vessel for "damaged goods" and so avoid customs difficulties. Applying arithmetic to the figures given in the deposition, we can estimate that each man in his crew received between twenty-seven and twenty-eight pounds of silver. Since Thomas More had a crew of thirty-nine men and one boy, he must have taken home upwards of a thousand pounds of silver.

In bypassing New York, Thomas did not escape legal redress entirely. Between July 1683 and April 1684, no fewer than four suits were brought against him in Boston's Inferiour Court of Pleas, all of them for proceeds allegedly withheld from the salvage. Nevertheless, only the first plaintiff won his case; the others had to be content with the shares they had received.

Thomas's mission was a harbinger of things to come. Soon, all over the Caribbean, sea captains were combing the shallows for sunken treasure, the most successful of whom was William Phips.

The nephew of a man by the same name, Phips had grown up near Pentagoet and had often heard the tale of how that fort was retaken in 1654 by the likes of Richard More.[11]

When Thomas More came home laden with booty in 1683, Phips was newly inspired and sailed off to investigate the same Spanish wreck in the Bahamas for himself.[12] Though thwarted on his first venture, he eventually succeeded beyond his wildest dreams and returned to England with 37,538 pounds of pieces of eight, 25 pounds of gold, and 2,755 pounds of silver, of which he received a share of one-sixteenth.

One might explain the sudden craze for sunken treasure as a response to Randolph's antismuggling crusade: unable to make money by the usual methods, New Englanders resorted to unusual ones. The rush was on for quick money, and lots of it.

Such was the mentality of John Collier, at any rate, when he returned to Salem in the autumn of 1683. Fresh from his stint as a New York marshal, Collier became involved in a scheme to divest a Salem sea captain, George Corwin, of his riches. In the midst of the burglary, Collier lost his concentration and suggested that he and his cohorts burn down a few wharves at the harbor instead. Among the perpetrators who convinced him to proceed with the original plan was David Geffard, Mr. Pilgrim's slave, who managed to escape to Barbados, probably with his lover, Richard's slave Judeth, and some percentage of the five-hundred-pound take.

Collier, for his part, was left to consider his actions in the Salem jail, apparently forgotten by his former employers. A valiant effort came in August, in the form of his appointment to aide-major and mustermaster of New York, but it was not enough to free him. For the moment, Randolph and Andros had more important matters to attend to than the incarceration of a deranged henchman.

IN 1684 the political crisis in Massachusetts had progressed so far that the very charter of the colony was in jeopardy. In July Randolph was writing to Samuel Shrimpton, warning him, in a case of trenchant if unwitting foreshadowing, that "Mr. Mathers the bellows of sedition and treason, has at last set his fools a-horseback. If they do not mend their manners, some of them may ride to the Devil."[13]

Many colonists were accordingly preparing for that ride in advance—especially the old-timers, who had their land rights to worry about. In the early days, property had been acquired rather informally, and who could say whether the king would require them to produce deeds?

In the months before the charter was revoked, Richard deeded to his daughter Susanna Dutch, recently the mother of a girl, his land in the South Field next to Elinor Hollingsworth's tavern. The following September, when some property belonging to the Conants—the original leaders of Salem—came into question, he was called upon, as one of the oldest souls in the colony, to confirm the ownership of the Conant estate in Maryland.

This deposition, given to Massachusetts governor Simon Bradstreet, fairly rings with the sound of a people asserting their identity against an intruding version of history:

> The Deposition of Richard Moore Senr. aged seaventy yeares [sic] or thereabouts. Sworn saith that being in London att the House of Mr. Thomas Weston Ironmonger in the year 1620 He was from thence transported to New Plymouth in New England . . . [14]

Richard then went on to describe in schematic form the wild peregrinations of Weston, from Plimouth to Maryland and then up to Marblehead, where he deposited his daughter with the Mavericks, where she lived until marrying John Conant. . . . Those events, having transpired so very long ago, must have seemed like a dream in 1684. What had become of all that excitement, all that freedom? What had become of Massachusetts?

The answer came a little more than a month later, on October 23, 1684, when Edward Randolph revoked the Massachusetts charter. For the next seven and a half years, the colony would have no local government of its own but would survive at the pleasure of the king and whomsoever he appointed to act on his behalf. This made for turmoil and, finally, explosions, in which Richard proved to be one of the casualties.

The first man appointed by the king to assume the government of Massachusetts was Joseph Dudley—the same man who had heard testimony in Richard's lawsuit over the bell. Dudley had moved up through the legal structure in the interim, serving as a judge and an ally to Edward Randolph, until he had proven himself loyal to the Crown's interests.

Upon his commission in May 1686, Dudley's second act, after forming a Commission of the Peace, was to order "that a Warrant be sent to the Constables of the several townes to convey John Collier, a distracted Person, to the Select Men of Salem, to provide for him as formerly, wch. was accordingly done."[15]

A "distracted Person"—make that a man intent on setting fire to the wharves of sea captains—was now on the retainer of Joseph Dudley's government.

THE WEALTHIER FIGURES in Massachusetts were able to find positions under Dudley. William Phips snared a post as the provost marshal. Shrimpton found his way onto a committee assigned to resolve the navigation and trade dilemma, as did William Brown Jr., Captain John Higginson (the son of the minister), and Richard's old nemesis John Saffin. In addition to navigation cases, this committee was authorized to look into matters of general disorder and grievances in the towns.

Richard may have continued on under Dudley as a surveyor of damaged goods, thereby benefiting with his more prestigious colleagues in the ongoing smuggling game. But a combination of personal and political problems soon squeezed him harder than he could manage.

On October 5, 1686, Richard's wife, Jane, died, at the age of sixty. Richard had outlived three wives and two sons, and his surviving children had either been banished or were raising families of their own. Only Richard Jr. continued to spend time around the house, but even he was often at sea, and for much of the time, there was no one on hand to tend to Richard and his tavern in his old age.

Indeed, one can hear something close to timidity in Richard's plea to a Dudley court that December to have his tavern license renewed, on the grounds that he was "one of the First Comers to the land." When had it ever been necessary to point that out?

Richard's isolation was made worse by the intensifying political climate. On June 3, 1686, Edmund Andros was commissioned to replace Joseph Dudley as governor of a new entity: the Dominion of New England, which included Massachusetts, Connecticut, Rhode Island, and Plimouth Colony. Dudley was not out of the picture, however. Andros appointed him as chief justice of the superior court, which included the General Sessions of the Peace and the Inferior Court of Common Pleas.[16]

Andros was an imperious and arbitrary leader, whose commission gave him almost absolute power. On Easter 1687 he forced his way into the South Church Meetinghouse to attend an Anglican service there. Cotton Mather groaned to see maypoles and swordfighting stages in the streets. Meanwhile, there was no clear indication as to when a new charter would arrive.

But Andros could not control the smuggling trade any more than Dudley could. Shrimpton continued to prosper under the new regime, as did Belcher, as did anyone who knew the game of currying favor.

As long as the money continued to flow, the various factions were content to play it fairly safe. Then in August 1687 Dudley overstepped himself. Presiding over a trial against several contentious Ipswich figures, he admonished the defendants with the infamous words: you "must not think the laws of England follow us to the ends of the Earth . . . you have no more privilidges left you, than not to be sold for Slaves." Heaping insult on injury, he then turned to the jury and demurred, "We expect a good verdict from you." From that moment on, the colonists were united in their hatred of the Andros government.

During previous crises, Richard had always been able to maneuver his way to safety and even to benefit from his troubles. In each of those cases, however, his success had depended on the ability to outwit his opponents. Never before had he been faced with an enemy who was able simply to change the rules at will.

For all his imperial might, Andros was running an underbudgeted autocracy, and as everyone expected, he now began to fund it by openly contesting the property rights of many New Englanders. Seeing what was coming, Richard began to shield his property by selling it, or parts of it, to influential figures. John Higginson Jr. sat on the committee to investigate trade and navigation—Richard sold him a "parcel of flats" and his wharf in October 1687. William Brown had risen to the position of councillor to Andros—on May 15, 1688, Richard sold him and his brother the "homestead he was now possessed of."

Richard's ship was perhaps in greater need of protection than anything, and he took steps to safeguard it as well. Andrew Belcher had been involved in some capacity with the *Swan* since King Philip's War. On October 18, 1687, Belcher arrived in Boston from England with the announcement that he was to be the assistant of the recently knighted Sir William Phips, who was still in England preparing his grand salvage in the Caribbean. Within a year, the *Swan* was being described as Belcher's ship, which indicates that he had bought a majority share in it.

So far, Richard had done what anyone in his position would have. And none of it made a bit of difference.

Phips returned to Boston on June 1, 1688, amid such tension

that his wife "was ready to faint as word was brought in by the Coach-man of Sir William's being spoke with at Sea."[17] Lady Phips's fright was understandable enough. Her husband had received an appointment as high sheriff of New England for the price of some "hundred of guineas,"[18] which effectively nullified the powers of Andros's high sheriff, a man named Sherlock, who was wont to impanel "juries of Strangers who had no Freehold in that Countrey, and extorted unreasonable fees."[19]

Not only did Andros refuse this patent, but Phips found his life threatened in the bargain.[20] "The infamous government then rampant there," wrote Cotton Mather, "found a way wholly to put by the execution of this [Phips's] patent, yea, he was like to have had his person assassinated in the face of the sun, before his own door, which with some further designe caused him within a few weeks to take another voyage to England."[21]

In a moment of haughty defiance, Phips then made the mistake of telling Randolph his getaway plan, letting slip that he intended to depart on his own frigate, attended by the *Swan*. Of course, there were few better places to ferret out details about the *Swan* than in Richard More's tavern, and because he had built it from pine rather than oak, there were plenty of knotholes in his chamber floors through which one could "bear witness."

It does not matter who started the process, except to note that a distracted person was presently about Salem, cultivating his grievances against smugglers and sea captains and especially men who tried to strip sheriffs of their power. This much can be surmised, and the man put in his place. But my main concern is with you, the watcher from afar.

How did you fit into these developments? Did you just happen to be at Richard's tavern of an evening when you heard something irregular going on behind closed doors? Did you understand who John Collier was, and how he fit into the picture? Were you among his cronies on the Corwin burglary? Was there talk of Thomas More's riches buried somewhere under the floorboards? Or were you merely roused to action when a certain would-be assassin, frustrated in his attempt to bring down Phips, offered you a reward for informing on the old captain instead?

I wonder, wonder and shuffle my papers, with their own diminutive winds . . .

13

Hypocrisy Unmask'd

Whence cometh it, that Pride, and Luxurie
Debate, Deceit, Contention, and Strife,
False-dealing, Covetousness, Hypocrisie
(With such like Crimes) amongst them are so rife,
That one of them doth over-reach another?
And that an honest man can hardly trust his Brother?

—Michael Wigglesworth,
"God's Controversy with New England"

SHORTLY BEFORE JULY 1, 1688, Captain Richard More was summoned to appear before several justices of the peace, each of them appointed by Joseph Dudley, for committing the act of adultery with a married woman. After the three witnesses delivered the testimony and the judges handed down their sentence, Richard was taken outside the courthouse, to a spot beside the adjacent watch house, and tied to the whipping post there. After receiving his lashes, he was sent on his way, with the instructions to affix the letter A—the infamous scarlet letter—in a conspicuous position on his upper garments, that he might broadcast his crime whenever he showed himself.

A First Comer, a mariner and an old man—whipped before his peers! That was a humiliation that would not soon be forgotten. Yet it also left the church authorities in a perplexing situation. To recognize the court's verdict was to recognize the enemy, while to ignore it was to ignore the letter on Richard's shirt whenever he went abroad in the street.

Certainly, they were not eager to cast Richard out. As was the custom, the elders had spoken to him privately on several occasions about his well-known tendency toward "lasciviousness and at least some degree of incontinency," but they had never worked very hard to prove their case. "For want of proof," as they put it, "we could go no further." In fact, they probably would never have done anything had the courts not forced the matter into the open. Richard, after all, represented the Ancient Days, and it was best not to show the Ancient Days in a less than exemplary light at a time when the colony was under such virulent attack.

Therefore, the church did what it usually did when at a loss as to how to proceed: it brought the matter before the congregation during a Sunday lecture. Though there was, undoubtedly, some coercion from the elders, it was Richard's peers who decided to bring him to account in a specially scheduled meeting: "Two brethren accordingly went to him to bring him before the congregation that afternoon."

And so Richard stood before the inquiring gaze of his fellow Salemites, the letter *A* already emblazoned on his breast, considering what he might say. Should he tell them that he had done much worse, sired a child in bigamy and abandoned his secret wife? Should he reveal that an Englishman going by his name, sitting at his rightful table, eating his rightful food, was presently lavishing his mistress with gifts and suffering not the slightest consequences? Should he disparage the court that had convicted him, with its packed juries, its extortionists, its illegitimate sheriffs—all well-established infamies that the congregation would gladly share in condemning?

In the end, Richard spoke "in some relenting way"—an apt turn of phrase that suggests a subtle mixture of protest and surrender: *Yes, it's true, but*...A public debate was not the same thing as a public confession, however, and the congregation voted to admonish him. The floor then reverted to the pastor, no longer the infirm John Higginson but the Reverend Nicholas Noyes, who had served alongside Joseph Dudley during the Great Swamp Fight and who, within a few short years, would lead the campaign against the witches of Salem.

Eyeing Richard with the gravity required of the moment, Noyes charged him with "a scandalous breach of the seventh commandment not fit to be named made worse by previous warnings and his old age, etc." Then he delivered Richard from the Lord's Supper, as the Puritans called the rite of Communion, and commanded him to repent of his deed.

Richard had been excommunicated.

THE MOST CURIOUS ASPECT of Richard's excommunication is the reticence that pervades it. The elders who spoke with him privately are not identified, nor are the "brethren" who fetched him from his house, nor even the woman who committed the deed with him. The specific variation on his breach of the Seventh Commandment (Thou shalt not covet thy neighbor's wife) is itself considered unfit to be named. The only clear fact is that the sin had been committed by Richard and that it was extreme enough to warrant his expulsion from the church.

Very few transgressions fit this description. The absence of the married woman's name in the pronouncement strongly indicates that she was not a church member.[1] But this in itself did not constitute an especially grave sin. Adultery with an Indian or a black, or even with one's own sister—all these were all also punishable, but none qualified as unspeakable. One cannot speculate that Richard's bigamy had been declared, because the charge would then not have been adultery. As for bestiality, even old Governor Bradford had not hesitated, in the straitlaced days of the 1640s, to enumerate the species of animals favored by a boy for venting his urges.

By process of elimination, we are left to consider that the unspeakable was, in fact, unfounded. It is quite within the spirit of the times that the charges would have been trumped up, on the basis of old and well-founded rumors, as a payback for Richard's role in the imminent retreat of William Phips. Alternatively, the court may have committed procedural abuses against Richard, much like those others had suffered, that rendered the case essentially void. In the end, it is impossible to say, but given the excesses of the Dudley courts and the church's peculiar insistence on ambiguous wording, I for one can only advocate shifting the crime away from the defendant and onto the judge.

Subsequent events would seem to support no less.

AFTER HE LEFT the meetinghouse and walked back the route he had come, past the gravestones of his family, to the gloom of his tavern, Richard had ample time to contemplate what he had just been told. He would have been expected to do so. The Puritans thought less than clearly about many things, but they knew their Scripture within a fraction of an inch.

The passage cited for Richard's repentance was Revelation 2: 21: "And I gave her space to repent of her fornication; and she repenteth not." The reference is to Jezebel "which calleth herself a prophetess, to teach and seduce my servants to commit fornication." Those who lie with Jezebel are to suffer the death of their spawn. Yet offsetting this morbid suggestion is an encouragement, delivered at the end of the chapter: "But that which ye have already, hold fast till I come."

Hold fast? It was almost as if the church was telling Richard not to repent at once but to wait until the moment was right. This makes sense when one considers the political situation of the moment.

On July 6, five days after Richard was cast out, the swashbuckling William Phips was sworn in as high sheriff of New England. Had Phips's commission been recognized, Richard might have held out some hope of overturning his conviction. The following day, however, Andros overruled Phips's patent for appointing his own sheriffs and, worse, began serving writs of intrusion—warrants for seizing land—against many in the merchant class, including Samuel Shrimpton. Down but not defeated, Phips put new speed into his plans to depart to England, where he intended to set Randolph "forth in his colors" and make the opposition to his patent known.[2]

There would be no immediate reversal of fortune for Richard. On the contrary, with the threat of assassination still hanging over Phips's head, Richard seems to have stepped his divestment. On July 10, as the *Swan* was being loaded up with silver from colonists who feared losing their estates to Andros,[3] Richard deeded the "dwelling house in which he lived"—a structure in the outlying area of his main house—to his son Richard Jr. If he were to die, or to have a sudden need to disappear, at least his son would have a place to live.

The *Swan* and Phips's frigate, the *Rose,* set sail for England on July 16—just two weeks after Richard's excommunication. Had he gone with them, he would have been able to add one more adventure to his vast and varied experiences. On its way out, the *Swan* encountered a pirate named Peterson off the coast of Rhode Island and exchanged fifty-seven pounds in money in return for fifty hides and forty "elephant's teeth"—an expedient method of laundering assets, given the situation at home.

But Richard did not leave Salem, nor did he meet his maker by staying. In August he and Richard Jr. sold a patch of the land surrounding the dwelling house to Peter Osgood, a local tanner. Then Richard sat down to a pot of wine in what was left of his home and watched the colony go haywire around him.

It was not a world he could easily recognize. Wigs were coming into fashion. The first newspaper was published in Boston and immediately quashed. The French and Indians were attacking to the north and to the south. Meanwhile, Andros had received a new and stronger commission, publishing it "with great parade from the balcony of the townhouse"[4] before whisking himself off to take the government of New York and New Jersey under his wing.

Where would it all end?

In a freak occurrence, as it turned out. In February 1689 rumors began to fly that William of Orange, a Protestant, had invaded England to usurp the papist King James II. Everything in New England hung on the outcome: if James were deposed, the Puritans had a chance again. When positive news of William's invasion was brought in that April, a group of merchants, including Samuel Shrimpton, posted an announcement:

> We judge it necessary that You forthwith surrender, and Deliver up the Government and Fortifications to be preserved, to be Disposed according to the Order and Direction from the Crown of England, which is suddenly expected may Arrive.[5]

On the eighteenth, an armed mob captured the frigate on which Andros hoped to flee and stormed the fort at Castle Island. A group of men, again including Samuel Shrimpton, lured Andros to the Town House in Boston, where he was held captive. Apprehending Randolph as well, they put a pistol to his head, marched him to the fort, and forced him to demand the soldiers' surrender. Dudley, who had been out of town, was chased down and reunited with his confreres in the Boston jail, which Randolph was soon sarcastically referring to as "the common jail at New Algiers." And there they remained until they were sent off to England in chains to answer for their misdeeds.

Although the charter had not been reestablished, Massachusetts had overthrown a tyrant and reasserted its hold on its own affairs.

Hold fast till I come.

WITH THE OUSTING OF ANDROS, a Committee of Safety was formed that represented Richard well—Belcher and Shrimpton were prominent members, as was Simon Bradstreet, the former governor and longtime moderate in matters of shipping and trade.[6] Though provisional, this committee saw to it that the old order would not vanish quickly. It asked the towns of Massachusetts to send delegates to a convention, and in early May 1690 the convention voted to restore the former colonial government to Massachusetts, with Bradstreet as governor.[7]

It was precisely at this time that Richard began approaching the church elders about his chances of being readmitted to the congregation. His argument can be guessed at easily enough: the reviled Andros government was out, and with it the judges who had arrayed themselves against First Comers such as Richard. Now that the colonial government had been reinstated, the least Richard deserved was an appeal.[8]

An appeal, and maybe even more. When Andros was brought before a court in England, he faced an avalanche of charges, most of them connected to the illegality of his administration. But among the lesser charges—robbing ship captains and outlandish abuses at trials—was the complaint of Richard's son-in-law, the sea captain Joshua Conant. According to Conant, Andros had hired ten Frenchmen for the purpose of taking Boston for France. That, certainly, had to be accounted for in the larger scheme of Richard's affairs.[9]

Spiritual forgiveness was another matter, however. The Reverend Higginson understood Richard's feelings well: he, too, had lodged charges against the Andros government for its tyrannies. But whatever the calumnies of Andros and his men, the church elders knew that the legal charges against Richard were not wholly unfounded. For years his circumstances in London had cast suspicious shadows around him. More to the point, it was

Richard's criminal record that had prompted the church to cast him out. To reverse that decision, would it not require an equivalent reversal from an authorized court?

While the church parsed these matters of the soul, Richard's earthly concerns continued to weigh him down. Randolph may well have been speaking of the Swan's heady adventure when, writing to the governor of Barbados from jail in 1689, he noted that "some, that have their estates abroad feare they have done more than they can answer, believing other governments will treat them as revolters from their allegiance, and give them neither protection nor lett them depart til they have orders from home [England] how to treat them."[10] In the rush to send money out of the colony, a lot of elephant's teeth had been stranded elsewhere.

That was the feeling not just in Richard's house but throughout the colony. In the desperate search for money, a military committee including Shrimpton and Phips was formed on March 24, 1690, for an attack on that old chestnut of an enemy: the French at Nova Scotia. To this end, Phips enlisted the Swan, under the command of Thomas Gilbert and presumably washed clean of its pirated goods by now, in the attack. This gave Richard some hope of regaining, according to his share in the vessel, what he had lost in the dark days of 1688.

Once the fleet had sailed, Richard turned his attention toward his deteriorating circumstances. In May he deeded land that he had already mortgaged to a neighbor. This sale was not an attempt to appease powerful townsmen. By this time, he was simply losing his land to poverty.

Then tragedy struck.

Richard's niece, Christian Woodberry, had some years earlier married into the Trask family in Beverly and moved in next door to Bridget Bishop—the widow of the man who had organized the Salem Common petition. Before long, Christian began to complain of the commotion that came out of Bishop's tavern—they played shovelboard at all hours, drank to excess, who knew what else.

Eventually things had gotten so bad that she enlisted the help of the Beverly minister, John Hale, in trying to get the tavern shut down. In 1686 or 1687 she had asked that Bishop be barred from the Lord's Supper.

But nothing had sufficed to quiet the Bishop tavern, and in the end it undid her neighbor. On June 3, 1690, Christian committed suicide with a pair of dull scissors. It was later determined that these "skissors" were so small that only a Devil could have inflicted a fatal wound with them. For the moment, the episode was only cause for "the astonishment and grief of all, especially her most near relations."

It was an especially awkward moment for her uncle Richard. Barred from appearing at her funeral (as he was barred from all religious functions), he could only mourn at a distance, his sin on his breast, listening to the pealing of the bell *that should have been his*.

Under the shadow of Christian's death, news of Phips's success at Port Royal was a diminished joy. And the good tidings were blotted out completely when Phips set out again, the *Swan* still among his number, on a foolhardy assault on Quebec. Even before this mission proved a total failure, it was clear that Massachusetts would not have enough money to pay the returning soldiers. Belcher offered to put some of his money in advance, but even that was not going to be enough. (Though, frankly, Phips might have found it in his heart to loose a few gold coins, too.) As a result, Massachusetts took a deep breath, issued the first paper money in North America, and watched as it inflated out of sight.

Salem certainly looked like a ruined thing: no charter, the economy in disarray, and even the church split in two—after years of petitioning, Salem Village had won permission to have its own wholly independent meetinghouse and had taken on Samuel Parris, a recent arrival from Barbados, as its pastor.

Yet amid all the commotion, Richard had taken the church's opinion to heart. In 1690 he was called upon no fewer than three times to depose on another set of ancient land claims: the various properties Richard Hollingsworth had bequeathed upon his death. Richard had previously used court dates to further his own ends—one recalls how he cornered Edward Prescott during the Quaker trials, ending up with a ship in the bargain. This time he would do much the same, in hopes of clearing his reputation.

One cannot underestimate the force of nostalgia at that time. The following year an aging captain named Joshua Scottow chose to write a tract called *Old Men's Tears at Their Own Declension*. In this jeremiad, Scottow claimed to have consulted some of the oldest men in the colony. These men, Richard among them, could easily have told him a story or two that would have raised the hackles of any sentient being. Yet Scottow did not compose a tale of betrayal, death, and dishonor. His pamphlet was sentimental and general, one man's attempt to redeem the past with warmed-over regrets. Like the church elders, he would bury history in the fertile sod of legend.

And so would Richard. Entering the court with his sailor's gait, he again revived the old memories and the long-gone faces. It was clearly an emotional performance. So dear was the memory of Richard Hollingsworth to his heart that he first referred to him as his father, then corrected himself and called him his father-in-law.[11]

Here was a man who had been there when the first Indian had walked into Plimouth and greeted them in English, when mutiny had cleaved the Old Colony, when civil war had wracked England, when Jamaica had failed, when Quakers had courted death. . . . John Hathorne, who recorded Richard's words, surely noted the irony in the moment. His father, William Hathorne, had lived through many of those same events and had even been an administrator to the Hollingsworth estate. What did it mean when such a repository of lore—a First Comer, no less—could be marked as a criminal? What indeed had become of Massachusetts?

ON APRIL 26, 1691, Richard again made the short walk to the
Salem Town meetinghouse to face his destiny. This time, however,
he was not accompanied by pious escorts but by a garrulous
friend who, over a pot of wine, had decided that the time was
right for him to make amends as well.

The church recorded the event as follows:

> Old Captain More having lyan under the Churches censure, al-
> most 2 yeares whereby he was debarred from the Lords Supper
> comeing severall times to the Elders, and at last publickly in a
> writing and partly by speech professing his Repentance for his
> offences against God and his Church was in charity accepted
> and by the vote of the Church forgiven and restored to his for-
> mer state.[12]

Public confession was a highly developed tradition in New England. The penitent was expected to wear his worst clothes for
the occasion and to give strong outward signs of contrition. When
these signs reached a certain emotional pitch, it was said that the
confessor was "blubbering"—one town had gone so far as to limit
the time in which blubbering could be done.

When Richard took the floor, he surely did everything that was
expected of him. He wept and rent his clothes until the spirit of
the Lord was in the air and the congregation was only too glad
to reinstate him to his former position among them. Then, somewhere in the midst of the enthusiasm, Richard delivered his document to the Reverend Nicholas Noyes and his elder partner, John
Higginson, who had first arrived in Salem on Richard's ship thirty
years before.

This was an unusual thing to do; one is hard pressed to find
another example in colonial Massachusetts of a penitent submitting a piece of writing. It is not hard to understand why. Unlike
a speech, the written word did not put the sinner to the test of
the community's conscience: it left no chance for a spontaneous,

and thus authentic, emotion to surface. A confession in writing was, in fact, something close to popery.

The records of the provisional government, cobbled together in a matter of months, have understandably not survived the centuries with any great comprehensiveness. Nevertheless, his delivery of a "writing" to the church could only have reflected a legal action: the overturning of the sentence that had been imposed on him by a discredited court.

All in all, it was an acceptable compromise. The church knew of Richard's wandering eye, perhaps even knew of his bigamous marriage decades earlier. But if the Dudley court had wanted to tar a First Comer—and a mariner—on flimsy charges, well, that was another thing altogether. Let him pull the letter from his coat; they had not surrendered it without a fight.

Richard, for his part, had cause for satisfaction, too. He had failed to avoid the admonition of his peers, just as he had failed to get his bell back, but at least he had seen to it that his accounts were squared. Richard More would not be left to stand as an insult to the colony's history.

Or would he? When the Reverend Noyes accepted Richard's document, it was yet another indication that the church wanted to bury its past. History, however, had its own burials in mind.

The friend attending the lecture with Richard, and following him in airing his fervent remorse, was one of his longtime tavern customers, Giles Corey. When Corey took his turn, he too wept and shook and otherwise demonstrated his contrition. This display was convincing enough that he was accepted into the church for the first time.

Richard left the meetinghouse with, literally, a clean breast: no more would the mark of adultery hang from his shoulder. At that moment, the world seemed to have returned to some semblance of sanity. Certainly, no one in the congregation that day, Richard as much as the next man, could have predicted that before two winters passed, Giles Corey would be lying in a Salem field, groaning in agony as one of his neighbors lay stone upon stone on his body, with no expectation of stopping until he was dead.

14

Hysteria

Nothing was more common in those days than to interpret all meteoric appearances . . . as so many revelations from a supernatural source. . . . But what shall we say when an individual discovers a revelation, addressed to himself alone, on the same vast sheet of record! In such a case, it could only be the symptom of a highly disordered mental state, when a man, rendered morbidly self-contemplative by long, intense and secret pain, had extended his egotism over the whole expanse of nature, until the firmament itself should appear no more than a fitting page for his soul's history and fate!

—Nathaniel Hawthorne, *The Scarlet Letter*

IN THE WINTER OF 1691, two girls—Betty Parris, age nine, and her cousin Abigail Williams, age eleven—were wiling away the cold days by amusing themselves as best they could. As many children had done before, they were dropping egg whites into a glass to see what shapes they made. One of them, they thought, formed the recognizable shape of a coffin.

As the winter wore on, they were joined by others, Abigail Williams and Ann Putnam, then Mercy Lewis and Mary Walcott. For a while these games remained innocent. Then, sometime about December 1691, Betty Parris began to exhibit strange symptoms: pinching sensations, knifelike strafings, and body contortions. Gradually other, more disturbing symptoms appeared. Betty felt that she was being choked, and was beginning to "see" things.

Betty's father was Samuel Parris, pastor of the Salem Village church that had separated from the one in Salem Town. Parris had not taken well to his flock, nor was he particularly well liked by them, and this uneasy relationship had made him overly severe in his sermons. Yet he did not leap to conclusions with his daughter. He called in a doctor, who looked her over for signs of physical illness. Finding none, the physician was the first to explain Betty's malady as evidence of "the Evil Hand."

At that point, the problem was still confined to the Parris home. But when Betty had not recovered after some six weeks, a neighbor, Mary Sibley, decided to take action. Sibley went to Parris's slave, Tituba, and another slave named Indian John, and asked them to help bake a "witchcake." This concoction, of English tradition, was made of rye meal and the girl's urine. It was then fed to a dog, who, bewitched by the cake, would presumably identify the witch who was afflicting young Betty.

The result was disastrous. When Parris found out about the witchcake, he gave Sibley a tongue lashing and declared that because of her actions, "the Devil hath been raised among us, and his rage is vehement and terrible; and when he shall be silenced, the Lord only knows." Then he delivered an apocalyptic sermon, telling his congregation that "for our slighting of Christ Jesus, God is angry and is sending forth destroyers."

Whether the dog ever made a meaningful sign is unknown, but the cake had its effect nonetheless. By this time, Betty's friends had also become distressed, and in their fevered state they began to name their afflicters. The guilty parties, they claimed, were Tituba herself, Sarah Good, and Sarah Osborne—two local women of low station. Warrants for their arrest were served on February 29, 1692, and they were summarily brought before two Salem magistrates.

The nightmare had begun.

FROM THE PERSPECTIVE of Richard's waterfront home, the witch-hunt was still a distant affair in March 1692. Set inland from Salem Town by several miles, Salem Village was made up largely of planters, whose concerns scarcely registered above the slapping of the tide against the wharves. Even as the spring wore on and the crisis began to spread, the situation was not altogether alarming. Old Captain More had seen it all before: the landbound would go crazy for a while, and he would simply have to mind his step until they came to their senses.

But this time was different. During previous crises the Massachusetts officials had wielded an absolute moral authority over their enemies, with the power to banish, even to take life when they saw fit. The men in power in 1692, for all their success at overthrowing Andros, were not in this position. With the introduction of freedom of worship into the colony in 1687, they could no longer "warn out" suspicious characters or impose the sentence of exile on a whim. On the contrary, conditions had forced them into a patchwork pragmatism, which saw them alternately glorifying the Ancient Beginning (their raison d'être) and lowering their moral standards for anyone who helped keep the colony stocked with goods. This, of course, was exactly why they had restored old Captain More—First Comer, expert mariner, and common adulterer—to his place in the community.

Samuel Parris, slighted at being relegated to Salem Village while the luminaries broke bread in Salem Town, was quick to declare such behavior unacceptable. One of his earliest sermons, delivered on November 24, 1689, opened with a warning: "When a man undertakes civil government and disposing justice to the wicked, out of a pretence of zeal for God's service and honor, but yet in truth aims at himself and his own private interest, such a one is deceitful in the Lord's work."[1]

That charge was aimed not at rag-picking women with witchcraft on their minds but at the government officials who had taken over after the fall of Andros. Having leveled the charge, Parris had served notice that Richard's protectors were no longer untouchable. He had also opened the floodgates for an entirely new kind of moral authority to rush in.

Under Andros, the Massachusetts colonists had been encouraged to give up their squabbling for the fine art of informing, with a heavy dose of false witness for good measure. This arrangement apparently encouraged Salem youth to boldness. Betty Parris, Abigail Williams, and the others did not make their accusations in a vacuum: they had learned, one might say, at your knee. Not that they could follow the machinations between the extremists, the moderates, and the popish intruders. When something went awry, they simply did as they had been taught—point a finger and fabricate—leaving the likes of Nicholas Noyes, who had recently insisted on Richard's excommunication, with a sudden need to look as though he knew what he was doing.

All the protective mechanisms that had kept Richard from harm were no longer in place.

WHEN TITUBA was brought in for a hearing on March 1, she did not deny her familiarity with witches. On the contrary, she constructed an elaborate tale of midnight meetings and animals capable of changing shape at will. Pressed for names, she positively identified the other two women already under suspicion—a relatively safe admission—but also mentioned a woman who dressed in silk and a tall, top-hatted man from Boston. This last reference opened the way for respectable persons to be pursued, and on March 11, Ann Putnam accordingly accused Martha Corey, a woman of good standing in the church, of tormenting her through supernatural means.

That Giles Corey had married Martha after the death of his wife Mary indicates that his taste in women had not changed. Like Mary, Martha held strong opinions and was not afraid to air them. This worked to her advantage in ordinary disputes, but very much against her in the current situation. The magistrates hearing the case were working from a well-established tradition in which evidence—even of the sort being proffered by the girls—led to confession, and confession to redemption. The sequence held true even in the worst of the trials: those who confessed were often not sentenced but set free instead, while those who denied the accusations were found guilty.

Martha Corey was among the more forceful deniers. Called on at her home, she wondered aloud whether her accusers, being so gifted in sight, had described the clothes she had been wearing. At her examination, Hathorne asked how she knew that the children had been instructed to describe her clothes. She replied that her husband had told her. This claim did not hold up well. Giles, who had come to the hearing with her, denied having told her anything. The Reverend Noyes had no doubt as to what her testimony that day meant: "I believe it is apparent she practiceth witchcraft in the congregation; there is no need of images."

And so it went. After the examination of Martha Corey, the dam burst, and many of Richard's other acquaintances were accused. Giles Corey discovered that perjury was no safeguard and was thrown into the Salem jail as well. Following him were Phillip English and his wife, Mary, daughter of William and Elinor Hollingsworth. Bridget Bishop was brought in and her breasts and pudenda inspected for telltale marks of witchery. One deponent gave testimony that lumped all these suspects together in a ritual with a mysterious "black man" that had led to the murders of four people, including Richard's niece Christian Trask.

For Richard, the situation was becoming precarious. His First Comer status, so often his currency, no longer counted for much: no lesser a man than John Alden, son of the *Mayflower* passenger, had been brought up from Boston and imprisoned with the rest. After May 23 Richard could not even avoid the reminders of the trials if he stayed shut up in his house. On that day, a mere look out his window revealed the sight of his next-door neighbor, Peter

Osgood, recently appointed constable, leaving home to arrest Sarah Pease, Benjamin Procter, and Mary de Rich on charges of witchcraft.

The hysteria had reached Richard's doorstep.

IN ONE of the curious coincidences of history, Massachusetts received its new charter just as the witch trials reached critical mass. It is perhaps equally curious that, in the deal reached between the colonists and the Crown, the man appointed as the new colonial governor was the hardboiled treasure hunter William Phips.

Phips arrived in Boston on May 14, with concerns quite distant from witchcraft. Ever the New England mariner, his interests ran more to kickback schemes: condemning seaworthy ships, selling them to a friend for a pittance, then putting the boat on the market at its real value, with everyone taking a cut. When a customs officer once felt emboldened to take him to task for these shady practices, Phips personally caned him on the courthouse steps.

The witchcraft problem was clearly serious, however. By the time of his arrival, the jails were swelling with occupants, and he could not avoid their presence entirely. After consulting various people with greater legal experience, he set up a special court, called a court of oyer and terminer. Then he vanished to points north to fight the French—that is, to make good on his colossal failure at Quebec.

The organizing of the new court had the immediate effect of bringing the crisis closer to Richard—from the meetinghouse in Salem Village to the courthouse in Salem Town. Now the tumult was centered only a few blocks away. The accused were marched from the Salem Town jail to the courthouse, clattering down the cobbled street, to the whispers and fearful glances of onlookers. And still the accusations spread.

The first to be tried was Bridget Bishop, the flashy, stylish tavernkeeper who had supposedly sent Richard's niece to her death.

As Bridget walked past the Salem Town meetinghouse, a great uproar arose within. Investigators fearful of her magical powers entered the building and "found a board which was strongly fastened with several nails transported into another quarter of the house."

Witches, rearranging the very house of the Lord! Witches, who in attending church in Beverly, had said her prayers beneath Richard's bell!

Was it all sorcery, from beginning to finish—his whole life, and everything he had known within it? Richard could have been excused for thinking so. That summer even faroff events seemed to portend the illusiveness of all things. News came that Port Royal, the thriving pirate's town in Jamaica, had been destroyed in an hour by an earthquake. Closer to home, Plimouth Colony, where he had buried his sisters and brothers, called for its final Day of Humiliation and was quietly subsumed into the colony of Massachusetts.

On June 8, 1692, Bridget Bishop was taken in a cart to Gallows Hill and hanged alone from a great oak tree, to trouble the world no more with her trickery. That was an image not easily shaken from the public conscience, and during the recess before the next trial convened, the judges privately began to disagree about the nature of the proceedings. Bishop had been convicted largely on "spectral evidence"—accounts of wild congress with supernatural beings. This was not simply a legal matter, but a theological one as well. The matter hung on a single question: Could the Devil take on the shape of an innocent person?

Phips, in town briefly between forays to Canada, considered the dilemma and decided it best to put the question to the ministers. Their answer, gravely considered, came out flatly against the inclusion of spectral evidence. The "daemon," they asserted, "may assume the shape of an innocent." As for evidence, more was needed than "the accused person being represented by a spectre unto the afflicted."[2]

The document in which these statements were contained was kept secret from the public, however, and could therefore be more easily disregarded by the judges. Certainly they showed no outward change of heart in the cases that followed. August brought the hangman's noose to eight Salemites, among them John Proctor, onetime habitué of Richard's tavern. September was even worse. Nine of the accused were tried and condemned on the seventeenth.

Of these Giles Corey's case was perhaps the most dramatic. After compromising himself in his initial testimony about his wife, he was brought before the court to explain more about what he knew. Though he tried to be factual about Martha, he succeeded only in fanning the flames. He found it hard to pray when she was near, he offered, and wondered at her own proficiency in prayer. One night he had come upon her at the hearth, kneeling silently and without apparent purpose.

From this and other testimony, Martha was carried away, screaming, "You can't prove me a witch!" But Giles's account had seemed unconvincing to some. Was he as much a wizard as his spouse was a witch? John Hathorne put this question to him directly in a court session of April 19. As the accusers writhed and twitched in their seats, the magistrate turned to the old man and asked, "What? Is it not enough to act witchcraft at other times, but you must do it in the face of authority?"

"I am a poor creature and cannot help it," Corey replied.

Corey, it turned out, still had some of the old unregenerate spark in him. When another of the magistrates, referring to one witness's fanciful account about a black hog, asked him what had frightened him, he snapped to attention.

"I do not know that I ever spoke that word in my life."

Thereafter, Corey remained contemptuous of the entire proceedings and refused to recognize the court; when brought before the magistrates again, he stood speechless. Under English law, a defendant who "stood mute" could not be tried. He could, however, be tortured, using an arcane medieval method called *pein fort et dure:* to be pressed to the brink of death with stones. The theory behind this procedure was that the increasing load would force a confession, and thus an end to "muteness."

The torture took place on September 16 or 17, in an open field beside the jail. Being located in the center of town, the site was easy to reach, and a large crowd turned out to witness the event. Richard could not have missed the commotion from his house and may well have hobbled the two blocks to look on in confused terror as his friend met his grisly fate.

As the stones were laid on, several tried to convince Corey to relent, including one Captain Gardiner of Nantucket. To the last, Corey was not swayed. His final words, according to legend, were simply, "More weight." The rest was simply grotesque. "In pressing," wrote a contemporary, "his tongue being prest out of his Mouth, the Sheriff with his Cane forced it in again, when he was dying."[3]

The day after Corey died, the hysteria reached a peak as seven women and one man were carted off to Gallows Hill for a mass execution. They stood on ladders, nooses about their necks, intoning the Lord's Prayer before the swift end came. Looking upon the figures swinging from the trees, before they were rudely cast into the small chasm that served as a grave, Reverend Noyes remarked, "What a sad thing to see eight firebrands of hell hanging there."

How far would Salem go to purge itself of its demons? Would it stop at nothing? If so many could be carted off so easily to their deaths, Richard had plenty to fear. After all, no one questioned whether the Devil could assume the shape of a guilty person, and Richard's guilt had never been fully expunged. In his dilapidated old hut, he sat on secrets that no one had dared name, with nothing to prevent the wind from carrying them into the bedrooms of young girls . . . and perhaps in his old age he could not even keep his memories straight and so was subject to a much more insufferable form of spectral evidence: the confused imagery of old age, in which the faces of women past and present, marriages beneath the sign of Robin Goodfellow and the cries of Salem teenagers, and the image of a witch named Elizabeth Richardson, mingled and haunted him.

BUT THE SEA IS larger than anything we can ever know, and already it was bringing a wind of its own to sweep the nightmares away. On the same day that those eight prisoners were sentenced to die on Gallows Hill, Thomas Gilbert arrived in Boston aboard the *Swan*, having taken a French flyboat, judged a "rich ship," as a prize. And with Gilbert came William Phips, who learned with disgust that his own wife, the Lady Phips, was presently under suspicion of witchcraft.

Enough was enough. With the return of Phips, several influential figures felt brave enough to denounce the trials, and the spell of conformity was broken. In October Phips dissolved the court of oyer and terminer and, on November 25, 1692, set up a new superior court to try the remaining cases. This new court did not admit spectral evidence and, as a result, found no way to convict any of the remaining accused.

Spectral evidence: peel it away and one arrives at the hard bite of something solid. On the same day that Phips organized the new court, Thomas More, Richard's son, appeared in the very same building to lay claim to his share of the booty taken aboard the *Swan*.

Richard had grown old making halfhearted statements, always fearing the exposure of his secret. And now here was his son, the very first in a list of claimants, writing in bold strokes:

Know all men by these presents, that I Thomas More of New York in New-England Marriner have appointed constituted and made and in my stead and place ordained and Deputed my trusty and welbeloved friend John Child of Boston in New-England aforesd. Taylor to be my true and lawfull Attorney for mee in my name and to my only proper use benefit and behoofe to Ask Demand sue for recover and receive all that the residue of my Share (I having received Six pounds) be it more or less & all my Shares taken in and with the Prize St. Jacob late taken from the French with my part of Share in all other Prizes or Stores of War, whether Goods Merchandizes, Ammunition or Provision, had made or to be had or made in and by virtue of the late Expedition of their Majesties Ship Swan and Briganteen Elizabeth and Sarah under the Command of Capt. Richd. Smitson, Capt. Thomas Gilbert and Capt. Benjamin Eems.[4]

The French had knelt before Richard's son, just as it had been prophesied in the passage of Revelation cited for him to contemplate: *And he that overcometh, and keepeth my works unto the end, to him I will give power over the nations: And he shall rule them with a rod of iron.*[5]

The ledgers had at last been balanced, and the meaning of Richard's life laid bare. The witness of a century, he was the only man alive to have seen firsthand the Puritan dream in its transit from brave beginnings to desperate denouement. That dream had encompassed a great hope, for a return to mercy and sincerity and justice and honesty, and many a courageous heart had been crushed in the attempt to reach it.

Of course, beneath the hope lay reality, which Richard had also seen firsthand. From his delivery into the hands of William Brewster, it had been a bitter struggle for material security from start to finish, with all the attacks and reprisals that attend such struggles. When the difference between dream and reality had become too great, the dream had become a disguise, a form of theater meant to conceal the baser designs of human beings intent on survival. And when that mask had grown too heavy even for the churchmen to bear, it had been the mariners—the men the Saints had always depended on—who stepped in to save them from themselves.

Never mind a place at the Lord's table. The preachers, in empowering one of his own, had left the way open for something better. In the end, Richard could nurse at the deepest consolation of all: the delicious and inalterable pleasure of revenge. Who knew but that this latest plunder might even contain a bell?

That December, when the witch trials had ceased and the town sat hard and cold on the land, a spectacular celestial body was seen throughout the New England sky. Dashing at first like a meteor (which it may well have been), it broke into seven pieces, each of which whirled against the blackness of the universe for some three minutes before dissolving again and leaving the colony in silent awe.

That, too, had been foreseen in the Great Book: *And I will give him the morning star.*[6]

Aftermath:
Stone Remains

RICHARD MORE DIED soon after the witch trials, on some
unwritten day between March 19, 1694, and April 20, 1696,
and was laid to rest beside his family members in the Old
Burying Ground.

Perhaps from time to time you passed his grave and remembered him—his weather-beaten face, his flowing beard, the knife thrust through his belt, the peculiar language he brought from the sea—and thought, too, of everything his presence on the streets of Salem had meant. Perhaps you knew that his was the only individual gravestone given to a *Mayflower* passenger. But you could not have known the significance that voyage would take on. Indeed, you could not have known how manifold the consequences of your time would be, spiraling through the ages—the tenuous link between you and me.

After the witch trials, your government was no longer defined by religion, and you increasingly thought of yourself as a Yankee.

The terms Saint and Stranger, both of which had applied to Richard in their turn, fell out of use. As far as you could see, the entire myth of the Ancient Beginning had been forgotten, as if an embarrassment.

But then, gradually, the spirit of the Puritan fathers reasserted itself. In the early 1700s a group of Plimouth men, tired of the dissolute atmosphere in their local taverns, formed the Old Colony Club and began observing their own Day of Thanksgiving. After a time, their tenacity saw the holiday established as a New England tradition. Then, after the colonies had a real revolution and joined to form a united nation in its own right, a man named Abraham Lincoln decreed that Thanksgiving would be celebrated in the South as well as in the North. Today, it is the one holiday characterized by simplicity and straightforwardness—exactly the virtues valued by your preachers.

The smuggling tradition, meanwhile, continued full bore, and its spirit—the unfettered flow of commercial goods—blossomed into an American way of life, as still can be witnessed in its most virulent form on the day *after* Thanksgiving, traditionally the biggest shopping day of the year. The contradictions between the Saints and the Strangers did not die with the Massachusetts charter.

That much can be said for the customs. Of course, almost all the artifacts that Richard touched or beheld are gone. The bell in the Beverly meetinghouse may yet ring in some steeple, or it may not—no one knows. Salem's South River has long silted up, sewing shut the water before the old wharves. The meetinghouse is gone, the gallows gone, along with the trees on the neck and the houses they made—all crumbled to dust. In the 1960s the Shipton mansion, in which Richard was born, was dismantled and shipped to a concern in Texas that sold it piecemeal to interior decorators. The echoes of Jacob Blakeway's laughter, tossed off casually while occupying his landlord's home, still lie trapped in the beams of various fancy houses scattered throughout America—perhaps in a room in which one of your descendants sits, reading these lines. . . .

And what do these splinters tell us of the man?

There are those who would argue that Richard's life story was suppressed in order to preserve the sanctity of the *Mayflower* story and the rectitiude of the First Comers. Those who hold to this line, however, must join league with the sanctifiers of your generation, who not only burnished the origins of the colony but protected Richard from those who would have exposed his transgressions. The moral luminaries did not want to punish Richard, but to hide him.

The sullying of the origin myth thus devolves onto you, who turned Richard in despite all efforts to the contrary. Yet here a painful truth must be admitted: in shaping the tale of an accused man, the role I am most suited to inhabit is that of prosecutor— more specifically, seeker of the verdict he wanted to hear—of the immortal villain Joseph Dudley.

It was I who assumed the worst about Richard More, who deprived him of any right to his thoughts, much less to his privacy, who tracked him down with unflagging dedication, hoping to reveal his true colors, and enlisted your help in the chase. You saw Richard More at his most vulnerable, and I prodded you to see more, past even what could be seen. The church did not pry; it accepted his shortcomings as the result of his hobbled beginnings and protected him accordingly. He had come from them, had come even before them, a mistake woven into their origins. But I have done differently. I asked you to see him naked, to inspect his lineaments and features for any likeness to imperfection—until only imperfection could be seen. And so you have.

Before me sits a stone from Richard More's childhood soil at Larden Hall. From time to time I gaze on it and wonder at the mystery of a seashell imprinted on a stone nicked from a landlocked county. With that image before me, I think back on what I have written, and though the story keeps shifting in my mind's eye, in the end there is nothing I can do: the pious and the permissive, the minister and the makebate, the scholar and the sailor alike, can only despise me for what I have done. Richard More was neither pilgrim nor beast; he was simply a man who wanted to redeem his mother, to make it "all one before God," and I have tried—without success—to deny him that privilege.

Notes

1. SWAN SONG

1. See Lorne Campbell's articles in *Burlington Magazine*.
2. Cumberlege, *Shakespeare's England*, p. 22.
3. There were many family connections between the two men. Samuel's grandfather Robert More had leased land from Sir John Zouch and then lived to marry his widow, Susan Davenport, causing the elder Richard More to call Lord Zouch "a kinsman" (communicated to me by Donald Harris, from his personal files). Katharine's ancestry also included Zouches several generations further back.
4. *Dictionary of National Biography*, vol. 21, p. 1332.
5. In September 1624 the king wrote to the duke of Buckingham that "I am well, and having changed my purpose in resolving to stay here till Monday, so earnest am I to kill more of Zouche's stags." Akrigg, *Letters of King James VI & I*, p. 439.
6. According to Sir Anthony Weldon, "Zouch was one of the 'chief and master fools' who assisted the king in his pastimes." See Dashwood, c. 2.
7. Cumberlege, *Shakespeare's England*, p. 108.

8. Unless otherwise noted, information specifically relating to Samuel and Katharine More's marriage derives from Samuel's Declaration.

9. The Shropshire Records and Research Centre (hereafter referred to as SRR) 1037/10/6 & 7.

10. Wilson, Philip, *Childbirth*, p. 69.

11. Wilson, *Childbirth*; Atkinson, " 'These griping greefes,' " p. 91.

12. Ibid., p. 92.

13. Donald Harris disagrees with me on the sequence of events here, and locates the first confession in June 1616, when Katharine and Jacob appeared before the bishop of Hereford.

14. SRR 1037/10/8 & 9.

15. On the face of it, the peculiar wording of this agreement (why mention Katharine's father and not Katharine herself?) was simply an attempt to downplay the question of patrimony. But the agreement was a separate action entered on the same day as the disinheritance, and therefore almost certainly initiated by someone with the well-being of Katharine's children at heart. Her father, Jasper More, had died in 1614, so it could not have been his doing. This points to the involvement of Katharine's uncles, Matthew and Reginald Smale.

Both men, Londoners by choice, had experience with family legal disputes. In 1608 (by which time Katharine was twenty and easily old enough to remember), they had gone before the Star Chamber, along with Katharine's father, to defend themselves against charges brought by their sister, Mary Horton. During this trial, Mary accused Jasper More and Reginald Smale of "conspiring and plotting together for nothg." If Katharine sensed any of her own troubles lying ahead, she could have done worse than calling on Matthew or Reginald, both of whom were childless, for assistance (The Public Record Office [hereafter referred to as PRO]: STAC8 175/12). (Reginald Smale remained close enough to his sister, Elizabeth More, to bequeath her "Sixe of my silver spoones wch were my mothers" in his will of 1623. See Campbell, *Burlington Magazine* [June 1987], p. 371.) More to the point, the Smales had their own motives for interceding at that particular moment. When Jasper More and Elizabeth Smale married in 1572, *their* marriage settlement required Jasper, or his heirs, to pay Matthew Smale, or his heirs, the sum of fifty pounds a year, so long as Jasper had living male heirs "of the body." For the moment, Jasper's son-in-law Samuel may have served this role (even if he was not strictly of Jasper's body), but there was no guarantee that Samuel would ever have legitimate children of his own. In fact, the laws of the time prohibited a divorced person from remarrying until his or her former spouse had died.

16. "14 Junii 1616, tam pr(a)efatus Jacob(u)s Blakeway quam antedicta
Katherina More comperuerunt, quibus articulo sive crimine incontinen-
tiae vitae sive adulterii iudicialiter objecto; fatebantur se insimul
plur(i)es et iteratis vi<c>ib(u)s incontinentur vixisse ac adulteriu(m)
una commississe." This translation differs from the one given to Donald
Harris in that it mentions charges already having been brought. My
translator, Holt Parker, knew nothing of the context surrounding the
sentence.

17. Conversation with Marian Roberts, archivist of the More family papers.

18. Smith, *Appeals to the Privy Council*, pp. 35–36n.

19. Cumberlege, *Shakespeare's England*, p. 41.

2. RELIGIOUS COMPANY

1. Potter, *English Law*, p. 205. Sir Richard Zouch, the playwriting cousin
to Lord Zouch, acted as the surrogate to Sir Henry Marten, LLD, Master
of the Court of Canterbury, on September 20, 1625, when he annexed
the codicil to Lord Zouch's will that made Sir Edward Zouch sole ex-
ecutor (PRO: PROB11/146, LH 295).

2. The signatories were the bishop of Ely (Nicholas Felton); Sir James
Hussey of Magdalen College; Sir William Bird of Saffron Walden, doc-
tor of civil law; and Dr. Barnabe Gooch of Magdalen College (PRO:
DEL 5/6 fo. 85). Sir William Bird, one of the signatories to Katharine's
Definitive Sentence was a commissioner to the Island of Jersey in March
1617 and in the 1620s received referrals—jointly with Henry Marten—
from legal advisers regarding appellate cases (Smith, *Appeals to the
Privy Council* pp. 25–26n, 29n).

3. *Calendar of State Papers (hereafter referred to as CSP) Domestic Series, 1611–
18*, pp. 89, 420.

4. *Acts of the Privy Council of England* (hereafter referred to as *APC*), *Col.*,
p. 38.

5. PRO: CO 1/2.

6. *APC, Col.* pp. 26–27.

7. Kinsbury, *Records of the Virginia Company*, vol. 3, pp. 135–36.

8. *APC, Col.*, pp. 10–12, 33–34.

9. Sams, *Conquest of Virginia*, p. 577.

10. Kinsbury, *Records of the Virginia Company*, vol. 3, pp. 84, 86.

11. Lord Zouch had dealings with the Merchant Adventurers of London,
the company that organized the *Mayflower* voyage, as early as May 5,
1619—more than a year before the famous ship departed. *APC, Dom.*,

vol. 4, p. 442; vol. 5, p. 55. This would seem to suggest that Samuel had a long period in which to consider sending his children away on the *Mayflower*. However, this option could not have been presented to him until the last moment, as I have argued.

12. In his Declaration, Samuel explicitly states that he was in Bath when the appeal was dismissed.

13. Conversation with Marian Roberts.

14. Even Lord Zouch, normally the rudder of all things seaworthy, was not likely to be of much help: Henry Mainwaring had written to him on June 19: "Hopes his Lordship improves at the bath," but the following year he was still so ill that he had to break protocol in the House of Lords and speak without rising. Foster, *House of Lords*, p. 193.

15. Carter, *English Legal Institutions*, p. 245.

16. Conversation with Marian Roberts.

17. *C.S.P., Domestic Series, 1619–1623*, p. 164.

18. Paul Harris later married into the duke of Buckingham's family.

19. This biographical sketch is culled from various sources, chiefly V. C. Sanborn, "Pickering vs. Weston, 1623," *Proceedings of the Massachusetts Historical Society* (hereafter referred to as *Mass. Hist. Soc. Proc.*), 54, pp. 165–178; Ford, "Captain Wollaston, Humphrey Rasdell and Thomas Weston," *Mass. Hist. Soc. Proc.* 51, pp. 219–32; and Peter Wilson Coldham, "Thomas Weston, Ironmonger of London and America, 1609–1647," *Genealogical Society Quarterly* 62, no. 3 (September 1974), pp. 163–72.

20. My rendition of the preparations for the *Mayflower* voyage are condensed from many sources, which can be found in the bibliography. Suffice it to say, they are largely in agreement with one another.

21. The sequence in which the children were assigned can be inferred from the mutually supporting logic of their age order and the locations of their guardians at various times. Winslow was in London when the other guardians were not; therefore, he took the eldest. John Carver was in Southampton when Brewster was not; he received Jasper More, the second-eldest. Brewster being the last of the guardians to join the party, took Richard and Mary More. That Brewster took the last two children also suggests that there were no other suitable takers, i.e., Richard was not highly desirable as a child.

22. Burgess, *John Robinson*, p. 255.

23. Ibid., pp. 254–55.

24. *C.S.P., Domestic Series, 1619–1623*, p. 175.

3. THE PROMISED LAND

1. Robert Cushman wrote a letter from Dartmouth on August 17, 1620, to Ed. Southworth at Henige (Heneage) House in the Duke Place (Duke's Place), in the ward of Aldgate, London (where Weston was living). Heneage House had been a religious house of some kind until the Dissolution (in 1531), when it passed from the hands of Sir Thomas Audley to Thomas, duke of Norfolk. Thus Duke's Place. The Separatists living in London took advantage of this building's religious status, as the law required them to worship in their local parish, and they could not attend a real church without violating their principles; they worshiped here when they were in London.

   Before passing to Thomas Heneage, Duke's Place had belonged to the abbots of Bury St. Edmund, and on January 2, 1622, a new priory was consecrated on its site by George Abbot, a bishop and a High Commission judge of the Puritan persuasion, assisted by Sir Henry Martin, the bishop's Vicar-General in Spirituals. Again we see early connections between the More divorce and the *Mayflower* voyage (Burgess, *John Robinson*, p. 257n).

2. William Butten, the servant-apprentice to Dr. Samuel Fuller, died three days before land was sighted, but apparently did not rate in the cosmology either way.

3. Winslow, *Mourt's Relation*, p. 71.

4. Related to the author by a member of the Wampanoag tribe in June 1982.

4. A MOTHER'S WISH

1. Barnabe Gooch's simultaneous roles as a judge in Katharine's appeal and a patentee on land around Plimouth are strong indications of Katharine's awareness that her children were about to be sent to the New World.

2. Katharine's petition has since perished, but the extant response—Samuel's Declaration—speaks of "eleven years complete" since their marriage. Since Katharine and Samuel married in February 1611, the Declaration must have been written sometime about February 1622, and the petition shortly before that.

3. Six or seven men arrived in Wessagusset on the *Sparrow* in May, with a larger contingent arriving on the *Charity* and the *Swan* in June or July.

Estimating a sailing time of about a month and a half, the *Sparrow* thus left England sometime in March, and the other two in April or May.

4. *C.S.P., Colonial Papers*, p. 30.

5. In 1623 the council sent Robert Gorges, son of the powerful Ferdinando Gorges, on a voyage to New England in order to settle Wessagusset for itself.

6. Donald Harris has surmised, with some insight, that a gratuitous payment of three hundred pounds made by Richard More of Linley to his son Samuel on June 24, 1622, was really paid to Katharine, in return for which she renounced all claims to Larden Hall.

7. The identity of this minister has gone largely unresearched—understandably so, since he has not seemed central to the story of Lyford's betrayal. But Richard More's maternal line included Pembertons, so it may not be a total waste of time to distract ourselves with a family portrait.

In identifying Jane Pemberton, who was Richard More's great-grandmother through his mother, Katharine, as the sitter for Holbein's miniature, art historian Lorne Campbell leaned heavily on the information provided by the coat of arms that was affixed to the painting's back. This coat was quartered, meaning that it combined the symbols of several families into one pattern, much the way later generations turned maiden names into middle names. Of the arms represented, one belonged to the Pemberton family—three pails—and another to an unknown family—three dragon heads. Noticing this, Campbell then looked for these motifs among other Pembertons.

A related Pemberton family, he found, lived in Rushden, Northamptonshire: Jane's brother Robert mentioned his "cousin Robert" of Rushden in his will, and this Rushden Robert wore the arms of the three pails and three dragon heads. Campbell also came upon a third Pemberton line, of St. Albans, Hereford, which wore the arms exactly as Rushden Robert did. The St. Albans Pembertons included Roger Pemberton, who was born in 1555 and died in 1627 in England. Roger Pemberton had a sister named Alice, who married a London merchant named James Williams; their son was Roger Williams, who, a decade after the trial of Lyford and Oldham, would be famously driven out of Salem for his heresies and would go on to found Rhode Island.

It is clear at least that Richard More, as a descendant of Jane Pemberton, was a distant relative, a sixth cousin apparently, of Roger Williams. Could Williams have been related in turn, then, to the Reverend John Pemberton, who, as a contemporary wrote, was "a great opposite" to Plimouth Plantation?

The search is complicated by the large number of Pembertons about whom almost nothing is known. One *Mayflower* historian has speculated that Lyford's confidant was the John Pemberton of Durham County, who matriculated at Broadgate's Hall, Oxford, on March 8, 1605 (*Clarke's Register of the University of Oxford*, vol. 2, p. 278), but support for the claim is missing. Roger Pemberton, on the other hand, had a son named John, who was born in 1587; he married Katharine Angell and had a son Thomas who accompanied Roger Williams to America. This John Pemberton described himself as a London grocer (meaning, an importer of spices), but it was not completely odd for a grocer to take up the calling, especially a nonconformist one.

Could he have been the man to whom Lyford addressed his letters? It seems so. What relevance the fact held for Richard is another matter. A sixth cousin is not a first cousin, and even if his mother had rifled through the family tree and hit upon the Pemberton grocer of London as a conduit for her maternal distress, it is unlikely that Richard ever knew of it. The fates were sending opportunities his way, but they remained invisible.

8. Willison, *Saints and Strangers*, p. 245.
9. Morton, *New Englands Memoriall*, p. 54.
10. Morton, *New Englands Memoriall*, p. 56.
11. One of the tasks of the ruling elder was "to open and shut the doors of God's house," Perley, *History of Salem*, vol. 1, p. 162.
12. Morton, *New Englands Memoriall*, p. 57.
13. Morton, *New Englands Memoriall*, p. 57–58.
14. Willison, *Saints and Strangers*, p. 251. Apparently, an oblique reference to Roger Williams.

5. TO SEA

1. Inferred from information (printed on a website without attribution) that says of the Allerton line, "the majority are large framed, rather over than under middle height, fair complexioned with dark hair and eyes, many have brown or sandy hair and some blue or gray eyes, but few, if any, have been known who were of a distinctly blond type."
2. It is not known whether Samuel was ever counted among the Merchant Adventurers, since his investment was to revert to the children. However, I believe the circumstances required that he deal with Allerton regardless of his status, for the reasons I have stated above.
3. Pentagoet was later renamed Castine.

4. Both England and France had claimed the right to the same territory and had already fought over a nearby settlement in 1613.

5. Present-day Augusta, Maine.

6. Among the early laws governing European vessels were the laws of Oleron, which, among other things, outlined a prototypical version of workmen's compensation.

7. The Old English was *gearn*, from the Old Norse *görn* (gut), which derived, it is thought, from the Latin *haruspex*—a diviner who read the future in animal entrails (*Webster's Third New International Dictionary*).

8. Quoted form Willison, *Saints and Strangers*, p. 276.

9. The Warwick Patent was signed by fiat by the earl of Warwick on January 13, 1630. An astonishingly brazen document, it covered most of present-day New England and extended westward all the way to the Pacific (assuming it was there somewhere). So stated, the patent included Plimouth Colony's territory, which in itself proved to be no problem, but a patent established only the ownership of land, not the government of those who lived on it, which was covered by a charter—and in all the confusion of the *Mayflower* passage, Plimouth Colony had never received a charter. So Allerton was again sent to England, this time to negotiate a charter for Plimouth with the earl of Warwick and his associates. Allerton succeeded in getting a charter drawn up, but it was never signed. His detractors claimed that a clause he had inserted made the terms untenable.

10. *C.S.P. Colonial Papers*, vol. 1, p. 140. Also, from the *Plymouth Colony Records*, vol. 1, p. 11: On February 4, 1639, "Willan Phybs" awarded Josias Winslow Sr. fifty acres in an unspecified location, as affirmed by Thomas Willett. This award was granted in Plimouth.

11. A full census of Plimouth Colony from this time is not available. However, in the 1627 list of inhabitants, Richard was the only one whose name could be whittled down to these initials. The spoon was found in a house now beneath the parking lot outside Plimouth Plantation known as the R.M. site, and is thought to date to the 1630s. Deetz, *In Small Things Forgotten*, pp. 133–35.

12. Strictly speaking, La Tour was entitled only to the territories of Sable Island, Port Royal, Minas, and the land inward of Sable Island for one hundred miles, while another Frenchman, Isaac de Razilly, was supposed to have authority over the rest. Williamson, *History of Maine*, p. 250.

13. Ibid. p. 250.

14. Thomas Morton, Allerton's brief guest in Plimouth Colony, was one of

the key advocates of dissolving the Massachusetts charter.

15. Both William Vassall and Isaac Allerton had close ties to Matthew Craddock, the first (and momentary) governor of Massachusetts Bay Colony. A stronger tie lay in the *Lion*, which Allerton used for much of his trafficking across the Atlantic and which the Vassall family owned.

6. PROVIDENCE AND DESIRE

1. SRR 445/281.
2. The elder Richard More's tenements on Ratcliffe's Highway were confiscated in 1623. At that time, he asked for a "remission of fine." The outcome of this episode is unknown. Information kindly supplied by Donald Harris.
3. William Vassall was a signatory to both the Massachusetts Bay charter and the Cambridge Agreement in 1629, the latter along with John Humphrey. Ironically, the Cambridge Agreement, which moved the entire government of Massachusetts to the New World, worked against him when he sought certain rights for non-freemen.
4. William Vassall's brother was Samuel Vassall. See *C.S.P., Colonial Papers*, vol. 1, pp. 197–199.
5. The most politically charged debate was over ship money, a tax charged by the king that was technically meant for raising a fleet but in reality functioned as a form of harassment.
6. Some thirty years earlier, the earl of Warwick had bought a large chunk of King James's naval fleet, and he had been using these ships as sea rovers ever since.
7. Allerton mentioned this crop in 1632, as recorded in a separate letter in the *Colonial State Papers*. The crop is not specifically named, but it may have been sugar cane, just then being cultivated in the Caribbean for the first time. *C.S.P., Colonial Papers*, vol. 1, p. 155.
8. Many passengers tried to leave secretly because of the political atmosphere, and some succeeded. But the king was just as anxious to abort a Puritan exodus and, unable to actually stop the ships, required an oath of allegiance of all outbound passengers. This is why many of the records of emigrants have survived.
9. Owned by William Woodcock, a member of the Providence Island Company and a close associate of Nathaniel Rich, the *Blessing* was pledged to the Providence Island Company in May 1635. Another of Woodcock's ships had been pledged earlier by February 20, in antici-

pation of twenty passengers sailing to Providence. *C.S.P., Colonial Papers,* vol. 1, pp. 197–207.

10. Passengers had the option of sending their names into the clerk or appearing in person. I have inferred that Richard and the Vassalls appeared in person because of the chaotic order in which the names of the Vassalls appear on the clerk's list.

11. Many of the last-minute meetings were held in Stondon Massey, at Jessop's Farm, home of the company secretary, William Jessop. See Newton, *Colonizing Activities of the English Puritans,* p. 177n. That Stondon Hall was also used for meetings is inferred from two facts: it was the residence of Nathaniel Rich, the key organizer of the Providence Island Company, and it was formerly the home of two generations of the Hollingsworth family. See Reeve, *Stondon Massey Essex,* pp. 37, 39. There was, at that time, a property in Stondon Massey known as Jessop's Farm.

12. The Katharine More who lived at Stondon Place married into the family of the Renaissance composer William Byrd in 1591 or 1592, when Richard More's mother was only five or six years old. Harley, *William Bryrd,* pp. 100–01.

13. The Hollingsworths were generally a rough crew; they fill the record books of the sixteenth century with property seizures and acts of violence against law-abiding citizens. Only John Hollingsworth stayed out of the fray, becoming a curate in the family's free chapel—that is, unregulated church—near the Thames, in Stanford-le-Hope.

14. Reeve, *Stondon Massey Essex,* p. 37.

15. Richard Hollingsworth may have been born on February 25, 1595, to George Hollingsworth, in Shustoke, Warwick (*International Genealogical Index* [*IGI*]). This man may have been the George Hollingsworth who died only three years later in Woodham Ferrers, a village not far from Stondon Massey. The evidence is by no means conclusive, however.

16. *Collections of the Massachusetts Historical Society* (hereafter referred to as *Mass. Hist. Soc. Coll.*), 5th series, vol. 1, p. 482.

17. One of the *Blessing* passengers, Barnabe Davies, traveled under the employ of William Woodcock, the owner of the *Blessing,* to take care of his property in Connecticut.

18. Unlike the order of entries for the Vassall family, the Hollingsworths appear on the passenger list for the *Blessing* in strict order of age, eldest to youngest. Unless the Hollingsworths queued up in such a fashion (which seems overworked as a plan), they must have sent their oath of fealty by courier.

19. The Thomas and Elizabeth Hunter listed in the *International Genealogical Index* (hereafter referred to as *IGI*) as the parents of William Hunter, baptized in London on March 6, 1624, may have been the parents of the Hunters traveling with the Hollingsworths, but definitive proof is lacking. As support for this theory, we may note that Christian Hunter had siblings named Thomas and Elizabeth.

20. SRR 1037/2/52.

21. Richard is not likely to have gone to his Duxbury land to live upon arriving in Boston—not with Christian anyway—because, with Brewster living next door, they would have had to marry immediately, and they did not marry for another full year.

22. Perley, *History of Salem*, vol. 2, p. 363.

23. Richard could not have sailed on the *Desire* to Providence Island, because he is recorded in Plimouth and Salem during the time when the voyage was made.

24. Quoted by Hall, *Antimonian Controversy*, p. 218.

25. Plimouth received its first full-time permanent minister, Ralph Partridge, several months or more after Richard's wedding.

7. A FAMILIST AFFAIR

1. Sherwood, *American Colonists in English Records*, p. 43.

2. Jeaffreson, *Middlesex County Records*, vol. 2, p. 27.

3. My identification of Elizabeth More rests on a series of interlocking facts. First and foremost, it is a matter of record that Richard More had a child named Elizabeth, who was baptized in Stepney on March 2, 1646. From this point, it becomes a question of discovering what happened to this daughter.

In April 1646 a Richard Moore was called to appear in a London court for an incident in which he assaulted a child about eight years old (Jeaffreson, *Middlesex County Records*, vol. 3, p. 97). If this child was Elizabeth More, as I believe it was, then she would have been born about 1638. The woman named Elizabeth who married Richard Clarke was born about this time—exactly where is not known—and it has been asserted that her surname was More. Her story is, therefore, of interest:

Sometime in 1660, 1661 or possibly before, [Richard Clarke] married an Elizabeth, whose last name is unknown, either in Salem or after arrival in Southampton. There has been some discussion as to whether his wife was Elizabeth Moore, the daughter of Thomas Moore. This does not seem feasible as she was born 31 January 1646/7 which would have made her very young to be married in 1660, and she is supposed to have married Simon Grover, so Elizabeth's surname remains a mystery.

This information, kindly supplied to me by Harman Clark (personal communication and Web site, members aol.com/clark/rich1.htm), refutes only the possibility that Elizabeth was related to the Southold More family, not the assertions—now untraceable—that her maiden name was More. If Richard More's daughter did go to Salem, she would have been old enough to marry Richard Clarke in 1660 or 1661.

Of course, one must still explain why Richard's daughter was not baptized at birth, but this is not as difficult as it might seem. Elizabeth More could not be baptized until her parents were married, and it is quite plausible that Richard, a sailor, impregnated a young woman during a brief call in an English port and left before learning the fruits of his accomplishment. The evidence here is quite compelling as well. Between the years 1635 and 1645, Richard apparently was in England often and within close proximity of Benjamin Woolnough on more than one occasion.

The picture that emerges is of a man who returned to London after some years away, to discover that he had fathered a child by one of the local girls. At this point, Richard came under moral pressure to marry Elizabeth Woolnough so that their daughter could be baptized. The lapse of some months between their marriage and the baptism may be simply a matter of Richard's having been at sea between the two dates.

Further circumsantial support for this hypothesis comes from the interpolation of later events. Richard's decision to settle out of court when charged with defamation by John Saffin in 1657, even though the settlement involved no change of terms, is explained in the body of the narrative as evidence that he feared the exposure of incriminating evidence against him. And finally, there is circumstantial evidence in Richard's history of landowning. When he moved into Salem Town in 1649, he did not sell his property farther out on the neck. This property remained in his hands until 1661. That is the furthest cutoff date given for the marriage of Elizabeth—to Richard Clarke, as they appeared in Southampton, Long Island, in that year as husband and wife.

4. In 1630, when Richard was still an apprentice to Allerton, someone named Richard Moore was apprehended in Southampton with a ship-

ment of illegally imported tobacco. The proverbial bagman, this Richard had been instructed to get his cargo up to Surrey, allegedly without being told what it was.

5. PRO, E190/824 and E190/824/6.

6. Virginia State Library, Virtual Archives, Survey Report 5900, p. 2.

7. PRO HCA 13/54; HCA 13/59.

8. *Plymouth Colony Records*, p. 23.

9. Robert Lemmon eventually married one of the widow More's daughters, making the association between Richard and the Southold Mores even closer.

10. *Plymouth Colony Records*, vol. 12, p. 23.

11. Richard deposed in 1684 that Thomas Weston had put his daughter Elizabeth in the care of Moses Maverick and his wife, Remember (Allerton) Maverick, at Marblehead. Remember, like Richard, had come over on the *Mayflower* and was the daughter of Richard's onetime guardian Isaac Allerton. In this same deposition, Richard named the locations of Weston's property and the principal tenants on them after Weston's death in 1646. The overall impression of the deposition is that Richard was well apprised of Weston's doings over a period of years. From this, I have inferred that they did business together. Likewise, their nearly simultaneous appearance in Maryland has led me to assume that Weston introduced Richard into the Maryland seagoing culture. Records of the Provincial Court of Maryland, Liber W.R.C. No. 1, folio 627.

12. In the 1580s Dr. Thomas Gerrard's grandfather had signed one of the earliest deeds for land in North America, and he was the son of one of the original adventurers in the Maryland colony. One of his relatives, Gilbert Gerrard, was a member of the Providence Island Company. Once in London, Gerrard listed among his expenses a sum "for 21 soapes paid to the seamen for so much borrowed on board." Brown, *Archives of Maryland*, vol. 4, p. 108.

8. THE DOUBLE LIFE OF RICHARD MORE

1. Jacqueline Eales, *Puritans and Roundheads: The Harleys of Brampton Bryan and the Outbreak of the English Civil War* (Cambridge: Cambridge University Press, 1990), pp. 59–63, 169.

2. Taken from Samuel's account, in the original manuscript. SRR 445/284.

3. The sect of the moment in the summer of 1645 was the Levellers, heavily represented in the New Model Army. The Levellers' leader, John

Lilburne, believing that the revolution had gone astray, had resigned from the army two months earlier; many of the rank and file were soon to follow in what ultimately became a mutiny. The stated demands made by Lilburne included returning land to the peasants and honoring the natural rights of man, but these goals were becoming alloyed with demands for back pay and whatever other liberties its more creative adherents could conjure.

Lilburne was not deaf to the concerns of mariners like Richard, either. A few years later he was able to write: "Monopolising Companies, Excise and Customes, do exceedingly prejudice Shiping and Navigation and Consequently discourage Sea-men, and Marinners, and which have had no smal influence upon the unhappy late revolts which have so much endangered the Nation, and so much advantaged hour Enemies." See John Lilburne, *Englands New Chains Discovered* (1648).

4. Robert Moore was baptized on October 8, 1604, in the parish of More. He served many years in the navy, doing a stint as midshipman in the prize *Mary* (under George Ayscue) when Scilly and Barbados were taken and in the engagement with the Dutch off Portland. He was buried March 9, 1658.

5. *C.S.P. Domestic Series*, vol. 2, p. 512.

6. See Hill & Frere, *Memorials of Stepney Parish.*

7. Lindley, *Civil War London*, p. 48.

8. According to one source, "most of his time was probably spent in and around London where he became well connected in parliamentarian circles." Conal Condren, in manuscript form, kindly supplied by Donald Harris.

9. Winslow was involved in the continuing attempt to salvage Plimouth's land rights in Kennebec, which at the time of his arrival in London was populated by "certain loose people who have factories upon the river ... and are under no government." *C.S.P., Colonial Papers*, vol. 1, p. 378. While in London, he also decided a case involving a neighbor of Richard Hollingsworth's in Salem and later lobbied for ship masts to be imported from New England—a task for which Hollingsworth was well equipped.

10. Winslow arrived in England in October 1646.

11. Jeaffreson, *Middlesex County Records*, vol. 3 p. 97.

12. PRO HCA 13/60.

13. Richard must have been present for the baptism of Joshua More, because at that time the church required the presence of at least one parent who was also a church member, and Christian More did not

join the church until a later date. Later still, the church revised its policy to allow children of non-church members to be baptized. This new policy was the much debated Halfway-Covenant.

9. THE BELL

1. Of the seven children born to Richard and Christian More, Joshua is the only one who does not turn up later in any capacity. His survival to the age of five has been inferred from a report that Richard had five children by 1650, but after that—nothing. In fact, there isn't anyone from that time and place with whom he could have been confused. The inference is that Joshua did not live past early childhood. Not for nothing had Richard and Elizabeth married under the sign of Robin Good-fellow!

2. Richard More bought this house from James Hyndes on October 3, 1649. Anderson, *Great Migration*, p. 1284.

3. This fact must refer to Richard's wife, because his daughter Christian was not baptized until September 5, 1652. Pierce, *Salem Church Records*, pp. 14 and 23.

4. The plan to import tar and masts from New England was formalized in November 1652 but did not substantially materialize until June 1653.

5. From a pamphlet published by Captain William Bray in 1652. Winslow was much criticized in the London press and vented his spleen often in turn. Another of his adversaries was Samuel Gorton, gone to London from New England to plead his case for a set of perceived heresies. Winslow petitioned the earl of Warwick never to allow "Samuel Gorton this pestilent disturber of our Societies any more to go to New-England."

6. *C.S.P., Domestic*, vol. 7, p. 32. For Joshua Woolnough's mad run at owning royal property, see also *C.S.P., Domestic*, vol. 6, pp. 408–09; *C.S.P., Domestic*, vol. 7, pp. 300, 369, 385; and related references to Hampton Court, ibid., pp. 99, 223.

7. Most modern accounts record only three ships in the Sedgwick fleet when it left London, with Richard's ketch being added in New England. However, John Hull, a contemporaneous businessman much involved in the comings and goings of ships, remembered four ships arriving from London, and the same four ships sailing back. Since Richard was captain of the fourth, unnamed ship that sailed on *Acadia* it seems that he must have sailed with the fleet from London and back to London as well. Hull, *Diaries*, p. 176.

8. On July 1, 1652, Edward Prescott was the freighter for the *Blessing* for

a voyage to Barbados. At that time, an insurrection was under way in Barbados, and the Crown was intent on putting it down. One of the crew sailing against Barbados was Robert More, Richard's "legal" uncle. Ayscue's fleet arrived off the coast of Barbados on October 10, 1651, and anchored at Oistin's Bay.

9. Prescott's attorney appeared before the administrators on June 27; Richard followed on June 29. *Records and Files of the Quarterly Courts of Essex County, Massachusetts* (hereafter referred to as *EQC*), vol. 1, p. 349.

10. Perley lists the name of Richard More's ship as the *Susan*, but it is my belief that this ship was named the *Swan*. On January 24, 1667, eight years after the earliest record of his part ownership of the vessel, Richard More executed a bill of lading for the *Swan*, on the account of Colonel Augustin Warner (Anderson, *Great Migration*, p. 1287). On June 28, 1675, William Woodberry was described as the master of the *Swan* (*Massachusetts Archives*, vol. 67, p. 211). William Woodberry was the son of Humphry Woodberry, who was Richard's brother-in-law (having married Christian Hunter's sister, Elizabeth) and a regular at Richard's tavern (*EQC*, vol. 7, p. 251). The document of June 28, 1675, is also of interest because it demonstrates how similar the words *Susan* and *Swan* looked in the handwriting of the era—which is to say, all but identical.

Richard More's *Swan* was involved in King Philip's War. A series of disbursements list William Woodberry as serving aboard the *Swan* between November 20, 1675, and June 24, 1676 (Bodge, *Soldiers in King Philip's War*, p. 197), during which time it sailed to Wickford, to supply provisions for the English troops. It is of crucial importance that Andrew Belcher was involved in this same supply mission (Bodge, *Soldiers in King Philip's War*, pp. 197–98). In the 1680s a ship of English build called the *Swan* was commonly referred to as Belcher's ship. As Belcher typically bought shares in ships rather than owning entire vessels (Batinski, *Jonathan Belcher*, p. 9), the question emerges as to whether "his" *Swan* of the 1680s and 1690s was the same as Richard's ship of the same name. My belief that it was rests on the appearance of Thomas More—the name of Richard More's second son—aboard the *Swan* alongside William Woodberry at Wickford (Bodge, *Soldiers in King Philip's War*, p. 197) and Thomas's reappearance in connection with Belcher's *Swan* in 1692 (Suffolk Deeds, Lib. XIV, pp. 222, 223).

11. According to C. J. D'Entremont, Jean Armounet is the first recorded master bellmaster in the French New World, his bell at Quebec having been blessed in 1664. The Port Royal bell therefore was almost certainly cast in France.

12. These figures are combined from three sources: Sedgwick, "Robert Sedgwick; A Sketch"; Rawlyk, *Nova Scotia's Massachusetts*, pp. 24–25; and Hull, *Diaries*, pp. 175–76.

13. The Sedgwick fleet of four ships sailed from New England on November 14, 1654 (Hull, *Diaries*, p. 176). Recruits were raised for the attack on Hispaniola on December 12, 1654, and Winslow made out his will on December 18. On December 27, 1654, the *Augustine* had not yet arrived from New England with "the masts" (*C.S.P., Colonial Papers,* Vol. 7 1654), p. 588.) On the same page, an entry on December 25: "the fleet is dispatched."

14. Bridget More had lavish tastes, which would lead her husband to borrow money more often than he wanted. In later years the English Richard wrote to Bridget, who was staying in London, complaining, "I have payd considerable summs for you and heare of greater in severall places which [you] runn into without my knowledge or directions." To her reply, not extant, he wrote, "I received your letter in answer to one of mine. I did not expect such language from you." Kindly supplied by Donald Harris from his unpublished text *Some Shropshire Sequels.*

15. Perhaps Cromwell's suspicions were rooted in the fact that the English Richard's brother-in-law, Isaac Pennington, was a leading figure in the burgeoning Quaker movement. Pennington's stepdaughter later married William Penn.

16. *Massachusetts Archives,* vol. 100, p. 50: "... pd Capt Jno Leverit and Mr Richd Moor [and?] ye Duch Designe ..." in the amount of forty-six pounds and twelve shillings. The date has been erroneously given as 1653 in some accounts.

17. Sedgwick was paid for services and provisions left in the French garrisons on May 9, 1655, ·in the amount of 1,793 pounds, 7 shillings, 8 pence. *C.S.P., Colonial Papers,* vol. 1, p. 424.

18. Richard bought this property from John Horne, a local carpenter, tavernkeeper, and deacon. See the map and discussion in Perley, *History of Salem,* vol. 1, pp. 312–14, in which the dates given for the respective properties held by Horne and James Hyndes also correspond to the years when Richard bought them. I have inferred from this that Richard sold his land on the neck in 1661.

19. Joseph Wickes was apparently the brother of the Thomas Wilkes, or Wickes, who co-administered the Hollingsworth estate and awarded Richard a share in the *Swan.* Like his brother, Joseph was deported from England for his father's activities during the Civil War.

20. Brown, *Archives of Maryland,* vol. 49, p. 119.

21. John Saffin's attitude toward slavery was also to become notorious in later decades; he wrote the first pro-slavery texts in the English New World, beginning in 1701.
22. *Mayflower Descendant*, 11, p. 167–168.

10. THE QUAKER CRISIS

1. *Brown Archives of Maryland*, vol. 41, pp. 327–29.
2. George Bishop, *New England Judged by the Spirit of the Lord*, p. 87.
3. *EQC*, vol. 1, p. 351.
4. That Richard felt justified in bringing the debt before a Massachusetts court, even though it had been incurred out of the colony, certainly suggests that their mutual claims on the Hollingsworth estate were involved.
5. Prescott was tried for the hanging of Elizabeth Richardson in October 1659, in a case brought in a Maryland court. Prescott managed to beat the charges by claiming that the ship's master, John Greene, had instigated the hanging against his wishes, and he was able to produce evidence of Greene's appointment to that post. The plaintiff, John Washington, declined to appear at the trial, pleading a baptism for one of his sons (Brown, *Archives of Maryland*, vol. 41, pp. 327–29). John Washington was the great-grandfather of George Washington, so we may forgive his concern for his progeny.
6. Brown, *Archives of Maryland*, vol. 3, p. 360.
7. Richard More mortgaged his warehouse to Henry Shrimpton on September 20, 1659. Anderson, *Great Migration*, p. 1284.
8. Richard More was on the committee as of August 2, 1659 (Green, *Calendar of the Proceedings of the Committee for Compounding*, vol. 2, p. 745.)
9. Erikson, *Wayward Puritans*, pp. 117–18.
10. Another source, written in 1661, is George Bishop, *supra*.
11. The minister preceding Higginson in Salem was Edward Norris.
12. Phillips, *Salem in the Seventeenth Century*, p. 199.
13. Fernow, *Records of New Amsterdam*, vol. 5, p. 335.
14. Ibid., p. 170.
15. Lemon's will was allowed on June 25, 1667, at which time Richard More proved it on oath. The will was unsigned.
16. Anderson, *Great Migration*, p. 1287. A close inspection of the record reveals the nature of this transaction. Although there was no sugar production in the Carolinas at this time, the settlers came almost entirely from Barbados, where sugar production was in full swing. In fact,

the Cape Fear settlers had made an arrangement whereby they would pay for their land with sugar grown in the Caribbean. Compare Waring, *First Voyage*, p. 17; Salley, *Warrants For Land in South Carolina*, p. 42.

17. Samuel More died on May 7, 1662, and was buried in More Parish in Shropshire (Cockell, *Registers of More*, p. 30).
18. Hull, *Diaries*, p. 158.
19. Richard sold this land to Thomas Pitman. Anderson, *Great Migration*, p. 1284. There is no record of how Richard acquired it.
20. It had become increasingly difficult to survive under the Navigation Acts, especially after England imposed taxes on goods going either way. Unfortunately, the Massachusetts General Court was incapable of silence where England was concerned, even when its insolence jeopardized the livelihood of the mariners and merchants. When one Salem man with views "dangerous to the government"—meaning that he was willing to live and let live—was elected selectman, the General Court rejected the decision. It was this rejection that Richard objected to.
21. The town of Salem voted to build a new meetinghouse on August 17, 1672. The new building housed both the courthouse on the second floor and a schoolhouse on the first floor. It is presumed that the downstairs served as the meetinghouse. Perley, *History of Salem*, vol. 3, p. 76.
22. Richard's old seafaring friend Robert Lemon had been in charge of ringing the Salem meetinghouse bell in 1662 and 1663. *EQC*, vol. 7, p. 132.

11. BATTLES LARGE AND SMALL

1. Perley, *History of Salem*, vol. 3, p. 80.
2. *Massachusetts Archives*, vol. 30, p. 188a.
3. Samuel and Thomas, his first sons, are not mentioned in the deed. Caleb, Richard Jr., Susanna, and Christian (his daughter) are. By this time Joshua More was presumably long dead.
4. *Massachusetts Archives*, vol. 67, p. 211. A document dated June 28, 1675, and signed by "John Leverett Gov," gives William Woodberry as "mr of ye Swan."
5. Ibid.
6. The number of Thomas Mores living in North America in the seventeenth century makes positive identification of Richard More's son difficult. The latest indisputable sign of him comes in 1670, when "Thomas Moore of Salem" petitioned an Ipswich court for an ordinary to be opened (*EQC*, vol. 4, pp. 314–15). This could not have been the Thomas Moore of the family from Southold, England, as they had moved out of Salem by 1661.

The Thomas Moore who served aboard the *Swan* in December 1675, as shown in Bodge (p. 197), would certainly seem to be the same man as Richard More's son, as he served alongside William Woodberry, Richard More's son-in-law, on a vessel that belonged to Richard More of Salem. By that time, a Captain Thomas Moore had conveyed pressed soldiers—Andrew and John Brown—from Boston to Kennebec in September 1675 and then returned to Boston (York Deeds, VI, 72; XII, 1, 24; VI, 109–10). This suggests a move to Boston.

There was a Thomas Moore living in Boston before December 4, 1675, when he bought land and buildings near the "Second meeting house," abutting property he already owned, from Alice Howard (*Suffolk Deeds*, Liber IX, p. 157). A fire started in this Thomas Moore's house on November 26, 1676, and spread throughout much of the town (Sewall, *Diary*, p. 28). Thomas appears to have left Boston, or to have been planning his departure, by January 1678, when he sold his original property by the seafront (*Suffolk Deeds*, Lib. X, p. 48). However, he kept his ties with New England.

In 1683 a Thomas Moore took part in a salvage mission of a Spanish wreck with a number of captains from New York (Cristoph, *Dongan Papers*, pp. 68–78). Moore apparently did not bring his vessel into New York, as the other captains involved did. In Boston several of Thomas's crew sued for unpaid shares from the salvage (*Abstracts & Index of the Records of the Inferiour Court of Pleas*, pp. 42, 44, and 48). Among these plaintiffs was John Prescott, who had signed the petition for an ordinary with Thomas More of Salem in 1670 and who had owed Richard More a debt, paid in the form of land sometime before January 20, 1678.

The salvage mission in which Thomas Moore took part inspired William Phips to search for sunken treasure at the same spot (Randolph, *Edward Randolph*, vol. 3, p. 262). Phips was not successful in his hunt for some years, but when he was, the prize was among the largest taken for that time and place. And on November 25, 1692, after Phips parlayed his riches into power, Thomas Moore revived their earlier association by claiming a share in a prize taken by the *Swan* in French waters (*Suffolk Deeds*, Lib. XIV, 222, 223).

7. Bodge, *Soldiers in King Philip's War*, p. 192.

8. It is interesting to note that Dudley was expecting either "Goodale or Moor" (Bodge, *Soldiers in King Philips War*, p. 192) but was aware only of Goodale's arrival (ibid., pp. 193–194).

Also of note: Caleb, Richard's third son, may have played a role in King Philip's war as well. A "Caleb More" delivered an account of the capture of King Philip, probably written by Richard Hutchinson of Salem, to London. See Lincoln, *Narratives of the Indian Wars*, pp. 103–106.

9. Both Samuel Sewall and Cotton Mather recorded this fire as beginning in the house of Thomas More.

10. *EQC*, vol. 6, pp. 256–58.

11. Richard married Jane Crumpton sometime around 1678, although the exact date is not known.

12. Virginia State Library, Virtual Archives, Survey Report 6002, p. 17.

13. Ibid., p. 19.

14. *EQC*, vol. 7, pp. 71–72.

15. In 1676–77 Richard More Jr. sailed to Barbados as master of the *Hopewell*. See Sherman et al., *Mayflower Pilgrim Family Genealogies*.

16. When Richard Knott pressed charges against Joseph Gillam in an Essex County court, Richard More acted as surety for Gillam. *EQC*, vol. 6, pp. 328–30.

17. The case of Richard Knott's servant, Job Tookey, is one of the more discouraging in the Essex Quarterly Court records.

18. *EQC*, vol. 7, pp. 323–24.

12. UNDER WATCHFUL EYES

1. Sheppard, *Passengers and Ships*. See also *Pennsylvania Genalogical Magazine* 3, pp. 2–67.

2. For the original account of Richard More and John Collier in New York, see Cristoph, *Andros Papers*, pp. 170–1, 211.

3. According to the *IGI*, a John Collier was born in Barbados on February 19, 1658, in St. Michael's Parish. In Plimoth Colony, William Collier had a son named John, who died as a child. Currently, there is no definitive answer to the origins of the John Collier discussed here.

4. Although Perley gives this as "waves," "warcs" seems much more probable. Perley, *History of Salem*, vol. 3, pp. 184–188.

5. Randolph, *Edward Randolph*, vol. 3, p. 343.

6. Collier was in Salem two months later, in June 1680, when he was on hand to witness the abuse of a dog at a local widow's home. *EQC*, vol. 7, p. 424.

7. By May 29, 1682, Randolph had seized "a Ship belonging to one Mr Shrimpton." Randolph, *Edward Randolph*, vol. 3, p. 143. In early September 1682 he seized the pink *Good Hope*, owned by Samuel Noell and Andrew Belcher. Ibid., p. 205.

8. On January 26, 1683, Collier delivered a mittimus to William Moore, regarding the pink *The Golden Hind*. He seems to have accomplished this task ably enough, because on September 15 he was appointed to

act as marshal on an Admiralty Court in New York that was trying the crew of the *Chameleon* for piracy and other possible crimes.

9. For the original account of this expedition, see Cristoph, *Dongan Papers*, pp. 68–78.

10. The probability that this Thomas More is the son of Richard is quite high, because one of the plaintiffs against him later in Boston was John Prescott—the same man who surrendered land to Richard More and who joined Thomas More of Salem in petitioning for an ordinary in Ipswich in 1670. See *Abstracts & Index of the Records of the Inferiour Court of Pleas*, pp. 42, 44, and 48.

11. William Phips was the son of James Phips, who had a brother William Phips. A gunsmith by trade, the elder William Phips deposed in the deliberations on Edward Ashley, describing how Ashley had sold firearms to the Indians. This William Phips was indentured to Plymouth Company but in 1639 returned to Bristol, England; thus, the Willan Phybs documented in a land award to Josiah Winslow on February 4, 1639, as witnessed by Thomas Willett.

12. Randolph, *Edward Randolph*, vol. 3, p. 262. In a letter to Sir Robert Southwell dated from Whitehall, August, 19, 1683, Randolph wrote: "Since mine to you of ye 28th last the Rose frigott of 20 gunns, an Algereen prize is fitted out to sea and bound to the Spanish wreck off the Bahama Islands under the conduct of one Phips a New England man who upon his late successfull returnes in that undertaking is intrusted by his Matie & commissionated for the whole business."

13. Randolph, *Edward Randolph*, vol. 3, p. 310.

14. Records of the Provincial Court of Maryland, Liber W.R.C. No. 1, folio 627.

15. *Mass. Hist. Soc. Proc.*, 13 (2d Series), p. 230.

16. John Saffin probably appeared in some judicial post as well, though one cannot be certain of this. Saffin had been elected as an officer of the Massachusetts Bay Commonwealth just before Andros arrived. On May 20, 1686, he was appointed along with two other men to hold vital government documents for safekeeping while Andros governed. In 1687, however, Saffin exercised his tendency to attach himself to powerful families and married Rebecca Lee, the daughter of the Reverend Samuel Lee, who had come with Andros.

17. Sewall, *Diary*, p. 169.

18. Mather, *Magnalia Christi Americana*, vol. 1, p. 160.

19. *Andros Tracts*, vol. 1, p. 74.

20. On June 30, 1688, Sir William Phips wrote a letter to Andros asking that "all sheriffs be dismissed and receive their deputations from the

Provost Marshall"—the provost marshal being Phips himself. Randolph, *Edward Randolph*, vol. 2, p. 72.
21. Mather, *Magnalia Christi Americana*, vol. 1, p. 160.

13. HYPOCRISY UNMASK'D

1. This opinion was expressed to the author by David Greene, editor of *The American Genealogist*, in a telephone conversation.
2. Randolph, *Edward Randolph*, vol. 2, p. 72.
3. *Mass. Hist. Soc. Proc.*, vol. 52, pp. 336–37. On July 10 Samuel Sewall shipped silver on his own account aboard "Andrew Belcher's" *Swan*.
4. Randolph, *Edward Randolph*, vol. 2, p. 73.
5. *Mass. Hist. Soc. Coll.* (Second Series), vol. 9, p. 478.
6. Also on this committee was Governor Simon Bradstreet, to whom Richard had deposed in 1684.
7. Hall, *Edward Randolph and the American Colonies*, p. 123.
8. Sometime in early April 1690, just prior to the restitution of the colonial government, the charges against Andros et alia were shipped with Epaphras Shrimpton to London, for consideration by the king. These charges included the complaint of Joshua Conant, the filing of which Richard More may have considered a prerequisite to taking any steps toward reinstatement by the church. See *Mass. Hist. Soc. Coll.*, vol. 45, pp. 650–53
9. *Andros Tracts*, vol. 1, pp. 150–51.
10. Randolph, *Edward Randolph*, vol. 4, p. 266.
11. Peabody Essex Museum, Phillips Library, Essex Quarterly Court Collection, 49-76-1.
12. Pierce, *Records of the First Church of Salem*, p. 171.

14. HYSTERIA

1. From Samuel Parris's ordination sermon at Salem Village (November 19, 1689), reprinted in Boyer and Nissenbaum, *Salem-Village Witchcraft*, p. 190.
2. Starkey, *Devil in Massachusetts*, p. 157.
3. Boyer and Nissenbaum, *Salem-Village Witchcraft*, p. 108.
4. *Suffolk Deeds*, lib. 14, pp. 222, 223.
5. Revelation 2:26–27.
6. Revelation 2:28.

Partial Bibliography

RESOURCES FOR PRIMARY DOCUMENTS

The Massachusetts State Archives, Boston, MA
The Public Record Office, London
The Phillips Library, Peabody Essex Museum, Salem, MA
The Shropshire Records and Research Centre, Shrewsbury, Shropshire
(SRR)
The Virginia State Library, Virtual Library

BOOKS

Abstracts & Index of the Records of the Inferiour Court of Pleas (Suffolk County Court) Held at Boston, 1680–1698. Boston: Historical Records Survey, 1940.

Acts and Resolves, Public and Private, of the Province of the Massachusetts Bay. Vol. 1. Boston: Wright & Potter, 1869.

Acts of the Privy Council of England: 1617–1619. Vol. 4. London: His Majesty's Stationery Office, 1929.

Acts of the Privy Council of England: 1619–1621. Vol. 5. London: His Majesty's Stationery Office, 1930.

The Andros Tracts. Vols. 1–3. New York: B. Franklin, 1971.

The Archives of Maryland. Baltimore: Baltimore Historical Society, 1885.

Collections of Massachusetts Historical Society. Boston: Massachusetts Historical Society, 1792–.

The Probate Records of Essex County, Massachusetts. Salem, Mass.: The Essex Institute, 1916.

Proceedings of the Massachusetts Historical Society. Boston: Massachusetts Historical Society, 1879–1998.

Suffolk Deeds. Boston: Municipal Printing Office, 1899.

Akrigg, G. P. V., ed. *Letters of King James VI & I*. Berkeley: University of California Press, 1984.

Anderson, Robert Charles. *The Great Migration Begins: Immigrants to New England, 1620–1633*. Boston: New England Historic Genealogical Society, 1995.

Anderson, Roger Charles. *The Rigging of Ships in the Days of the Spritsail Topmast, 1600–1729*. New York: Dover, 1994.

Andrews, Matthew Page. *The Founding of Maryland*. Baltimore: Williams & Wilkins, 1933.

Atkinson, Colin B., and William P. Stoneman. " 'These Griping Greefes and Pinching Pangs': Attitudes to Childbirth in Thomas Bentley's *The Monument of Matrones* (1582)," *Sixteenth Century Journal* 21, no. 2 (1990): 193–203.

Bacon, Sir Francis. *Essays and New Atlantis*. Roslyn, N.Y.: Walter J. Black, 1942.

Baker, Emerson W., and John Reid. *The New England Knight: Sir William Phips, 1651–1695*. Toronto: University of Toronto Press, 1998.

Baker, William A. *Colonial Vessels: Some Seventeenth-Century Sailing Craft*. Barre, Mass.: Barre Publishing Co., 1962.

Batinski, Michael C. *Jonathan Belcher, Colonial Governor*. Lexington: University Press of Kentucky, 1996.

Bodge, George Madison. *Soldiers in King Philip's War*. Leominster, Mass.: n.p., 1896.

Bourne, Russell. *The Red King's Rebellion*. New York: Macmillan, 1990.

Bowman, George Ernest. "The Deposition of Richard Moore . . ." *Mayflower Descendant* 4: 194.

———. "The Only Mayflower Gravestone," *Mayflower Descendant* 3: 193–200.

Boyer, Paul, and Stephen Nissenbaum, eds. *Salem-Village Witchcraft: A Documentary Record of Local Conflict in Colonial New England*. Boston: Northeastern University Press, 1993.

Bradford, William, edited by Samuel Eliot Morison. *Of Plymouth Plantation, 1620–1647.* New York: Knopf, 1952.

Bray, William. *To the supreme authority, the Parliament of the Commonwealth of England: a serious charge against Mr. Edw. Winslow, one of the commissioners for compounding at Haberdashers Hall.* London: s.n., 1652.

Breshaw, Elaine, G. *Tituba, Reluctant Witch of Salem.* New York: New York University Press, 1996.

Brewster, Dorothy. *William Brewster of the Mayflower.* New York: New York University Press, 1970.

Brown, William Hand, ed. *Archives of Maryland: Proceedings and Acts of the General Assembly of Maryland, January 1637/8–September 1664.* Baltimore: Maryland Historical Society, 1883.

Bruce, John, edited by W. D. Hamilton and S. C. Lomas. *Calendar of State Papers, Domestic Series, 1625–1649.* London: Longman, Brown, Green, Longmans & Roberts, 1858–1897.

Burgess, Walter H. *John Robinson: Pastor of the Pilgrim Fathers.* London: Williams and Norgate, 1920.

Campbell, Lorne. "Holbein's Miniature of 'Mrs. Pemberton': The Identity of the Sitter," *Burlington Magazine* (June 1987), pp. 368–71.

———. Handwritten document of the descendants of Nicholas Smale. Held at the Clothworkers' Company in London, and lent to the author courtesy of D. E. Wickham.

Carter, A. T. *A History of English Legal Institutions.* London: Butterworth & Co., 1910.

Christensen, Erwin O. *The History of Western Art.* New York: New American Library, 1959.

Chu, Jonathan M. *Neighbors Friends or Madmen.* Westport, Conn.: Greenwood Press, 1985.

Cockell, Edgar William, transcr. *The Registers of More, Shropshire.* London: Shropshire. Parish Register Society, 1900.

Connolly, James B. *The Port of Gloucester.* New York: Doubleday, Doran & Co., 1940.

Christoph, Peter R. *The Dongan Papers, 1683–1688.* Syracuse, N.Y.: Syracuse University Press, 1993.

Christoph, Peter R. and Florence A. *The Andros Papers, 1674–1680.* Syracuse, N.Y.: Syracuse University Press, 1989–91.

———. *Books of General Entries of the Colony of New York, 1674–1688.* Baltimore: Genealogical Pub. Co., 1982.

Crump, Helen Josephine. *Colonial Admiralty Jurisdiction in the Seventeenth Century.* London, New York: Longmans, Green & Co., 1931.

Cumberlege, Geoffrey, ed. *Shakespeare's England*. Vol. 1. London: Oxford University Press, 1950.

Cumming, Valerie. *A Visual History of Costume: The Seventeenth Century.* New York: Drama Book Publishers, 1984.

Currier-Briggs, Noel. *Colonial Settlers and English Adventurers.* Baltimore: Genealogical Pub. Co., 1971.

Dashwood, J. B. *The Thames to the Solent by Canal and Sea.* London: Longmans, Green & Co., 1868.

Deetz, James and Patricia. *In Small Things Forgotten: An Archaeology of Early American Life.* New York: Anchor, 1996.

D'Entremont, C. J. *The Story of the Acadian Bells.* As printed on the website http://users.andara.com/~grose.

Dow, George Francis. *Records and Files of the Quarterly Courts of Essex County Massachusetts.* Salem, Mass.: Essex Institute, 1919. Referred to within as *EQC.*

————. *Everyday Life in the Massachusetts Bay Colony.* New York: Dover, 1988.

Dow, George Francis, and John Henry Edmonds. *The Pirates of the New England Coast: 1630–1730.* New York: Dover, 1996.

Earle, Alice Morse. *Curious Punishments of Bygone Days.* Bedford, Mass.: Applewood Books, 1896.

Erikson, Kai T. *Wayward Puritans: A Study in the Sociology of Deviance.* New York: Macmillan, 1966.

Fernow, Berthold, ed. *The Records of New Amsterdam, from 1653 to 1674.* New York: Knickerbocker Press, 1897.

Foster, Elizabeth Read. *The House of Lords, 1603–1649: Structure, Procedure, and the Nature of Its Business.* Chapel Hill: University of North Carolina Press, 1983.

Gill, Crispin. *Mayflower Remembered: A History of the Plymouth Pilgrims.* New York: Taplinger, 1970.

Goodwin, John A. *The Pilgrim Republic: An Historical Review of the Colony of New Plymouth.* Boston: Houghton Mifflin, 1879.

Grant, W. L., James Munro, and Almeric W. Fitzroy, eds. *Acts of the Privy Council of England, Colonial Series.* Vol. 1 (1613–80). Hereford: printed for His Majesty's Stationery Office by Anthony Brothers, 1908.

Green, Mary Anne Everett, ed. *Calendar of the Proceedings of the Committee for Compounding & c., 1643–1660.* London: Eyre and Spotswoode, 1889–1892.

————. *Calendar of State Papers, Domestic Series.* Vols. 8–11 (1603–25). London: Longman, Brown, Green, Longmans & Roberts, 1857–1859.

———. *Calendar of State Papers, Domestic Series*. Vols. 1–13 (1649–60). London: Longman & Co., 1875–1886.

Hall, David D. *The Antinomian Controversy*. Middletown, Conn.: n.p., 1968.

Hall, Michael Garibaldi. *Edward Randolph and the American Colonies: 1676–1703*. New York: W. W. Norton, 1960.

Hansen, Chadwick. *Witchcraft at Salem*. New York: Signet, 1969.

Harley, John. *William Byrd: Gentleman of Royal Chapel*. Aldershot, Hants, England: Scolar Press, 1997.

Harris, Donald F. "The More Children of the Mayflower: Their Shropshire Origins and the Reasons Why They Were Sent Away with the Mayflower Community," *Mayflower Descendant* 43, no. 2 (July 1993), pp. 123–32; 44, no. 1 (Jan. 1994), pp. 11–20; 44, no. 2 (July 1994), pp. 109–18.

Hill, George William, and Walter Howard Frere. *Memorials of Stepney Parish*. Guildford, England: Billings & Sons, 1890–1891.

Holly, H. H. *Sparrow-Hawk: A Seventeenth Century Vessel in Twentieth Century America*. Boston: Nimrod Press, 1969.

Hugill, Stan. *Shanties from the Seven Seas*, Mystic, Conn.: Mystic Seaport Museum, 1996.

Hull, John. *Diaries of John Hull, Mint-Master, and Treasurer of the Colony of the Massachusetts Bay*. Boston: J. Wilson & Son, 1857.

Jeaffreson, John Cordy, ed. *Middlesex County Records*. London: Middlesex County Records Society, 1888.

Kinsbury, Susan Myra, ed. *The Records of the Virginia Company of London*. Washington: Government Printing Office, 1906–35.

Langdon, George D. *Pilgrim Colony: A History of New Plymouth, 1620–1691*. New Haven: Yale University Press, 1966.

Lincoln, Charles H., ed. *Narratives of the Indian Wars, 1675–1699*. New York: Charles Scribner's Sons, 1913.

Lindley, Keith. *Popular Politics and Religion in Civil War London*. Aldershot, Hants, England: Scolar Press, 1997.

Marsh, Christopher W. *The Family of Love in English Society, 1550–1660*. Cambridge: Cambridge University Press, 1984.

Mather, Cotton, edited by Kenneth B. Murdock. *Magnalia Christi Americana*. Books I and II. Cambridge: Harvard University Press, 1977.

Miller, Perry. *The New England Mind: From Colony to Province*. Cambridge: Harvard University Press, 1953.

Miller, Perry, and Thomas Johnson. *The Puritans*. New York: Harper & Row, 1963.

Moody, Robert E., ed. *The Saltonstall Papers: 1607–1815*. Boston: Massachusetts Historical Society, 1972.

More, Samuel. *A true declaracon of the disposinge of the fower children of Catherine More* . . . Photographic reproduction of Wagner's transcription, courtesy of Donald Harris.

Morton, Nathaniel. *New-Englands Memoriall.* New York: Scholars' Facsimiles & Reprints, 1937.

Newton, Arthur Percival. *The Colonizing Activities of the English Puritans.* New Haven: Yale University Press, 1914.

Owen, David R. *Courts of Admiralty in Colonial America.* Durham, N.C.: Carolina Academic Press, 1995.

Patterson, A. Temple. *Southampton: A Biography.* London: Macmillan, 1970.

Perley, Sidney. *The History of Salem.* Vols. 1–3. Salem, Mass.: S. Perley, 1924–28.

Phillips, James Duncan. *Salem in the Seventeenth Century.* Boston: Houghton Mifflin, 1933.

Pierce, Richard D., ed. *The Records of the First Church of Salem, Massachusetts, 1629–1736.* Salem, Mass.: Essex Institute, 1974.

Potter, Harold. *An Historical Introduction to English Law and Its Institutions.* London: Sweet & Maxwell, Ltd., 1932.

Randolph, Edward. *Edward Randolph.* Vols. 1–7. New York: Burt Franklin, 1967.

Rawlyk, George A. *Nova Scotia's Massachusetts: A Study of Massachusetts–Nova Scotia Relations, 1630–1784.* Montreal: McGill–Queen's University Press, 1973.

Reeve, Edward Henry Lisle. *Stondon Massey Essex.* n.p.; n.p., 1906.

Rous, John, edited by Mary Anne Everett Green. *The Diary of John Rous, Incumbent of Santon Downham, Suffolk, from 1625 to 1642.* New York: Johnson Reprint, 1968.

Sainsbury, W. Noel, ed. *Calendar of State Papers, Colonial Series: North America and the West Indies, 1574–1739.* London: Longman, Green, Longman & Roberts, 1860.

Salley, A. S., Jr. *Warrants for Land in South Carolina, 1672–1711.* Columbia: University of South Carolina Press, 1973.

Salzman, L. F. *The Victoria History of the County of Northampton.* Vol. 4. London: Oxford University Press, 1937.

Sams, Conway Whittle. *The Conquest of Virginia: The Third Attempt, 1610–1624.* Spartanburg, S.C.: Reprint Company, 1973.

Sedgwick, Henry Dwight. *Robert Sedgwick: A Sketch.* Cambridge: John Wilson and Son, University Press, 1896.

Semmes, Raphael. *Captains and Mariners of Early Maryland.* Baltimore: Johns Hopkins Press, 1937.

Sewall, Samuel. *The Diary of Samuel Sewall*. New York: Putnam, 1967.

Shakespeare, William. *Four Comedies*. New York: Simon & Schuster, 1948.

Sheppard, Walter Lee. *Passengers and Ships Prior to 1684, Penn's Colony*. Vol. 1. Baltimore: Genealogical Pub. Co., 1970.

Sherman, Robert M., Verle D. Vincent, Robert S. Wakefield, and Lydia D. Finlay. *Mayflower Pilgrim Family Genealogies Through Five Generations*. Vol. 15—James Chilton and Richard More. Plymouth, Mass.: Mayflower Society, 1997.

Sherwood, George. *American Colonists in English Records*. First Series. London, n.p., 1932.

Shurtleff, Nathaniel, and David Pulsifer, ed. *Records of the Colony of New Plymouth in New England*. New York: AMS Press, 1968.

Shurtleff, Nathaniel B., ed. *Records of the Governor and Company of the Massachusetts Bay in New England*. Boston: William White, 1854.

Smith, Joseph Henry. *Appeals to the Privy Council from the American Plantations*. New York: Columbia University Press, 1950.

Starkey, Marion L. *The Devil in Massachusetts: A Modern Inquiry into the Salem Witch Trials*. New York: Doubleday, 1949.

Stearns, Raymond Phineas. *The Strenuous Puritan: Hugh Peter, 1598–1660*. Urbana: University of Illinois Press, 1954.

Steel, D. J. and A. E. F. *National Index of Parish Registers, Vol. 1: Sources of Births, Marriages and Deaths Before 1837 (I)*. Baltimore: Magna Carta Book Company, 1967.

Sumner, William H. *A History of East Boston, with Biographical Sketches of Its Early Proprietors, and an Appendix*. Boston: William H. Piper, 1869.

Thompson, C. S. J. *Quacks of Old London*. New York: Barnes & Noble, 1993.

Vane, Gilbert H. F. *The Registers of Shipton*. London: Shropshire Parish Society, 1899.

Wagner, Anthony R. "The Origin of the Mayflower Children: Jasper, Richard and Ellen More," *New England Historical and Genealogical Register* 114 (1960), pp. 163–68.

———. "The Royal Descent of a Mayflower Passenger," *New England Historical and Genealogical Register* 124 (1970), pp. 85–87.

Warden, G. B. *Boston: 1689–1776*. Boston: Little, Brown, 1970.

Waring, Joseph I. *The First Voyage and Settlement of Charles Town, 1670–1680*. Columbia: University of South Carolina Press, 1970.

Williamson, William D. *The History of Maine from Its First Discovery to the Separation, A.D. 1820, Inclusive*. Vol. 1. Hallowell, Me.: Glazier, Masters & Co., 1832.

Willison, George Findlay. *Saints and Strangers*. New York: Reynal & Hitchcock, 1945.

Wilson, Peter Lamborn. *Pirate Utopias: Moorish Corsairs & European Renegadoes*. Brooklyn: Autnomedia, 1995.

Wilson, Philip K. *Childbirth: Changing Ideas and Practices in Britain and America 1600 to the Present*. New York: Garland, 1996.

Winslow, Edward, edited by Dwight B. Heath. *Mourt's Relation: A Relation or Journal of the English Plantation settled at Plymouth in New England, by certain English adventurers both merchants and others*. New York: Corinth, 1963.

Winthrop, John, edited by James Savage. *A History of New England from 1630 to 1649*. Vol. 2. Salem, N.H.: Ayer, 1992.

Index